## Endorsements for *After the Game*

"Spreadsheets don't create synergies—PEOPLE DO. It is much easier to teach the math behind valuation techniques than it is to create or maintain a cohesive team and lead it in the right direction."
—DONNA M. HITSCHERICH, Senior Lecturer, Director of the Private Equity Program at Columbia Business School

"I love *After the Game*. It resonates so deeply not only with me but any athlete at any level."
—BRIAN DE LA PUENTE, retired NFL player

"As a former athlete turned business leader, *After the Game* outlines the key characteristics one learns in sports and can apply to business."
— DANNY WADHAMS, former D-I athlete and owner of Flowing Tide

"Your mindset is everything as a business leader. Everyone wants to be part of a winning organization . . . After the Game!"
—SONNY THADANI, CEO of Robin and founding member of Accordion Partners

*After the Game* brings the reader the necessary and indispensable tools for any successful transition into business, entrepreneurship, or a trade with the knowledge that has been proven to be successful by some of the best athletes in the world. The classrooms, locker rooms, and fields of college and professional sports are constant proving grounds for individual growth, character development, and overcoming adversity. *After the Game* provides access to the training camp for success and wisdom of its application for the toughest business fields in the world."
—DEMAURICE SMITH, former executive director of the National Football League Players Association (NFLPA)

"When the final whistle blows on their sports careers, many athletes struggle to find their purpose. In *After the Game*, Jay Dixon provides the necessary insight to guide players through answering 'What's next?' *After the Game* is a necessary resource for both current and former athletes."
— STEPHANIE GEOSITS, board of directors for Soccer Canada and founder of All About Sports

"*After the Game* is an excellent road map that shows athletes how they can use their skillsets from sports to succeed in the business world and shows business leaders how athletes can make excellent employees and leaders. *After the Game* focuses on self-awareness and emotional intelligence, vital pieces to being successful and prosperous! This book will help a lot of people achieve the success that their heart desires!"

—MARQUES OGDEN, former NFL offensive lineman
and CEO of Ogden Ventures LLC

"As a former Los Angeles Dodger who transitioned into entrepreneurship, I deeply resonate with the message in Jay Dixon's *After the Game*. This book brilliantly bridges the gap between athletic discipline and business acumen. Dixon's insights are a practical guide for any athlete looking to redefine success beyond the field. A must-read for those ready to channel their athletic ability into entrepreneurial triumphs."

—TYLER ADKISON, former MLB player,
entrepreneur, and angel investor

"Whether you are leaving a career in sports, transitioning between companies or industries, or finally achieving that long-desired promotion, *After the Game* is indispensable reading for anyone experiencing a significant career change."

—PAUL INGRAM, Kravis Professor of Business
at Columbia Business School and Presidential Award
winner in Teaching Excellence

"As a seasoned talent executive, I am thoroughly impressed by *After the Game*. This book is a critical tool for former athletes to navigate the challenging transition from sports to entrepreneurship. The unique blend of mindset coaching and practical business acquisition strategies shown is innovative and necessary. *After the Game* is an essential read for anyone aspiring to redefine their identity and achieve entrepreneurial excellence post-sports career."

— STEVEN DEVALL, VP of Talent Partnerships
and Influencer Strategy at Vox Media

# AFTER THE GAME

## BRIDGING THE GAP FROM WINNING ATHLETE TO THRIVING ENTREPRENEUR

### BY JAY DIXON

Forefront
BOOKS

Published by Forefront Books, Nashville, Tennessee.
Distributed by Simon & Schuster.

Library of Congress Control Number: 2023922332

Print ISBN: 978-1-63763-267-3
E-book ISBN: 978-1-63763-268-0

Cover Design by Faceout Studio
Interior Design by PerfecType, Nashville, TN

Printed in the United States of America

"Enhancing the lives of athletes after sport."
*Champions of Business*

# CONTENTS

# PREFACE

## Bridging the Identity Gap by Harnessing the Unique Skills of Athletes

Throughout their journey, athletes are celebrated as the epitome of physical strength and mental fortitude. Yet when the applause fades and the spotlight dims, athletes face a profound existential question: "Who am I if I am no longer an athlete?" The transition out of a life defined by competitive sports can be extremely challenging, leading to what is often referred to as an "identity gap."[1]

The identity gap signifies the disparity between an individual's old identity (as an athlete) and their new identity,[2] which often feels uncertain and unsettled. Research shows that the vast majority of athletes experience this loss of identity and need more time, as well as social support, for a successful career transition.[3] Other athletes have reported a decrease in their social status after their college sports career ended.[4] Most simply believe their best days are behind them.

Athletes spend a significant part of their lives developing, honing, and ultimately being defined by their athletic identities. In fact, one study found that 78 percent of student-athletes identified as athletes first before their role as students.[5] Consequently, their life after sports can feel like losing a part of their core self, leading to struggles with self-concept, role confusion, emotional distress,[6] and even depression.[7]

Yet it's important to remember that athletes are equipped with a unique set of skills and characteristics nurtured through their sporting careers. Qualities such as resilience, dedication, discipline, teamwork, and goal-orientation are invaluable in the realm of entrepreneurship.[8] These skills can provide athletes with a significant advantage in business endeavors, providing a bridge to cross the identity gap and embark on new, fulfilling journeys.

The transition from an athletic career to entrepreneurship offers ex-athletes a chance to reframe their narrative, find new purpose, and use their intrinsic qualities to acquire and lead successful ventures. This book aims to guide former athletes through this journey, providing insights, strategies, and inspiration for a timely leap into successful entrepreneurship.

Just as athletes draw strategies and techniques from their coaches, this book is designed to serve as a mentor, helping athletes to understand and apply their athletic abilities off the field. It aims to support athletes to redefine their identities, not by losing their *athlete* self, but by adding a new dimension to it—that of an athlete-entrepreneur.

And just as we aim to give athletes a new identity, we also aim to create awareness of their unique skill sets and characteristics among the general public. Investing in exceptional business leaders is crucial for sustained success and growth of business. Research indicates that CEOs with a background in competitive athletics are statistically better leaders: 17 percent longer tenured, 12 percent lower debt, and 15 percent higher return on assets.[9]

Linking leadership characteristics with corporate performance is a large and growing field. The early professional background of CEOs before assuming their leadership roles bears significance in corporate decision-making. For example, Benmelech and Frydman (2015) examined the influence of military service experience on managerial decisions, financial policies, and overall corporate performance. They discovered that firms led by CEOs with a military background tend to adopt more conservative policies, demonstrate ethical behavior, make fewer investments, engage in fewer fraudulent activities, and exhibit better performance during industry downturns. While existing literature has explored various CEO characteristics, the specific impact of being an athlete on CEO decision-making remains largely unexplored.

The research-backed evidence demonstrates that athletes have the potential to drive financial performance, foster innovation, inspire teams, navigate challenges effectively, and create a culture of excellence, demonstrated further through the neuroscientific benefits of athletics. (For details, see Appendix: Unlocking the Neuroscientific Benefits of Athletics for Business Success: 10 Principles.)

Understanding the education athletics provides and the unique skill sets it develops is critical to business success for former athletes.

This book aims not only to inspire former athletes to lean into their skills and create awareness among the business community of their unique skill sets to thrive as leaders, but also to provide a fast-track way for athletes to achieve business success and enhance their mindset in preparation to become an entrepreneur.

———

This fast track is through acquiring a successful business, often termed "Entrepreneurship Through Acquisition" (ETA), and leveraging the soft skills for success. Studies show that ETA, which has been around for forty-plus years and historically has been taught at elite business schools, leads to a higher success rate than starting a business from scratch. According to various studies, the success rate for ETA is estimated at 50 to 60 percent and has been a growing trend among investors as an alternative asset class. With an estimated $10 trillion in assets held in twelve million privately owned businesses to be sold by 2040 by the baby boomer generation,[10] the opportunity is enormous.

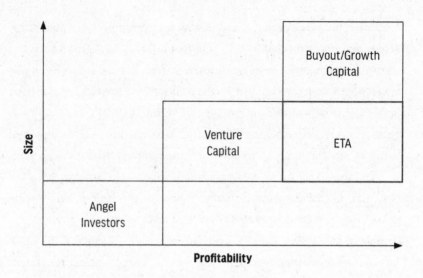

Acquired businesses generally have better financial performance compared to startups. Research indicates that acquired businesses tend to generate higher revenues and profits in the early years compared to new ventures.

ETA can result in faster time to profitability compared to launching a new business. Acquiring an existing business allows entrepreneurs to leverage the groundwork laid by the previous owner, which can accelerate the path to positive cash flow.

Those who are interested in starting a business from scratch should know that the success rate is relatively lower compared to ETA. According to the US Bureau of Labor Statistics, about 20 percent of new businesses fail within their first year, and around 50 percent fail within their first five years.[11] (Success rates can vary based on industry, location, and other factors.)

The difference in business, as in sports, largely depends on the guidance and laser-focused wisdom from coaches and mentors, the dedication and drive of the athletes and entrepreneurs, and the will to succeed, no matter the obstacle.

We invite you to delve into these pages, uncover the emerging entrepreneur within you, and start bridging the gap that stands between your past and your future. We believe this is one path to entrepreneurial success, and we are here to support you now, and perhaps even down the road.

Here's to the beginning of your exciting journey as an athlete-entrepreneur.

# *THE INVITATION*
## A Return of the Glory Days

I t's often said that athletes die twice. I'm on my second life and I have a mission.

When I was seven years old, I put on a football helmet. From that moment on, my identity was sealed. I was an athlete. A warrior. A passionate, disciplined, committed, optimistic, persistent, competitive, supportive, and motivated soul. It was my DNA.

When my helmet came off after my last bowl game, I felt like I'd died. For the next three years, I struggled in all areas of life. Relationships were ruined. I bounced around to different jobs. I numbed myself with unhealthy coping strategies and feelings of loss, an identity crisis, and distress.

If you played college sports, then you know the highs and lows of a season. You've felt the rush from a win ignite in your chest, and the crush of a loss bring you to your knees. You've known the mental and physical challenge of always pushing to improve, reaching for the next victory. Your coach's voice is constantly playing in your head, even off the field. Your whole rhythm of life is set by the seasons, the ongoing cycle of training, competing, and improving.

It's a familiar rhythm that continues until you wake to the day of your final game.

Do you remember that day? I imagine you do. It's a day most of us never forget. Whether it ended in victory or defeat—and whether you competed in high school, college, or at a professional level—there was a sense of finality that is inescapable. A final whistle blew. A final point was played. A final lap. A final putt. With a final goal scored, your personal goal came to an end.

And after that last game, you shed your identity as a competing athlete, along with your jersey or uniform. Your next step was into the real world with two looming questions hanging over your head: "What's next?" and "Who am I?"

These are hard questions for nearly all athletes. Playing football had been my focus most of my life. Since age seven, I'd lived, breathed, and dreamed of being a sports star. Life consisted of practices, teammates, and sweat. Lots of sweat. I followed my coaches with an almost militaristic fervor, and every August I couldn't wait to suit up and do battle again.

My early life didn't present many challenges. I can't paint some rags-to-riches story about meager beginnings. I was living in the affluence of Orange County, California, with the sun on our shoulders and Mickey Mouse's kingdom just down the road. I attended San Clemente High School, which generated numerous Division I football players from the program my year and many more before and after me. My goal was to rank among them, and as my senior year started, the "process" began. Big coaches started visiting the school in search of the next breakout talent. As some teammates began selecting colleges to attend, the colors and clothes from their newly selected schools started appearing at parties. I was still wearing surf clothes with my ego in check, with no real offers coming in to play Division I.

My goals were simple: a full-ride scholarship and playing time at a D-I school. I had no desire to be a walk-on and knew I had it in me to be a full-scholarship football player; the right team just hadn't found me yet. Every team has guys who simply won't make it. But I wasn't one of those guys. I saw it. I knew it.

The deadline for college commitments approached, and all I had coming in were partial offers at smaller schools. Nothing solid. My frustration grew like a weed. I remember putting on a pair of jump shoes—i.e., shoes with a platform that forces the wearer to rely heavily on their calf muscles, to increase speed and explosiveness—and just went 100 percent Forrest Gump, racing through my neighborhood like some predator was nipping at my heels. After a good three to five miles, I wasn't any clearer on my situation, but I knew the training couldn't hurt.

I decided to attend the local junior college, Saddleback College, to hone my game. Saddleback takes pride in its long history of building championship teams and individuals, often a stepping stone for those with similar goals as mine. The coaches had a plan for me to get to Division I—a plan that is universal in football: bigger, faster, stronger, and more fundamental techniques.

For the next two years, my world was, yet again, football. I lived in the weight room and on the field. I ate up everything I could related to football. I also studied hard because I knew that to be a D-I prospect, I needed to be the full package. Coaches and administrators love scholar-athletes, and I was setting myself up to be a lock for some lucky school.

One day, finally, my work paid off. Hall of Fame head coach Chris Ault and defensive line coach Marty Long were sitting in my living room, accepting a glass of iced tea from my mother. Growing up on the West Coast, everyone knew about Coach Ault and Nevada's "Air Wolf" and, eventually, the "Pistol" offenses, which made for high-scoring contests. Before the visit was over, a full ride was in front of me, an offer on the table.

Well, I was in. The trips I had lined up to visit other D-I universities were canceled. I simply told them I had accomplished what I needed.

At Nevada, as a mid-major Division I school, we had to be tough, disciplined, and play like a unit. Our coaches did such a great job of drilling those ideals into my head so thoroughly that I found myself repeating those same words years later as a businessman. I attended

Nevada for three years. I redshirted, but I earned more playing time as my seniority rose. By my senior year, I was a starter, and we opened up on ABC television at Nebraska. When I was a kid growing up in the '90s, Nebraska football was untouchable. They were winning national championships left and right, the darling of college football. One Christmas, my parents got me a Nebraska football sweatshirt. As a kid in California, I wore it nonstop as a prideful sign that I only intended to be the best.

Now, I was on Nebraska's field—the "Sea of Red"—with my team during warm-ups, listening to the crowd's deafening roar, hearing my name in front of ninety thousand fans over a loudspeaker, as a starter against the Cornhuskers.[12] Coach Ault came by and looked me dead in the eye: "It's your time, Dixon!" His confidence in me gave me a jolt, a fire in my soul, and fearlessness in my body. I played a majority of the snaps against a monstrous offensive line, battling, fighting, and using the energy of my teammates and coaches to continue to play. And although we lost, it was still a dream come true to have set my goal at a young age to play football at that level, and to be on the same field as my childhood dream team, knowing that I had achieved it. My body was beat, but my soul was alive.

It was the highest high I had ever felt.

But these moments of glory made it even harder to accept the end.

I remember after the last game of my college athletic career, walking off the field thinking, *I'm done. Now what?*

I was at a loss. The football calendar had dictated my life so profoundly that when I stopped playing, it felt like the earth had ceased spinning on its axis. I staggered around day to day, dizzy from the abrupt halt of my career and identity as an athlete. No more sweltering summer conditioning. No more locker room banter with my buddies. No more brassy crescendos from the marching band, pumping us up from the stands.

I wish I could tell you that the highs were enough to sustain my transition into post-college life. I certainly expected my professional career to operate like my athletic one. I knew I had potential; my success on the field had taught me that. But I no longer had a coach to point me toward a goal. I wasn't even sure what the goal was. And I've spoken with many others who have talked about this same struggle.

---

My first job was in sales, where I worked for next to nothing, with customers slamming doors in my face on the regular. It was a discouraging start that sent me looking for something else. I coached some high school football also. My next move was to land a corporate job.

*This is it*, I thought. I had traded my uniform for a suit and the locker room for a cubicle. In the beginning, I was fired up, hungry to succeed. But the work was monotonous and unfulfilling. I needed a win, a season, and a championship I could reach for.

I assumed that the next logical goal would be a promotion, so I jumped at an opportunity that was way out of my league. I insisted that the vice president promote me to a position at their new office, in order to establish a new business unit in downtown Los Angeles. It was a pretty prize for our executive team and critical for company success. He hesitated due to my age and lack of experience, but ultimately gave his support and assigned me the promotion. I thought for sure this would be the cure to my apathy, but the boost only lasted a few weeks. I soon realized I would never be fulfilled working in the corporate world, building someone else's business.[13]

After an abrupt departure from that job, I left my home in California with my partner, and after bouncing around, spending a few years coaching, we started a company on the other side of the country. I was convinced working for myself would be better than working for someone else, but also hesitant to take a risk. Thankfully, it did prove to be better. The hard work quickly paid off. I found myself hungry to continue growing the company, excited to emancipate myself from a typical nine-to-five "job."

Then an unexpected thing happened. A local entrepreneur and investor approached us out of the blue and offered to buy the company we'd spent only a short time building. It wasn't retirement money, but it sure was enough to take the pressure off a bit. The whole concept of *selling your business* was completely foreign to me, but I immediately recognized it as a big win. A championship win.

I saw the potential to repeat this formula of starting, growing, and selling small businesses. Better yet, I recognized it as a similar process to my athletic seasons and championships.

My drive ignited. My pulse quickened. There was nothing I loved as much as a challenge to help others. The sale of a business can be compared to a trophy on my shelf, proof that anyone can accomplish great things. After being a part of two more sales, I knew I had something. Better yet, I knew I loved to coach and advise others. I also knew that the core values I'd learned on the football field—analytical and creative thinking, resilience, motivation and self-awareness, and dependability and curiosity—would propel me forward in the business world. I had already learned more about how to be an entrepreneur from the football field than many of my peers would learn in business school.

Since that very first win, I have been obsessed with how people start, grow, buy, and sell small businesses, and fascinated with analyzing synergies among companies. I consulted with many entrepreneurs to successfully buy and sell companies. I found that buying and selling businesses was successful by leveraging the unique skills and traits I learned in athletics, not the spreadsheets, and classroom skills were much easier to learn considering the athletic characteristics I'd honed over many years. I further realized that mindset training was critical to leadership performance in business, as it was consistently displayed by the most successful entrepreneurs. My only regret is how long it took me to arrive here. I feel certain that if someone had sat me down at the end of college and explained how to harness all my potential and skills, I would have avoided a lot of pain and frustration.

Don't get me wrong—the standard job track offers a lot: financial security, promotions, and a predictable forty-year career that ends with retirement. There's nothing wrong with taking that route. I simply chose another path for my early career.

I was fortunate to overcome my trials as an athlete who lost their sport, redirecting my passion and skills into entrepreneurial ventures. I've suffered some losses, achieved many successes, and I still wake every morning with an excitement and passion for coaching others to succeed in the game of business.

---

My goal is to prevent you from suffering unnecessary mental pain and frustration when your career ends. It can be devastating to know you have great potential but have nowhere to apply it. Why is it so hard to translate your devotion and drive to the real world? Why is there a disconnect for some students between their athletic career and their business career?

My experience says a new framework, a new mindset, is needed to help you through the transition and to understand how business operates. You must learn how the "game" of business works both tactically and in your mind, understand some key business principles, learn how to think, and shift your approach to the way you work. I've also sketched out a timely model that has been buried in business schools called Entrepreneurship Through Acquisition (ETA), which I outlined in the preface, where an entrepreneur can fast-track their way to business success through buying an operating business. With the largest wealth transfer in history on the horizon—the transition of baby boomer businesses to new owners—there has never been a more opportune time to leverage your athletic skills into success.

I have laid out these principles and skills in the following fable of two fictitious former college athletes, Kai and Christina, whose challenges represent the same ones many student-athletes face as they blindly step out into the workforce, struggling with an identity gap of who they were as a high-performing athlete and who they are now, without the title and support system. You will also meet Success Coach Jack, who offers advice to these college athletes for their life after sports. His advice comes from the lessons I have learned through my own experience and from my mentors. Through their interactions, Coach Jack introduces Kai and Christina to new mindsets, teaches them the "game" of business, and explains the steps to buying, building, and then selling their own businesses.

I also firmly believe the pursuit of what's possible post-sports is defined by the ability to successfully apply the skills and characteristics you learn in athletics to business. Those skills and characteristics are what truly drive businesses, not the technical skills.

I've written this book to be a manual for those who I call an athlete-entrepreneur—an entrepreneur whose athletic past sets them up to succeed as champions of business. I'm convinced that many athletes need a professional life that promises dynamic challenges with big wins that benefit all parties.

My mission is to enhance the lives of athletes after sports. I want to enable athletes to enjoy this pursuit in their lives utilizing a time-tested, research-backed, and athlete-approved approach.

For some people, life on the bench is enough. It's a safe spot with a view of the action. But I know you didn't become an athlete to sit on the bench. You're most alive when you're on the field, playing your heart out with your team. You need to be in the game.

The end of high school, college, or professional athletics doesn't have to be the end of the game. I've got a spot for you on the team if you're willing to train and give your all. So, join me for an incredible adventure and wins you'll never forget.

PART I

# BUILDING THE
# DREAM TEAM

# 1

# *MEET KAI*
# *(JUST ONE MORE GAME...)*

As Kai Stafford turned his rented Jeep Wagoneer into the already packed parking lot behind Kyle Field in College Station, Texas, he glanced at the temperature on his dashboard. It was already eighty-two degrees at 10:00 a.m. on what appeared to be a perfect Friday morning in September. And according to the local weather report, the warm weather would continue for the entirety of this weekend's Texas A&M alumni events, hitting ninety-five degrees by early afternoon. Blazing heat and mild humidity, just the way he liked it.

He smiled as he turned down the radio and lowered his window to let the warm air circulate through the Jeep, punctuated now and then by the earthy, peppery scent of nearby cornflowers, sweet-smelling chrysanthemums, and other fall blooms. This was his first time back on campus since last year's alumni weekend. He had faithfully returned every year since graduation to reconnect with his friends and former teammates, and his first true love—*football.*

The Jeep crawled along, waiting to be directed to a space. As the gravel crunched under the tires, Kai took a deep breath and was instantly back on the football field. He could still conjure upon command the scent of freshly cut grass, dirt, and sweat.

In the 2012 game against Arizona, his team won 44–27 and a stadium of enthusiastic Aggies stormed the field—one of his most beloved memories. As a six-foot-three, 225-pound middle linebacker, Kai had just played his best collegiate performance ever, wreaking absolute havoc as he terrorized the offensive line and had sacks and tackles for losses that he had always dreamed of. *Damn, what I wouldn't give to be out there again*, he thought as he inched along behind the car in front of him, scanning the endless sea of vehicles. *Just one more game.* He gripped the steering wheel tighter, smiling as he remembered how deafening the stadium became after a great play.

Truth is, he'd give anything to feel that way again—unstoppable and confident—like his best days were right in front of him, here and now, as the master of his own destiny. Instead, since graduating and walking off the field after his final game, he'd slowly lost his fire and his identity as an athlete, unsure of his purpose as he struggled to fit into the corporate world, just another cog in a big, squeaky wheel. *I can't believe my best days are behind me.* He'd witnessed the same transformation from glory days to complacent haze in a few of his teammates, but they sidestepped it in conversation, choosing instead to focus on the highlight reels of their past lives, what was and what could have been.

As the car in front of him turned into an empty space, Kai flashed to another great play where he celebrated on the sidelines with his teammates, running up to kiss his beautiful girlfriend in the stands. She'd attended every game, his biggest cheerleader. Four years later, they were married.

Another beat and his smile wavered. *This weekend would be better if Robin and Mia were here.* He angled his left hand up and glanced at the gold band on his ring finger, sparkling in the sun against his warm, tawny brown skin. His wife, Robin, had opted out of the weekend trip for the first time in their marriage, choosing instead to take their two-year-old daughter, Mia, to visit Robin's mother and sister in Florida for a girls' weekend. It was one more point of contention in what lately seemed like an endless list of things to argue about.

"It's an unnecessary expense, babe," Kai said to Robin's unflinching glare, in a futile attempt to sway her decision. "Plus, I want to show Mia off. I got her that cute little jersey dress with her name on it."

"Now *that* was an unnecessary expense," Robin shot back.

"Oh, come on." His usually irresistible puppy dog look wasn't working this time. "It fits her perfectly. I got you that jersey to match, so we look like a unit! You know she loved going last year."

"She was barely a year old," Robin responded with arms crossed. "She doesn't remember it and she spent half the time asleep."

"Yeah, but now she can play with the other kids and run around." Kai tried his best to convince her to change her plans but got no response. "Maybe teach her some moves with the soft football I got her." He juked to the left, then right, avoiding an invisible opponent and trying to draw a smile.

*No luck.* Not getting the reaction he hoped for, he stepped in closer and put his arms around her, but she backed away from his advances and headed down the hallway.

"Baby, we've always gone to the alumni weekend together. What am I supposed to say to my boys when they ask where you and Mia are?"

"You can tell them the truth—that we're having a girls' weekend. No *boys* allowed." As she walked away, he knew she'd emphasized *boys* intentionally. "Plus, you can always work more, right?" she shouted from the laundry room. "To cover all of our *unnecessary* expenses."

*Ouch.* The barb landed.

Kai sighed deeply, easing the Jeep forward again, thinking about how abruptly their relationship had gone downhill not long after Mia was born. It was right around the time Kai's CPA firm was in the midst of a merger, and he had to fight tooth and nail to keep his position at Arthur Whitney.

When Robin was hospitalized during the seventh month of pregnancy with complications from preeclampsia, Kai's division had been performing a rigorous audit for the merger with no extra pay. He felt torn between working late hours to hopefully save his job or leaving every day at 5:00 p.m. to be with his wife for several hours after work. More times than he cared to recall, he chose to work late, because at least he felt like he had some control over the paperwork and processes, and it's what the company had asked of him. He had *zero* control when it came to his wife's medical situation. Although neither Kai nor Robin ever fully spoke their fears aloud, both were terrified of losing this baby, especially since they'd suffered a devastating miscarriage two years prior.

As Mia's arrival neared, Kai, who had always been a numbers guy, easily convinced himself that he could be more helpful in the office during the audit than bedside with his wife. Plus, Robin had her mother, sister, and a close group of girlfriends who were able to visit her daily when he wasn't able to make it.

To be fair, most days he popped in for a quick lunch break since the hospital was only five blocks from his firm. But he didn't come by every afternoon like Robin wished he would, like she'd often asked him to. At least a handful of times, he'd promised to stop by after work but ended up working until it was too late, working to ensure that his job—and their income—was secure. As a husband and father-to-be, he strongly felt his responsibility was to financially provide for his growing family, so he chose to stay at work until the point of exhaustion each day, calling to wish her good night on his drive home. Robin had often reminded him that a phone call or video call simply wasn't the same as his physical presence.

Robin was never worried that he was out cheating on her with other women while she was in the hospital on bed rest—she'd told him this during one of their calls—but he felt he was most definitely cheating on her with his monotonous job, and she wasn't sure which was worse.

Although the remainder of Robin's pregnancy progressed without incident and both Mia and Robin were perfectly healthy after the birth, the stress of the situation, including the financial onslaught of medical bills, took root in their relationship and had only continued to grow, with tendrils of resentment poking through the surface on the regular.

Thankfully, they had good insurance. And Robin's school, where she taught fifth-grade science, had granted her a medical leave of absence while she was hospitalized. But out-of-pocket and unforeseen expenses soon piled up. Diapers alone added up to a monthly car payment. And then daycare became another huge monthly expense.

He'd considered asking Robin to quit her teaching job to stay home with Mia for the first few years, at least until she went to preschool, but knew that wouldn't go over well. Robin loved teaching and loved her kids. She'd already decided she would go back to work after her maternity leave. If they had a second baby, he'd bring this solution up then.

But the damage had already been done. And it was deep.

Kai had chosen his job over his wife in her greatest time of need. That's what Robin saw, anyway, and she had repeatedly pointed it out over the last two years, especially when Kai frequently went out after work with a few coworkers to blow off steam at one sports bar or another, instead of coming straight home to be with Mia and Robin.

From her perspective, just two years after college, Kai started to lose motivation, struggling with anger and frustration, and withdrawing from the healthy lifestyle he used to love. The stressful pregnancy only exacerbated the issues, and by the time Mia arrived, Robin felt Kai was slipping away from her—becoming unhappy and overworked, instead of the energetic, driven athlete she once knew. She'd mentioned her observations a few times, hoping to help her husband, only to be quickly shut down.

Now, from Kai's point of view, he was doing what he should do as a husband and new father—taking care of business and working his way up the corporate ladder to provide a better life one day. He didn't understand why he constantly experienced resentment at home when what he really wanted was a thank-you for working long hours to ensure Robin and Mia were taken care of. His salary was twice as much as Robin's, so the more he worked, the better off they'd be.

Because of his long hours, he felt he deserved to go out with his buddies now and then and watch a few games on TV. He missed football, his team, and his old self with a dire ache and had never regained the confidence from those glory days, not even when he received a promotion to manager after the merger was complete. As the fog of depression slowly wrapped its fingers around his mind, choking out the joy in daily life, he became more withdrawn at home, and more anxious and robotic at work. He was in survival mode and didn't even know it, running on fumes and repetition, simply going through the motions. After clocking out late every night, he figured the least he could do was watch the games and support his team while downing a few beers.

Of course, Robin didn't see it that way at all. She wanted a husband and a helpmate—a partner who wanted to spend time with her and their daughter, instead of a workaholic who cared more about somebody else's company than he did about his family, and who always seemed to be complaining about his job and not getting rewarded for the extra work—but never took any actions to change direction.

In his view, she seemed to find every possible opportunity to remind him that while she had fallen in love with a fun, flashy, confident football star, she was now married to a stuffy money manager with a borderline drinking problem and a pessimistic view of life.[14]

Not that his life as a money manager held much more comfort. With the firm's restructuring and Kai's promotion, he was moved to another division under a CFO who had the personality of a dead fish and the EQ of one too.[15] Maybe even the IQ to match. No one liked Bryce, but as the nephew of one of the founders, he was a permanent thorn to contend with on the daily. He was always finding reasons to make employees look incompetent, no doubt to make himself feel more powerful, and creating more busy work in general. Bryce had been a regular student in college and never understood why anyone would waste their time in sports and not be completely focused on the classroom.

In Kai's mind, Bryce was one of the main reasons he worked so many hours. If only Kai could get the approval to implement better processes and procedures, the whole division could run much more smoothly, like a well-oiled machine. Like a team—the way it should be.

———

"Sir? Excuse me, sir." The parking attendant tapped Kai's arm and brought him back into the present.

"Oh, sorry, man. I was lost in my head. You caught me!"

The attendant smiled. "There's an open spot just over there." He pointed to a parking space with his orange flag.

"Thank you, man." Kai flashed a big smile and pulled into the spot. He quickly glanced up into the rearview mirror and straightened his jersey. "It's game time, baby!"

Ten minutes later, he spotted his crew from across the parking lot. They were already tailgating, grilling out, and playing cornhole next to a big tent. One of his buddies saw him and held up a beer to welcome him. The weekend was going to be lit!

Kai pulled his phone out to see if he had any text messages from Robin. *I wonder what my girls are up to today.* He had messaged her earlier and asked her to send pictures of their weekend adventures. He already missed his little family.

*Damn.* No response. His brow furrowed in disappointment. Then he quickly put on a big smile to greet his friends and former teammates. As stubborn as he was private, Kai refused to let anyone—even his closest friends—know that he and Robin were on shaky ground. Being stoic and not admitting his struggles had served him well in football, but now it was eating him up inside.

## 2

# MEET CHRISTINA
# (I MISS THOSE DAYS...)

Christina Bates, grabbing one of the few empty seats at the Big Dripper, one of the hipper coffee places in midtown Manhattan, settled in to do a bit of work. On this unseasonably warm Friday afternoon, only a few spots remained, and she relished the energy of the place as she sipped her cortado, checked email on her phone, and opened her laptop to an Excel spreadsheet.

She'd moved to Weehawken, New Jersey, three years before for a commissioned sales position for Peppley NYC, a huge office furniture wholesaler. She didn't love the job, but she did like meeting new people and finding out who they were, what they needed, and how she could help. As a problem-solving overachiever, she had always found sales easy.[16] And this position provided her with flexible hours, a remote work environment, and enough extra income each month to make a sizable dent in her college loans, which she was still paying off.

She preferred working in coffee shops in and around NYC because of the opportunities for networking—both personally and professionally.

She'd met some of her closest friends this way—standing in line to order—including Jane, the manager of her recreational soccer team with NYC Footy. And then there were a few guys she met that led to dates, some far better (and some far worse) than others.

Christina giggled into her mug recalling this past Saturday's date disaster. She'd met Nate earlier in the week outside a coffee shop near Rockefeller Park. He seemed like a nice enough guy. He'd played soccer in college as well, and they both like dogs. That was enough for her to exchange numbers and agree to dinner. But it had been downhill from there.

Fifteen minutes late with no apology, Nate didn't even say hello when he sat down in front of her, didn't offer to buy her a drink—not even a sparkling water—and talked about himself the entire time. She considered getting up and walking out in the middle of one of his lengthy monologues, but she had been looking forward to the shrimp pasta she ordered, so she accepted her fate for the next hour and turned it into a game, relying on her ability to ask *really good* questions. This was one of the qualities she'd long ago mastered—how to read people and ask open-ended questions to gain helpful information without offering much about herself unless specifically prompted.

All she had to do was ask Nate a question about his work or his interests and *boom*—she had a guaranteed three to four minutes to eat without having to offer anything about herself, other than a feigned, "Oh, that's interesting!" or a "Hmm, really?" now and then to provoke him further.

Thirty minutes into dinner, he hadn't asked her one question about herself. *Not even one.* She decided not to mention the glob of ketchup he had on his left cheek. She also decided dogs and soccer were no longer enough of a reason to give anyone her number, no matter how handsome.

———————

Christina watched the line of patrons grow at the counter and was glad she snagged a table when she did. She took another sip of the cortado, then checked the time—2:58 p.m.—and pulled her compact out to make sure she had no lipstick on her teeth, no milk on her lip, and that her blonde hair remained in place. She wanted to look her absolute best on the video call. She took a deep breath, put in her earpiece, flashed a bright smile, then logged into the conference call.

*Time to shine*, she thought to herself.

Not even fifteen minutes later, the conference call ended and she had another sale. This made five this month already. Her quota was six. If she completed seven, a bonus would be enough to fully fund her vacation budget for the summer.

"Hey, I didn't mean to overhear your call, but it sounds like congratulations are in order."

Christina turned to her right as a middle-aged man at the table next to hers smiled her way, a tall coffee in hand lifted toward her as a *Cheers*.

"Oh! Thank you," she said, as she returned the smile. "Almost hit my quota for the month."

"That's incredible. Sales, I assume?" the man asked.

"Yes. Office furniture," she laughed. "The most glamorous sales of all!"

The man offered a kind smile. "That's a tough world. I used to be in sales myself until I decided to make a shift so I could focus on significance instead of success."

*Interesting*, she thought. *Is he about to launch into an MLM pitch? God, I hope not.* "What do you mean by significance instead of success?" she asked, deciding to take the bait anyway.

"Well . . ." He shifted a bit in his seat to face her. "I struggled for years doing the corporate thing. Made a lot of people a lot of money. But no matter how many sales I made, or what title I held, I still felt lost. I had no real goals, no plan, and a lot of hangovers!"

They both laughed at that.

"Hangovers are the worst!" she nodded.

"Absolutely. But losing your sense of identity is worse."[17] His tone became more serious. "I'm so sorry, I didn't introduce myself," he said. "My name is Jack Merrick. I'm a Success Coach." He extended his hand for a shake, which she accepted.

"Christina Bates," she responded in kind. "Do you mean like a business coach or a life coach? Do you do corporate training?" She closed her laptop, now an active listener—or at least a captive audience for the moment.

He shook his head to indicate she was partially right. "More like individual business mentoring. And I only work with athletes."

She sat straighter in her chair, a huge smile at hearing the word *athlete*. "I played soccer for four years at UCLA!"

"Ah! D-I. You're a Bruin, huh?"

"Till I die," she smiled. "Did you play college sports too?"

"Football at Nebraska almost thirty years ago. Biggest meathead you ever saw," he laughed.

She nodded. "Hey, that's a great school."

"And even greater coaches," he offered. "My problem was that when I stepped off the field after my very last game, I completely lost myself. I felt like I had died. I had no direction. No motivation. No coaches. No team."

She sat back in her chair a bit, resonating with his confession. "Oh, I get that. When you walk across the stage at graduation, you're handed a piece of paper that somehow equates to your entire college experience. And come Monday morning, you're expected to start a whole new life but without the teammates and structure you've relied on."

"Exactly," he said, pointing at her. "The thing is, you can't just turn off your drive like that, or your competitive nature once your athletic career ends. You don't just assume a completely new identity overnight. You will *always* be an athlete."

She leaned in, truly interested now. "I've been playing since I was four years old. I still play in rec leagues now. I can't quit. It's my one true love. Besides coffee," she said grinning and lifted her mug. "I still play on weekends with my team but it's not the same as making a penalty kick in a championship game." She leaned back in her chair. "Man, I miss those days."

Jack leaned in, mirroring her. "Then *you know*. You know you can't just turn that part of you off. You can mask it somewhat in a corporate setting. Your drive likely comes out in other ways like being a hard worker, being competitive with your sales numbers, and having a solid daily schedule."

"One hundred percent," she agreed. "I'm certain that a big part of why I do so well in sales is due to the discipline I've been taught to have since I was little."

"And I'm sure your employer rewards you mightily for your hard work," Jack smirked, already guessing the answer to be a resounding *no*.

She rolled her eyes. "It is a good job. And I make decent money, especially with bonuses."

Jack stayed silent and nodded, as if waiting for a *but*.

"But it's not like I can afford to do everything I want. Maybe someday. That's the goal."

"You think you can reach your financial goals without a plan in place?" he asked.

His assumption and blunt question caught her off guard. "Well, I haven't really thought about what comes next."

His expression softened and he gave her a reassuring smile. "It sounds as if you are managing well but wish you had a better plan in mind. You are already successful. That's very clear. And you have an incredible amount of opportunities ahead of you. That's also clear. What you might consider is whether you want to continue to make a ton of money for someone else, or whether you want to begin building your own empire."

"Like . . . as a business owner? An entrepreneur?" Her voice cracked a little. She had zero desire to learn how to build a business. It seemed like such a huge investment of time, money, and heartache. She only knew one person in her family who owned a business, and he was always experiencing financial trouble. *No thank you*, she thought.

Jack shrugged his shoulders. "Someone ultimately makes the money from your hard-earned connections and excellent work. Why shouldn't it be you? I'm sure you could find a good use for more money than you're making now, right?"

"Well . . . yes. I could pay off my loans faster."

"Think bigger."

She took a deep breath as she thought. "Well . . . I could buy a place instead of renting."

He stayed silent, a sign for her to keep going.

"Uh . . . Oh! I could donate more money to an animal sanctuary I love." Her expression brightened at that. "And I'd travel more. Invest more. Volunteer more."

"So, what I hear you saying is that part of you making more money is the desire to take good care of yourself, as well as giving back to others and to causes you care about?"

"Yes."

"See? You're already seeking significance, like a true athlete-entrepreneur," he grinned.

Christina blinked, more confused than ever. But before she could ask a clarifying question about what an athlete-entrepreneur was, Jack looked at his watch and stood up to leave.

"I have to catch the subway, but it was so nice to talk with you. And congratulations again on your big sale today," Jack said, shaking her hand again. Then he reached into his coat pocket and pulled out a business card. "I'd really like to continue our conversation sometime if you're interested." He handed her his card. And then he left.

She looked around to see if anyone else had been listening to their conversation, but all the other patrons were absorbed in their phones or their work.

*What just happened?* she thought as she looked at the card. *And what exactly is an athlete-entrepreneur?*

His card read:

**Jack Merrick**

Success Coach

"Enhancing the lives of athletes after sport."

# 3

# *EVER HEARD OF A BUSINESS COACH?*

W here's the rest of your crew, man?" Derrick and Kai exchanged their customary hug-handshake combo.

"They're having a girls' weekend with Robin's sister and mom in Florida. Probably getting manicures right now." Kai smiled to dissuade any questions about his personal life.

"What?! Robin didn't want to hang with us this year?" Derrick seemed genuinely shocked.

"Said she wanted to visit family instead," Kai shrugged.

Derrick was the football athletic training student during Kai's junior and senior years, and they'd become good friends. When Kai graduated and moved to New York ten years ago, they'd kept in touch, and they always got a group of friends and family together for the alumni weekend celebrations. As Kai scanned the tailgating area and saw all his buddies and their wives and kids, it was clear that Kai was the only one who *didn't* bring his family along this year.

"So, what's up with work? That guy still making a mess of everything? What's his name—Richard? Chet? Harold?" Derrick pretended to adjust a fake monocle and raised his nose into the air to look as stuffy as possible.

"It's Bryce." Kai belly laughed at his friend's acting. "He's just a pain in the ass. Trifling and weak. I think his purpose in life is to annoy me. He's nothing like the coaches I looked up to for so long. Wouldn't even be able to survive as the water boy."

"I know some people like that," Derrick chuckled.

"Yeah, I mean my job is secure, thank God. At least I think so. Our division is doing really well. I've been working some long-ass hours making sure all our documents are uploaded in a new CRM, and I think by fall everything will settle down. Maybe I can finally implement some new systems and lead a team then, *if I'm allowed to*."[18] Kai rolled his eyes and took a long swig of his beer. "What about you? How's the new gig? Still love it?"

"I really do." Derrick grabbed Kai's shoulder and squeezed it in excitement. "It's my dream job and every day I'm thankful I get to head into the facility. It's not even work to me! Plus, that campus is gorgeous."

Kai made a mental note that Derrick's grip was as strong as ever. Maintaining the same imposing physique he had a decade ago, he'd undoubtedly benefitted from being around athletes and a weight room all day. Kai, on the other hand, had packed on thirty pounds, allowing his stressful career to take priority over his once-regimented daily workout and food-prep habits.

Derrick had accepted a head athletic trainer position at Georgia State University five months prior, and he'd only had the best things to say about it. Kai wondered if Derrick was in the honeymoon phase with his job. But it did sound like a great career move. Derrick's wife, Lachelle, was from Atlanta, and they were able to move closer to her family. Even better, their three young boys loved being able to see their grandparents nearly every weekend. That meant Derrick and his wife got to go on more date nights and even a few weekend trips. Kai was trying to remember the last time he and Robin went on a date night when his phone rang with a FaceTime call from his wife.

Kai excused himself from Derrick and answered excitedly. Mia filled the screen, showing off her purple glitter fingernail polish.

"There's my baby girl," he smiled wide, waving into the phone. "Your fingernails look so pretty! What color are Mama's nails?" Robin put her hand in front of the screen to show off perfectly manicured long, hot pink nails with gold-foil designs. "Looks good, baby!" Kai said, hoping for a quick conversation to catch up on the day's events. "What are y'all up to today?"

"We had brunch with Mama and Sissy at the beach. Now we're headed to the park to play and maybe go for some ice cream later," Robin said, now with Mia bouncing on her lap.

"Ice creeeam!" Mia clapped excitedly.

"Oh no, the sugar rush is coming," Kai chuckled.

"Hey, we gotta go," Robin said. "Say bye," Robin prompted Mia.

Mia waved and said, "Bye-bye," and then blew a kiss into the phone.

Kai mimicked his daughter's kiss back. "Have a good day, baby. I miss you," he said. Then to his wife, "I love you, Babe."

His sentiment was not returned.

"Bye," said Robin. Then she ended the call.

Kai looked over at Derrick, who suddenly seemed far too interested in his beer.

———

Two bratwursts, a half-rack of ribs, and five IPAs later, Kai and Derrick were relaxing in comfortable camp chairs under the tent when Derrick asked the big question.

"So . . . are you and Robin okay?"

"What?" Kai immediately took another drink. "We're fine. Why?"

Derrick lowered his voice a bit to make sure no one else heard their conversation. "Because she's not here with you now and she *always* comes to the alumni weekend. Remember when you said she was still nagging you about working too much? I'm just saying, I wonder if y'all might need some help."

Kai fought an unexpected surge of anger. "Help? We don't need help. I just need my wife to appreciate my hard work and to not be so damn cold all the time!"

Derrick kept quiet.

Finally, Kai relented. "Things just haven't been the same since Mia was born. I love that kid, man. She's my everything. I know people say marriage and kids change you. I guess that's right. And she might be an only child, too, with as little affection as I get these days."

"Maybe you *are* working too hard on something that doesn't feel right, man," Derrick offered. Kai raised an eyebrow at the accusation. Derrick put his hands up in defense. "Look, I'm not taking sides. That's not my business. But you do work a whole damn lot and have no skin in the game. Lachelle would be pissed if I worked the hours you do and didn't get rewarded."

Kai waved a hand, dismissing Derrick's words. "Gotta pay the bills. My parents harp on job security and sticking with a big firm."

"Have you ever thought about being a consultant instead? Doing your own thing? I've heard you can make a lot more money as a business owner and you call the shots. Develop your own team, and find a way to win. And *everyone* needs a CPA. Especially in New York City. You'd have plenty of business!"

Kai looked at Derrick like he'd sprouted horns and hooves. "Are you insane? The last thing I need right now is more stress, more work, more hours. Robin would up and leave me for sure."

Derrick thought about another approach. "Have you ever worked with a coach? Like a business coach?"

"No, why? What is a business coach going to do for me?"

"Might be nice to get the lay of the land from an outside perspective. If nothing else, it would probably help you with networking in case things *do* go south and you need to find another position."

Kai stared at his friend.

"I'm not saying that's going to happen. But you're a freaking genius with numbers, and you're a good networker. And I know you don't want to spend your whole career working for a damned idiot who makes your life hell. Your boss should be like your coaches: inspire you and make you better to fulfill your potential. Not crush your life. That's all." Derrick sat back, hoping his suggestion had landed.

"*Shit*," Kai chuckled. "I sure don't want to spend the next twenty years working with *Bryce*. Not even two more years! I mean, I could talk to someone, I guess."

"Cool. I know a guy. Name's Jack. Here, I'll text you his contact info. He's in New York too. Only works with people who are former athletes."

"Huh." Kai loosened up a bit. "That's a unique business model." Kai opened the contact card and saved it to his phone. "Thanks. I'll look into it when I'm back home."

# 4

# CAN'T TURN OFF THE DRIVE

Hey, that was an incredible corner kick!" Jane fist-bumped Christina as they strode off the field after the morning's triumphant game.

"Thanks! Bridget buried it in the back of the net so fast I didn't realize we'd scored again for a hot second."

Both women dropped down on the grassy sideline with the rest of the team, removing their cleats, sweaty socks, and shin guards. Only three weeks into the season, the Lady Jays were undefeated and were hoping to defend their championship from the previous season.

"Anyone wanna grab tacos at Sid's in a bit?" Jane asked a few teammates sitting closest to her. Sid's was the best option for fast, delicious, and inexpensive Mexican food near the field in Crown Heights. They prided themselves on having extra-strong margaritas.

Several yeses came back. Christina smiled. "Tacos are always a yes. Especially with a tall margarita."

"Plus, we have to celebrate your latest sale, Chris!" one of the players piped up, referring to Christina's meeting earlier in the week. Two of the other women clapped in congratulations.

She stood up and took a dramatic bow. "Why, thank you. A few more sales and I can afford some new cleats! And a looong weekend on a beach somewhere. I'm already working on the next lead."

She turned to face Jane, who was putting her gear in her backpack. "Hey, I wanted to tell you about a weird conversation I had at the coffee shop right after that sale."

"Oh? Another potential date? I hope he's better than the last dud. The Ketchup Catcher . . . that's a memorable nickname, you know? We could make a whole yearly calendar of all these epic fails!" Jane cracked herself up with the idea of a calendar of Christina's dating disasters.

"No, no. Not a date. This guy sitting at the table next to me. He overheard my sale and we started talking about what it's like to be an athlete and then graduate, and basically be thrust into the corporate world without much of a game plan."

Jane rubbed the back of her neck as the small crew started walking the three blocks to the restaurant. "Yeah, I know that particular pain. I didn't have a clue what I wanted to do, even with a degree. And neither did half of my graduating class, I'd bet. Half of them got married and started having kids immediately. I flopped around from job to job until I found something I really like, but it has nothing to do with my degree, you know?"

Christina nodded in agreement. "I mean, I have a marketing degree so at least I'm *kind of* using it now in sales. But like you said, I had no idea what direction to go in. I'd have loved to have a guidance counselor in college like we had in high school. Remember those?"

"I think that's called your academic advisor." Jane nudged Christina in the shoulder.

"Oh, I had one. But we only ever talked about which classes I should sign up for to get the degree I wanted. We never once talked about what I could use that degree for, or how to network, or even what kinds of marketing and sales careers were available. I felt completely lost for a while after graduation without any guidance or community."

Both women were silent for a bit as they walked, contemplating the huge transition that many graduates experience.

"I think I'd lose my mind if I couldn't play soccer anymore," Jane said. "No matter how hard my week is, soccer always levels me out and makes me feel like I'm on top of the world."

"Are we daydreaming about playing in the World Cup again?" Bridget caught up to the two teammates and heard the tail end of the conversation.

"I wish! I was just telling Jane I recently had a conversation with a guy about how hard the transition can be for athletes when they graduate or quit playing. It's a legit issue."

"No kidding. My cousin was badly injured during his junior year of rugby and it ended his career. Compound fracture and joint tears. It was nasty. He dropped out of school. His personality changed and he became reclusive and angry."

"Really?" another teammate asked. "That sucks."

"It's so sad. He was such an incredible athlete too. An all-around great guy. But I guess he lost all motivation and drive once he was hurt. He didn't know how to be anything other than a rugby player."

"You're right. That's not your typical coffee shop conversation." Jane leaned into Christina, circling back to their earlier communication.

"Not at all. The guy was super nice though. A little intense. Probably in his early fifties. He said he's a success coach and he works with athletes."

"Like an athletic performance coach for endurance?"

"No, more like a business coach for athletes. I think. He mentioned something about being an 'athlete-entrepreneur' but he left before I could ask him anything else."

She grabbed the business card out of her wallet and showed it to Jane. "What do you think? Should I reach out?"

Jane opened the door to the restaurant and the small group filed in, ready to celebrate the day's win with delicious food and drinks.

"Athlete-entrepreneur . . . like an athlete mixed with an entrepreneur?" Jane asked as Christina walked in second to last.

"I'm guessing that's what it means," Christina responded with a shrug. "Would make sense."

"Hmm. Well, couldn't hurt." Jane slapped Christina on the back and got in line behind her. "At the very least, you'll have another wild story to share after next Saturday's game!"

---

Later that afternoon, as Christina sat on the couch folding laundry, she thought about the conversation with Jack. He'd asked more personal questions than she was comfortable with, at least from a stranger in a coffee shop. But the term athlete-entrepreneur kept running through her mind. What exactly did Jack do? For some reason, she felt like she should reach out.

*I should at least look him up online*, she thought, putting her folded Nike socks in a neat pile on the coffee table.

Fifteen minutes later, she was even more intrigued. A quick Google search told her that he was a legitimate business owner—multiple businesses, in fact. He had a solid LinkedIn[19] following, and he'd been involved with the acquisitions and sales of several well-known companies. Then she watched two different video clips of him being interviewed where he specifically spoke about the importance of identity transitioning for athletes to help them bridge the gap between sports and what comes after.

He was passionate for sure. She saw the same intensity in the interviews that she experienced in person when Jack talked about not being able to turn off the athletic drive and lessons learned walking off the field of competition for the last time.

"Hmm," she said aloud, alone in her living room. She pulled the card back out of her wallet and put it on the coffee table, focusing on the phrase at the bottom: *Enhancing the lives of athletes after sport.* "What could it hurt?"

She sent a quick email to the address listed on the back of the card:

> Happy Saturday, Mr. Merrick. We met at Big Dripper
> earlier this week and I'd like to continue the conversation.
> By the way, what exactly is an athlete-entrepreneur?
> —Christina Bates

# 5

## SILENT TEARS AND SPOKEN HOPE

Robin heard Kai walk through their front door on the Upper West Side of Manhattan at seven o'clock on Sunday night. He rolled his luggage into the foyer and immediately gave Robin a huge hug. She hugged him back, burying her face in his shoulder. She was still processing her weekend in Florida with her family, and despite needing time away, she had missed him.

"Dad!" Mia heard her father's voice and came running out of her bedroom in her green dinosaur pajamas.

"My baby girl!" He turned from Robin's hug and lifted Mia high above his head, twirling her around.

Mia giggled and clapped as Kai started zooming her around the living room like she was Superwoman. Her beaded braids swayed and bounced, covering her face, and she laughed louder when Kai flew her over to the couch and gently dropped her onto the plush pillows below.

"Again!" Mia shouted with laughter as the two continued to play.

Robin smiled at the sight. For a moment, her little family was a happy unit again.

She'd had some hard conversations with her mother and sister over the weekend in Florida when Mia had been napping or out of earshot, namely about her homelife and Kai's ever-present moodiness. She was concerned about him but no matter how sweetly she tried to get him to open up and talk to her, he wasn't interested. He'd already scoffed at couples counseling the few times she'd suggested it. But the wake-up call for her had been harshly delivered two months prior when he'd come home from work so angry that he refused to go out to dinner for their long-awaited date night, requiring Robin to cancel their prized reservations and order in pizza instead.

Later that night, as she sat next to her husband on the couch in her black satin dress and perfect makeup, she couldn't help but wonder how things had gotten to this point. Seemingly unaware of her deep disappointment, Kai railed on and on about inter-office politics and the stupidity of the archaic processes he was being forced to use. He finally cooled down enough to acknowledge how nice she looked, but it was too little too late. She'd been looking forward to a nice night out for weeks.

Later that week, Kai was out with his buddies after work, like always, when Robin decided to tidy up their master closet before putting Mia to bed. She reached high up on a shelf to grab an extra laundry basket when she realized it had something in it. She carefully lowered it toward her and stared at an empty single-shot vodka bottle.[20]

*Dammit, Kai,* she thought. "What is going on with you?" she said out loud as she placed the basket on the carpeted floor, flipped the closet light off, and stormed into the kitchen.

Kai had always worked hard and played hard. It was how he approached life and it served him well in football. When he was out with his friends, they often put the same tenacity into partying as they did with sports.

As frustrated as he was with his work life and as frugal with household expenses, this created a lot of tension and more than a few fights. Kai consistently made excuses for his drinking and spending while directing snide remarks at Robin any time she wanted to buy a new outfit or get her hair or nails done. No matter how many times she pled her case, Kai never understood her perspective, swearing that he needed an outlet to reduce stress from work, even though he met his friends after work nearly every day for a few drinks and to shoot the breeze while watching sports across multiple TVs. By default, that meant the brunt of the household chores, including making dinner, feeding Mia, and putting her to bed, fell on Robin's shoulders. And she was sick of it.

Standing at the marble kitchen countertop, she considered several options. She could confront him about not being a college athlete anymore and ask him to grow up, or she could stay quiet and hope that he had a great anniversary night planned for the two of them. That would be the only way she'd allow this to blow over.

But the more she thought about the late-night partying and heavy drinking, the madder she became. She began to tally all the times in recent memory when he'd spent money on something frivolous and excused it away as something he needed, wanted, or deserved. Or when he'd made a big deal if she went shopping, even if it was for toys for Mia. She quickly lost count.

So why would he hide the vodka shooter? He wouldn't dare try to say it was a friend's, would he? But more importantly, what else could he be hiding? He was in control of the family finances and while they'd never been in the red, they'd had a few tight months. She wondered how much he was spending on numbing his frustration with alcohol.

Several years of pent-up frustrations came tumbling out of the recesses of her mind, one after the other.

*What should I say to Kai? Should I say anything at all?*
*Maybe I should give him an ultimatum—go to counseling with me*
*or I'm moving out until he figures himself out.*
*Could we move back home with my parents for a while?*

Awash in a barrage of thoughts and emotions, Robin stormed back into the closet and grabbed the bottle, placing it squarely on the dining room table where it wouldn't be missed when he came home.

She stood at the kitchen counter, watching her daughter who was engrossed in her favorite episode of a popular children's show in the living room. Robin took a deep breath and surveyed the house from where she stood, taking in all of the turning points and firsts that had transpired in this space since they moved in four years prior.

It had been their first home purchase together as a young married couple.

The space had witnessed the excitement of a positive pregnancy test and then the depths of despair a few months later with the unexpected miscarriage.

There had been Super Bowl parties, themed dinners, game nights, and also late-night fights over finances, miscommunications, and hurt feelings.

The second pregnancy test came packaged with both excitement and fear. The wall in the foyer still had a small spot of missing paint where the tape held one end of the sign for Robin's baby shower. She had been admitted to the hospital two weeks later due to complications.

Bringing a healthy baby home had been the biggest blessing. But the stress of life with a newborn and new expenses had only created more distance between them.

Robin began to cry silently, making sure Mia didn't hear her. This was not how she expected marriage to be. This was not acceptable. Not sustainable. Not healthy. Kai needed help. *They* needed help. Torn between all of the possible outcomes, she decided not to say anything to Kai and finally put the bottle back in the laundry basket in the closet on the shelf.

Although Kai tried to make up for his recent behavior, surprising her with flowers, their next date-night dinner was at a local sports bar instead of a nicer restaurant like she'd asked for. As they sat across from each other in a well-worn booth, he kept his attention largely on the big-screen TVs. She felt a sadness she could no longer dismiss or overcome.

In one last attempt to turn the night around, she pulled out a perfectly wrapped package from her purse and slid it toward him. He tore into it, ecstatic to unwrap a pair of expensive new sunglasses he'd been talking about. She had been keeping them a secret for date night, knowing he'd be happy, if just for a few minutes. And in her mind, that was worth the extra expense.

In return, he pulled a slightly warped envelope out of his back pocket. She opened it with one last hint of hope. He'd thought of her too! Was it a gift card for a spa day or to her favorite store? Maybe tickets to a show? Instead, it was a card that played a sappy love song when opened. He'd signed it, simply, "Love you, Kai."

"Thank you," she said with the best smile she could muster under the circumstances.

Kai squeezed her hand, then slid on his new shades and went right back to watching the game.

Minimal effort. Minimal cost. Where was his mindset? Wrapped up in his dismal work? That night she decided she was done with trying so hard to help him unpack whatever struggles he was going through.

She kept the topic completely to herself until the weekend she visited her family, instead of attending the alumni event in Texas with Kai.

On the Saturday night of their trip, after Mia was sound asleep, Robin was standing in her mother's kitchen while her sister, Sasha, was on her phone, researching times for a movie they wanted to see the next day before Robin and Mia had to catch their flight back home. Her whole family knew something was off—and had suspected marital troubles for a while—but knew Robin would share what was on her heart and mind in her own time.

Unable to keep the secret to herself any longer, she spoke. "I found a vodka bottle hidden in our closet." She kept her eyes focused on the countertop but knew her mother and sister were focused on her now, intently listening.

"I thought you said he promised to stop acting like he was in college and save money for a nice trip," her mother said, taking a few steps forward.

"He did promise!" Robin said, still looking downward. "I guess he lied again. I just don't know what's going on! He took me to a damn sports bar for our big date night and ignored me all night so he could watch his games. I got him those nice sunglasses he's been wanting and all he got me was a damn card! No apology. No acknowledgment that something is clearly wrong. All he wants to do is pretend he's still some big-shot football player! I'm sick of it!"

Robin's sister was at her side, a hand on her shoulder for support. But Robin kept staring at the counter.

"Things aren't getting any better and I don't know how to help my own husband. I think he's depressed but he refuses to talk to me. I can't say anything right! We end up yelling at each other and I know Mia can hear us. I feel like I'm failing as a wife. I'm losing him." She gripped the marble lip of the countertop to stay grounded, but then broke into tears, sliding onto the floor, a dam of emotions finally released. Her sister and mother instantly grabbed her and sat with her on the kitchen floor, rocking, crying, and wishing they could make her pain vanish.

After many tears and difficult conversations that night, the trio researched family therapists online and selected one they thought was best. Even if Kai refused to go to therapy, Robin was determined to get help for herself so she could be the best person, the best mother, and the best wife she could be under the circumstances.

After the rest of the family had gone to bed, Robin stayed awake late into the night, hoping that somehow, someway, things would still get better and that the great distance between them could be overcome.

She wasn't giving up on him. She hoped he hadn't already given up on himself.

———

Later that Sunday night, after unpacking from their respective trips, Robin joined Kai on the couch. Across the room, Mia sat at her little craft table, scrawling in her coloring book before bed.

"So how was the weekend?"

"Aww baby," Kai turned to Robin and placed a hand on her leg. "It was a great time. You shoulda been there. Lachelle made her potato salad again and Derrick brought his smoker. I could have eaten my bodyweight in ribs and wings!" He laughed, rubbing his round belly. "They all asked about you."

"What did you say?" Robin asked, feeling some remorse from not going as a family.

"Girls' weekend. No boys allowed." He turned away slightly, still feeling rejected from her choosing her family over the alumni weekend.

"How's Sasha and Miss Patricia? Mister Cole?" he asked, turning back to her. He'd always referred to his mother-in-law the same way her students lovingly referred to her in the many math classes she taught—and was still teaching—over her now thirty-five-year academic career.

"They're both good. Mama joined a gym and is doing water aerobics four times a week after work. She said Dad refuses to join her, but he likes her new swimsuits."

Kai laughed.

"But I didn't see him this time. Dad is still in Chicago for work for another week. And Sasha has one more semester to go before she's done with nursing school. She's going to start working at the local nursing home part-time."

"That's good. Good," Kai said, nodding. He stared off, still considering the conversation with Derrick about the coach, and whether it would be beneficial to talk with someone about work. He thought counseling was for weak-minded people but was intrigued by the sound of coaching. He had to agree that continuing to work under the current CFO, even for another year, was a terrible situation. Maybe talking to a business coach wouldn't be so bad. He hadn't felt like himself in a long time and wondered if his potential was being suffocated. Perhaps this guy could share some inspiration to put him back on track.

"What are you thinking about?" Robin ran her fingers through his curly hair, trying to reconnect with the man who had stolen her heart years ago.

"Oh, Derrick and I were talking about a business coach he knows who lives here in the city. D said he could see me doing my own thing consulting or running my own company. I don't know about all that, but I know I don't want to work with Bryce any longer than I have to."

"Ugh," Robin agreed. "We had an administrator like that a few years ago, remember? Thank God she left, but she sure did cause a lot of issues for a while. I think it's worth a call at least."

"Yeah. He gave me the guy's info. I might call him." Kai nodded to himself, still deep in thought about why a business coach would only work with athletes.

"Hey," Robin said, nudging him back to the present, "I think it sounds like a great idea. You should call. Never know what connections you could make. I mean, you're not happy at the firm."

"You don't think I'm happy?" Kai turned to face his wife, a little shocked.

"No. I don't. You always complain about work, about Bryce, about not being able to implement your ideas and processes and feeling like there isn't a team. And then you stay out late with your buddies complaining about work, numbing your feelings. And when you get home late, you complain about work to me!"

Robin crossed her arms and sunk back into the couch.

"I don't wanna fight tonight, Babe," Kai said, leaning over to kiss her cheek, hoping for an easy, uneventful night. She leaned away as he did so, and silence settled between them.

"Look. You're right," he finally admitted. "I'm not happy there. It pays the bills and then some, but I don't want to work someplace where I don't feel a part of a team chasing a championship. Every day is the same and it never feels like I'm making progress. The money is nice but it's not everything."

A small smile graced Robin's warm face. This was the first time he'd openly admitted his discontent with the CPA firm instead of merely grumbling about the many inefficiencies.

"Well . . . what else is there besides money?" she said, leaning in for a kiss, baiting his response.

"A queen for a wife and our beautiful child." He kissed her back.

"You gonna call the coach?" She gave him the look that said, *You'd better.*

"I promise I will call him this week."

"*Tomorrow,*" she nudged him.

"Tomorrow." Kai smiled and enveloped his wife in a big bear hug.

For the first time in what felt like months, the couple fell asleep that night without anxiety and signs of discord.

# 6

# *AN OFFER ON THE TABLE*

Two weeks later, on a Friday afternoon, Kai and Christina joined Jack Merrick at a corner table at a local diner. After introductions and pleasantries were swapped, Jack got right down to business.

"I've talked briefly with each of you, but I'm sure you still have questions as to who I am and why you are both here today."

Kai and Christina looked at each other, then back to Jack and nodded. Kai raised a finger. "And why you work specifically with athletes?"

"Good," Jack smiled.

"There's an epidemic that's affecting young businesspeople, former athletes, like yourselves, all over the world. It doesn't care about race, gender, social hierarchy, family of origin, or religion. And, specifically here in the US, I estimate that it's costing billions upon billions of dollars each year in lost revenue, in loss of purpose and motivation, in unattained dreams and goals, in strained relationships and broken families."

"Jeez," Christina mumbled, uncomfortably shifting in her chair. "What is it? What's the epidemic?"

"It's the very same thing you and I talked about in the coffee shop." She noted the intense gaze she'd witnessed weeks earlier, the same fiery spirit he embodied in the videos of his speeches.

"And what you and I discussed on the phone two weeks ago, Kai." Jack stared into their faces as intensely as any coach during a locker-room halftime speech, intent on getting his point across.

"It's the identity gap—what happens when an athlete's competitive days are done. When they walk off the field for the last time with no plan, no built-in community, no coach to help direct their path. Research says that 97 percent of athletes—*97 percent*—experience a loss of identity and need a longer period of time to adjust to post-sport life.[21] An overwhelmingly large percentage experience loneliness, difficulty in adapting to a new life, negative self-talk, and doubts. Athletes are used to the physical pain that comes from training, injuries, and exhaustion. But they're rarely equipped to deal with the mental pain that is created when that life abruptly ends and a new one begins with very little support or guidance. In short, they are not reaching their full potential— not in business, not in income earning, not in quality of life, and not in overall happiness."

Kai leaned forward, resting his elbows on the table and lacing his fingers together, contemplating Jack's words, offering a barely perceptible nod of understanding.

The Success Coach continued. "In the most severe cases, athletes who feel either hopeless or helpless to change their situation will choose to numb themselves with drugs, alcohol, gambling, or any addiction or distraction they can find that will dull the pain. Unfortunately, some end up in jail. Others will die by suicide."

Christina sat straighter in her chair. "I recently heard a news report that over the last few months, a handful of NCAA athletes have died by suicide. It's awful," she said. She glanced at Kai.

"I heard that report too. Sucks." Kai nodded in agreement. "I've seen that downward spiral happen to some of my teammates when they were done playing. It's like they didn't know who they were anymore.

A couple have been arrested for possession or other stupid things. Just doesn't make any sense to throw your potential away like that."

"I know I struggled with that transition after graduation. Thank God I didn't ever try drugs," Christina added, her expression tightening. "Although there was the occasional rager . . ." she muttered.

"So, Jack—what does this have to do with us?" Kai asked. "What does this have to do with business coaching? I'm not sure I'm following."

Jack smiled. "You and Christina are here because you both have immense strengths as former athletes—and current athletes." He smiled at Christina. "Once an athlete, always an athlete. And those strengths have gotten you fairly far into your early careers. You're each successful in your own right. But you're both disillusioned by your current work situations and you feel stuck with no real direction forward. Am I correct so far?"

Both Kai and Christina looked uncertain as to what the other knew about their situations, if anything. "Yes, I mean, since we last talked I've considered finding another job that pays better," Christina said.

"I'm not talking about another job, Christina." Jack leaned in, offering the slightest smile. "A simple *job* will never fulfill your drive and your gifts. Until you are the one steering your own ship, until you see the game of business, you will always feel discontent, like you could be doing more, creating more, becoming more. Like unfulfilled potential."

"Okay. But what does that mean?" She folded her arms and sat back, trying to understand the bigger picture.

Jack laughed. "I still get so worked up over this because it's my passion. But I can't expect it to be yours just yet. The two of you have both indicated that since the inevitable end of your college athletic experiences, you've struggled with a loss of identity and an uncertain purpose, a lack of high-level competition, and you miss being part of a competitive, like-minded community. You also dislike working for someone else, especially when you are not compensated extremely well or respected in the workplace." Jack looked specifically at Kai.

"I know that's right," Kai responded. He remembered his earlier phone conversation with Jack where he expressed his extreme displeasure with some of the unnecessary workplace politics he had to endure in order to do his job well.

Christina nodded. "That's fair. I do feel like I'm often running in circles at work without much direction. And my soccer league is great, but it's nowhere near the same level of competition or skill as my university team."

Jack nodded. "What I'm saying is that you can harness all of the incredible abilities and lessons learned over the many years of playing sports—and direct them into entrepreneurial pursuits instead of continuing to help your respective companies get further ahead while you're feeling more and more left behind."

He tapped the table with his index finger to make a point. "I run a program called an athlete-entrepreneur accelerator and I mentor ten people each year into becoming entrepreneurs by *acquiring an existing business*. I know for a fact that athletes have a head start when it comes to the skill set needed to succeed in business. Research proves it. Athletes are natural strategic thinkers. They have good negotiation and leadership skills, risk tolerance, adaptability, communication, networking, persistence, and vision. These soft skills are essential as an entrepreneur and a CEO. And I think you both have what it takes."

*Crickets.*

He knew they needed time to process the information, so he preemptively answered some common questions he'd been asked over his many years of coaching. "No, I'm not asking you to buy anything, pay tuition, or join a multi-level marketing company."

Christina smirked.

"And no, this is not an invitation to a cult."

Kai laughed out loud. "Damn, I hadn't even thought about *that*!"

Christina wasn't so sure. "What is an athlete-entrepreneur anyway?"

"Good question. An athlete-entrepreneur is someone who has built their own empire using the same tools, gifts, talents, and drive that sustained their athletic career. You are both here because I know you have an inquisitive spirit and the ability to succeed in the face of uncertainty."

"But why just us?" she asked. "I mean, I'm flattered, but what makes us stand out?"

Jack smiled at her confidence. "It's not just you. Of the nearly ninety former athletes I've had similar conversations with over the last six months, eight have already committed. I only have two slots left."

"Oh wow," Christina said. "You've been busy!" She tilted her head at the surprising statistics. Kai nodded in agreement.

"Hydrated and highly caffeinated!" Jack offered, grabbing his navy-blue insulated coffee flask. "I frequent every coffee shop within a twenty-mile radius."

"My buddy Derrick gave me your number. Did you talk with him, too? Why isn't he in the program?" Kai was curious now. He looked up to Derrick like a big brother and admired his passion and drive for his career.

"Derrick is a great guy, but he is a worker bee. Told me that himself. Some people need the safety of a predictable nine-to-five life. He's got a great thing going at Georgia State and he absolutely loves it. Nothing wrong with that. We need people like him just like we need people who have the guts to carve out a different life for themselves. People like you." Jack smiled.

"Not everyone is cut out to be an entrepreneur or uplevel their lives in a massive way," he continued. "When it comes to work, you have two options—you work for someone else, or you work for yourself and begin to build the kind of life most people only dream about."

Christina furrowed her brow. "I have an uncle who owns a detailing business, but he's always having money problems. Makes his family nuts."

"I'm not saying it's always rainbows and puppies," Jack said, leaning back in his chair. "I've lost in business before and it sucks, every time. But the highs of winning—closing a huge deal or helping other people achieve their financial goals in your business—you just can't beat it. And I can absolutely say I've won far more times than I've lost."

Jack saw that the two faces across the table still expressed concern, fear, and uncertainty. He recognized those looks of deep contemplation because he'd once been in their shoes, considering whether making the jump and doing the hard work would be worth it. It *was* worth it, of course. A million times over. This was all part of the process of coming to terms with one's doubts. But first, they needed to fully understand the offer, and the rules of engagement.

"So, let's discuss why *you're* here."

Kai took a deep breath. Christina straightened, ready for the catch.

"What I'm offering you both is the opportunity to join the athlete-entrepreneur accelerator program where you will learn the rules of the game of business and, ultimately, buy a company and run it as the CEO where you'll have a great salary and get shares in the business. I will teach each of you, and your cohort, how to purchase a business, scale it, sell it, and do it again. Along the way, you'll learn the importance of a strong mind, body, and spirit, the need for community, and why giving back is a gift both to yourself and to others. You'll learn how to go from being successful to adding significance. How to escape the rat race and achieve your true potential.

"It's a full-time commitment. You will be required to adhere to a structured daily schedule and a code of conduct, as well as study an in-depth curriculum. You will be spending your days learning across multiple areas, including mindset, identity, resilience, goal setting, communication, mergers and acquisitions, financials, and more. You will do this learning in groups as well as complete several hours of daily individual research and homework. The first three months will be especially tough. Think of it like business boot camp." Jack chuckled.

"Sounds like spring training for the brain." Kai smiled, liking what he'd heard so far.

"Not too far off, Kai." Jack nodded, "But it will require you to resign from your current positions. For the full two years, you will receive a salary but are required to acquire a business before the two years are up. The name of the game is acquiring a business as fast as you can. I've seen it done in less than six months."

Kai's eyes grew wide. He wanted to hear more but was already thinking Robin would never go for this. Too different. Too many unknowns.

"The first three months are spent primarily in the classroom. This is your test to see if you have what it takes to make the team. And then you'll be on the hunt for businesses to acquire. And if you are found to be underperforming at any point, you're cut from the team. This is not some offer to get paid well and sit around and do nothing. You have to earn your keep—through showing up consistently and early. Doing the work, the homework, the research, being engaged in the sessions and with the mentors and your peers."

Christina had so many questions spinning through her head that she didn't know where to begin or which one should come first.

"But if you stick with it," Jack was saying, "you'll be ready to buy your first business and scale it. Three to five years later, you'll be able to sell it for millions more than you bought it for or continue to acquire more businesses to expand your empire.

"If you're not interested, no harm, no foul." Jack held up his hands.

"And if you *are* interested," he leaned in, drumming his index finger on the table for emphasis, "I promise I will do everything in my power to show you how to become a successful entrepreneur, and to create your own future and fortune, instead of clocking in every day and knowing your talents are being optimized for the benefit of your boss alone."

"Do we have to move?" Kai asked, already calculating expenses and conversations.

"Not initially. The first three months of training will happen right here in NYC. If you ultimately decide to buy a business out of state toward the end of the program, depending on what kind of business it is, you might need to move."

Kai nodded.

"Where do we get the money to buy a business?" Christina looked uncomfortable. "I don't have *millions* in my savings account at the moment." A calculated risk-taker by nature, her sarcasm was a thin shield for her fear of the unknown.

"My team and I will buy it for you," Jack said, noting the duo's stunned faces. "I have a board that raises capital from investors to fund the search for businesses to acquire. It's becoming a popular alternative investment for the wealthy, versus venture capital, which is typically for early-stage companies, or growth capital, which is an alternative for large businesses. There's over twelve million small businesses planned to be sold by baby boomers. Investors see this opportunity.

"You'll also be writing a thesis on which type of company you'd be best suited to run. Then you'll do the research to identify one thousand of those businesses and begin reaching out to the owners, brokers, and others in the network to start the conversation."

Christina sighed. "That's so much information it's almost too much to consider at once." She was uncommonly stoic and perhaps a little pale.

"It's a lot to think about," Jack conceded, never breaking eye contact. "It's one of the biggest decisions you will make in your life. And that's not a cliché."

"What's the cost? To us, I mean," Kai asked. "This sounds good . . . but almost too good."

"No financial cost at all, other than making a big life change and trusting the process. I will demand your hard work. And it *will* be hard work, more mentally than physically. But part of the program is focused on fitness and nutrition. You can't sustain consistently high levels of mental acuity and continued focus without the proper fuel and daily movement."

"Our athletic trainer used to say you can't put cheap gas in a Ferrari and expect it to run well," Kai said, rubbing his belly—fully aware of the thirty-five extra pounds he'd packed on since graduation. "I could stand to lose a little." He smiled, thinking of how he'd practically lived in the workout room in college.

"You'll be a well-oiled machine in no time!" Jack laughed.

Christina was still on the fence. "Okay . . . but—but *why*? This just doesn't make sense. Why would you pay us a salary for two years of education and then buy a business for us? It's like winning the lottery without having bought a ticket, and I can't wrap my mind around it." She rubbed her temples. "That's . . . that's insane."

Jack let out a big belly laugh. "I've been called much worse!

"Look, the truth is that I've reached a place in life where I no longer have to work for a paycheck. And I don't say that to brag. It's simply the truth. I worked my ass off when I was your age and that allows me to live my passion each day, which includes giving back to young entrepreneurs. The model I'm going to teach you has only been taught to the elite business school students. But what those students often miss is the athletic education you received. Once I hit a certain threshold, I promised myself I would spend the rest of my time giving back to others like me. And it just so happens that I'm passionate about helping former athletes get back in the game. I can promise you that you'll never have another opportunity like this in your entire life." Jack tapped his fingers on a large leather zipper binder on the table to his right.

"No kidding." Christina stared at the wall beyond the table, finally allowing herself to contemplate a new reality.

"As athletes, we have to make quick decisions at times, but we do our best to mitigate risk and not make big decisions based on emotion alone," Jack said. "You do not need to give me your answer today. I want you to go home and think about it. Review all the documents. Weigh the benefits and the risks. Talk to your trusted circle of family and friends. And most of all, listen to that small voice inside. It always knows what to do." He opened the leather binder, pulled out two substantial legal-sized manilla envelopes, and handed one each to Kai and Christina.

Kai opened his, peered inside, and gave a thumbs-up before closing it again.

"When do we need to decide?" Christina asked, uncertainty lingering in her voice as she placed her unopened envelope on her lap.

"One week. Let me know by next Friday. And as I said, no harm, no foul. But I hope to have you on the team. *Both* of you."

# 7

# *A STEP CLOSER TO YES*

Later that afternoon, Kai told Robin about the meeting with Jack. As he suspected, Robin's reaction was less than favorable. But Kai had already reviewed the documents, reviewed the family savings and their expenses, and was certain that this could actually work. He knew he could say yes without taking a huge risk. He'd have to make sure Robin was on board though. There was no going forward without her buy-in.

As he pulled the now familiar documents out of their folder and placed them on the table, he detailed what each one contained and couldn't help but smile.

"You really do think this is a good idea?" she asked, curious but not yet convinced.

"I really do. Think of it like any other job offer, except this opportunity is extremely clear about expectations and timelines, risks and rewards. A program, a season, a championship to chase. I wish most employers handled their paperwork this way."

"I thought you said this was an opportunity to become an entrepreneur, not another employee." Robin searched Kai's expression for an explanation.

"Baby, the best route to entrepreneurship is through buying an existing business. The perception of starting something and making billions is just that—a perception. Think about it, 90 percent of startups fail and 60 percent of acquirers are successful. It's an unprecedented opportunity. I've honestly never heard of any program like this. I can't believe Derrick didn't say yes." He shook his head, making a mental note to check in with D the next day.

Kai began by walking through each document's purpose in detail and what it would mean for him as the mentee and for their family finances and the large expectations of his time. He would be required to invest a great deal of intentional hours and effort into the curriculum and coaching programs, and not unlike his role at the CPA firm, he might not be as available at home as Robin wanted him to be.

She wasn't thrilled about that. But she quickly admitted that she liked the idea of working toward financial independence sooner rather than later.

As Kai easily and thoroughly examined each clause and paragraph, he felt a passion he hadn't felt in a long time unless he was actively playing football or studying footage in preparation for the next game. He'd forgotten how much he enjoyed learning and teaching others what he knew, a gift he'd realized in graduate school when he was asked by several classmates to help them study for exams.

Somehow, this stranger in the form of a success coach had stirred up something in him that had been buried for years. Kai could feel his old self surfacing again—the spirited man who was going to change the world through skill and sheer determination. Who promised to always put his family first. If he made this program work for him and continued to apply the lessons and build relationships along the way, within only a decade's time, he figured, he and Robin's lives would be completely transformed. *A championship*, he thought.

They could buy their vacation dream home in the Caribbean, top off Mia's college fund, pay off their remaining medical bills, max out retirement accounts, have a healthy savings cushion, and face less financial stress. Robin could even retire from teaching. Maybe they'd have another child or two in grade school by then.

This was the excitement of something new they so desperately needed. Maybe it was the fact that someone else had recognized Kai as *still* being an athlete, which made him feel valued as a team player. Or maybe it was the ego boost from learning that Derrick, who Kai highly respected, had turned down the opportunity to work with Jack because he wanted to play it safe.

For the next three hours, the couple hashed through every financial concern and plan B they could think of. It would probably take a few years to reach their first financial goal of paying off their medical debt, but Kai believed he would be able to consistently bring in a higher level of income with a CEO salary and be fulfilled in pursuing his potential.

Robin volunteered to become a travel planner so they could take multiple vacations per year as they crisscrossed the world as a family. This is not quite what Kai had in mind, at least not yet, but he loved the way Robin smiled when she thought about what their new life could look like. "Cancun, baby!" she laughed, as she began dancing around the room, pretending to sip on a tall fruity drink with an umbrella.

By the end of the night, Kai and Robin had talked through a number of doubts and concerns. They ultimately decided that Kai should go for it, especially since he was certain he could easily and quickly get another CPA job if things didn't work out for some reason. He was willing to learn and challenge himself, to expand his horizons. And to commit to his part in upleveling the family goals.

He'd let Jack know on Friday that he was a *yes*. At least, he was 95 percent certain. They'd figure out the rest later, in terms of timing his departure from the firm.

## 8

# *GREAT ON PAPER, SCARY IN HER MIND*

**D**uring the half-hour bus ride home to Weehawken, New Jersey, from the meeting at the diner, Christina replayed the conversation over and over in her head as she tried to get to the root of her discomfort. Something just didn't sit right with her. It wasn't anything that Jack said about the mentorship program and the opportunity, but something she felt.

Could she really be an entrepreneur? *Sure.* She already had a flexible schedule and the ability to work remotely. She was basically halfway there, she thought. So, what was holding her back?

Back at home, she thought of her uncle who was always jumping from business idea to business idea but could never seem to grow or thrive without asking all of his friends and family for money. She knew she would never operate that way, so she couldn't hold on to that story as a reasonable example of why *she* shouldn't take a step forward.

She flipped off the TV and grabbed her journal. Sometimes when she had emotions or thoughts that needed to be processed, it seemed easier to put them on paper than to talk about them out loud.[22] She made two columns like she usually did when making decisions, dividing the page vertically in half. On the left she wrote *Yes: Reasons why I know I can succeed.* On the right she wrote *No: Reasons why I think I could fail.*

She started filling out the Yes column. Affirmations came to mind first, so she journaled a few of those.

## YES: REASONS WHY I KNOW I CAN SUCCEED

I want to be successful.

I am a leader.

I want to have a team atmosphere.

I want more flexibility with my time and the freedom to make my own decisions.

I am intelligent.

I'm a hard worker.

I'm great with people and with conversations.

I've never failed at any large work-related endeavor.

Next she started a column for no.

## NO: REASONS WHY I THINK I COULD FAIL

I don't know how to manage the financial or legal side of a business.

I have no experience in building company culture or a business team.

I don't know how to do the financial side of things.

I don't know how to source or vet a business opportunity.

I don't really know how to be an entrepreneur or what it entails.

I fear change and the unknown, especially when finances are involved.

I don't have a super healthy relationship with money.

Hours of reading and studying each week sounds a little overwhelming.

Will I have time to read all the books and other resources needed to learn?

I have a lot of doubts.[23]

As her thoughts started to spiral into panic on the page, she realized she needed to take a break. Logically, she knew that the root of all her concerns was fear. Fear of the unknown. Fear of the what-ifs. She even had a fear that if everything went incredibly well, her life could still be upended by success. And even though that sounded great on paper, it felt scary in her mind.

She began to pace around her living room, realizing she still needed two thousand steps to hit her daily count. As she moved, she remembered something she'd learned in therapy years before: that her fears were often an indicator of a deeper feeling—the feeling of being unworthy and unlovable.

She knew why those fears existed. She'd done enough deep work to understand that traumatic events in the formative years don't have to define your life as an adult. But still, the fear persisted.

Did she want to be successful?

*Yes.*

Did she believe she could learn anything she needed to in order to cover her blind spots and gaps in knowledge?

*Yes.*

Did she want a better quality of life and the ability to do more and save more?

*Absolutely, yes.*

She sat down, grabbing the folder from her coffee table, and opened it. She knew she couldn't make any decisions whatsoever until she had fully reviewed, understood, and then reviewed all of the documents a second time.

For the next two hours, she pored over the pages one at a time, flagging the most important areas with Post-it Notes and taking notes on a pad of paper for further review.

As she flipped the last page over into the face-down pile of reviewed documents, she was cautiously optimistic about the opportunity. The details were as clear as they could be, but her self-doubts and fear of the unknown were still clouding her view.

One of the requirements was that the mentees give up any vices before joining the program, whether it be drugs, alcohol, nonprescription pills, or any other coping mechanisms used for numbing and disconnecting. The mentees were expected to function at their very best. So whatever substances hindered their excellence would need to be stopped before joining.

Christina had never tried drugs but she did love a good margarita—or *three*—and often got tipsy when out with friends. It was when she felt she could truly be herself: fun, stress-free, and confident.

She stood to stretch her legs and continued pacing around her living room, letting her thoughts come and go. Could she lay off the alcohol for two whole years or more? *Sure, I can do anything*, she thought. But did she really want to? Alcohol made her fun, a version of herself she wished she was more often. It also added up mightily, according to her bank account, and in extra calories she was always fighting against in the gym and on the field.

She knew she couldn't say yes to an opportunity like this if it wasn't a "hell yes." Another helpful tip from therapy she used to gauge her genuine interests when making decisions: If it's not a *hell yes*, it's a *no*.

Jack's offer wasn't a full "hell yes" just yet. But she still had a week to decide.

Moments later her watch buzzed, letting her know she'd hit her daily step goal. She checked her phone and saw an invitation from some of her teammates to meet at a new tapas restaurant in thirty minutes. As she grabbed her purse and jacket, she decided she'd run this past a few of her friends over dinner and see what they said.

*I'll only have one drink tonight*, she thought as she closed the door behind her.

# 9

# *HEADS ARE ROLLING*

**M**onday mornings at Arthur Whitney were predictable, starting with an 8:30 a.m. meeting for all C-level staff, followed by a 9:30 meeting for managers. At 7:52 a.m. Kai was already at his desk, turning on his multiple screens, ready to push through another bland day when a coworker rushed right into his office, not even bothering to knock.

"Hey, Kai. Did you hear the news?" Camden's words held a foreboding tone.

"What news?" Kai said, caught off guard.

"Layoffs. HR has started notifying people. Jenkins and Sanders downstairs were already told to pack up their desks. I don't know what's going on or how many people will be let go."

Kai was stunned and spun around in his chair to face his friend. "We just finished the merger. Why would they be doing layoffs?"

"I don't understand it. Maybe the quarterly numbers aren't looking as good as we hoped."

Kai squinted, going over all the numbers in his mind. "Nah, man. They looked good as of last week. I checked myself! We're actually doing better than planned. This doesn't make any sense." Kai stood and began pacing his office, trying to understand what he was hearing. His anxiety heightened, his blood pressure rose. Beads of sweat began forming on the back of his neck.

"I don't know what I'm going to do if I'm axed," Camden said. "You know we just finished the kitchen renovation in the new condo, and I used my merger bonus to turn the spare bedroom into a California Closets dream space for Michelle."

"Oh nice. I'm sure she loves it," Kai offered, thinking about how much Robin would love a walk-in closet.

"She does, but we may be living in it and renting out the rest of the rooms to strangers if I'm on the chopping block."

Kai mentally tallied the funds in the family savings account, their checking account, his 401(k), Robin's retirement fund, and Mia's college fund. They'd be okay for at least three months, maybe four. He would have enough savings to cover six months, if they weren't still paying off medical bills. If he got a large severance package, that would make things easier for sure. But he still hated being caught off guard.

"I hope that's not the case, Cam. I sure hope not." Kai looked at his watch. "Hey, I have to get ready for the 9:30 meeting, but I'll let you know if I hear anything."

Camden nodded and exited Kai's office, heading down the hallway at a quick pace.

"Damn." Kai ran his hand through his now damp hair. He scanned his cherrywood L-shaped desk as he rested his forearm on the back of his office chair. He wouldn't need much time at all to pack up his things. Was he on the way out too? If so, how would Robin react to the news? Would this be a failure or a blessing? His eyes focused on the one framed picture he had brought to work—of their most recent family portrait taken on Mia's second birthday a few months back. He exhaled deeply, thinking about all the possible outcomes of the day ahead. He remembered the conversation with Robin and how just last night they were so excited for him to say yes to this new opportunity to work with the Success Coach. But he wanted it to be on his terms, his timeline, so he'd have more time to get everything in order. He'd have to see how the week went.

He made himself focus and finished running a few final reports for this morning's meeting. Every few minutes, he'd glance to his left, at the picture of his family, uncertain as to whether he'd be keeping his job. He'd survived the merger and even gotten a promotion, but he knew that didn't protect him. If anything, those who were newly promoted were often let go first because of the extra expenses of a higher salary.

At 9:20 a.m., Kai grabbed his laptop and headed down the hallway to the conference room. He could instantly feel the chaotic energy inside the room. He grabbed one of the few available seats left and nodded a brief hello to a few of his coworkers. Heated side conversations buzzed in the air as the group of managers waited for the CEO to walk in. Hopefully, there would be answers today. And hopefully, good news for Kai.

He looked around at the fifteen other managers. Not one of them looked confident. He took a deep breath and opened his laptop as the CEO entered the room and closed the door.

An hour later, the group of managers filed out of the conference room looking defeated, some angry, some scared, some completely shocked. The CEO had explained the layoffs were to remove the underperforming employees who remained from the merger and capitalize on the strong surge of new business coming in, thanks to the increased marketing budget. Letting go of a large number of employees during a surge of new business didn't make any sense, but Kai suspected there was a deeper reason, and this was the easiest explanation to disseminate through the company.

In all, thirty-two employees out of the 373 would be let go, and the emails, as Camden alerted Kai, had already started rolling out from HR before the workday had even begun.

Kai took a slow walk around the company to clear his mind, stopping at the snack machine along the way to grab his favorite sugary treat and a soda to help numb the anxiety he was feeling. He was only fifteen feet from his office when Camden rounded the corner, a full box of trinkets in hand, escorted by security. Kai almost dropped his snack.

"What the hell?" Kai said in disbelief. But Camden was not allowed to stop and talk. As he walked past his friend, Camden quickly leaned in. "You're safe, man. I saw the list."

"Keep walking, no talking," the grumpy security guard instructed as he tried to ensure Camden didn't speak to anyone else on the way out.

This scene replayed several more times in front of Kai's office over the next few hours until the large space was eerily quiet. Four people from his division had been laid off and abruptly asked to leave the building immediately. No time for goodbyes, tears, or conversation.

Kai was so frazzled he couldn't focus on his work. *How does he know I'm safe? What list?* he thought. He picked up his phone to text Camden and saw he already had three messages from him.

*You're safe.*
*For now.*
*See you later at Peter's?*

Kai almost did a double take. What list had he been talking about? He wanted to know who else was on the list and texted Camden back.

*Peter's at 5:30.*

He wanted to ask more questions but would wait until he could ask in person. No need to leave a trail of written communication about sensitive matters like this. But it did run through his mind. *What if they only kept me because I recently got a promotion?* What if there was a second wave of layoffs planned?

His work ethic was unmatched. He was always on time—most often early—and had only ever received praise for his stellar reports, his gift of numbers, and his ability to problem solve on the spot. And except for the one time a few years back when his former manager reported him to HR, he'd never had any notable issues at work.

Three years earlier, as a first-year employee, Kai had suggested a slight revision for internal processes and presented it to his manager but was quickly shut down and told he was wasting time by dreaming up fantastical ideas that would never work. But Kai was certain his process would save a great deal of time, and therefore money.

After the second time he received a swift no, he reached out to the CEO to present his idea in person. Kai's idea was accepted and put into process immediately, validating Kai's talents while making him a target for the manager's passive-aggressive disapproval. Kai had lived with that annoying rain cloud over his head, especially since receiving the promotion and directly reporting to Bryce, who was no better than the previous manager but had far more clout.

By 4:30 p.m., the remaining employees in the south wing of the building resembled scared mice, quiet as possible, working away on their computers and refreshing email constantly, hoping they weren't next. Kai couldn't stand it any longer. He messaged Cam that he was leaving early, grabbed his coat, and headed out.

He had to know the details of the layoff and if there would be a second wave soon.

By the time Kai exited the building, he was convinced he would never be safe at this job, even if he made it through multiple layoffs.

# 10

# *I CHOOSE ME*

On Wednesday morning, Christina sat in a tiny office in one of her favorite coworking spaces, preparing a slide deck for her next presentation. Today's sales call was basically a done deal. The buyer had already given her a verbal yes the previous week, and this call was mostly a formality to discuss numbers, fabrics, and colors.

Christina had received an email notice over the weekend that another sales member on her team, Shawn, was going to be joining this morning's sales call with her, alongside one other staff member, a back-office manager she hadn't encountered before. Christina assumed it was because she'd been doing so well at hitting her numbers, they wanted to use her as a teaching model. Shawn's numbers had been steady over the last eighteen months, but nothing spectacular.

She sat straighter in her chair as she thought about the good example she was setting for Peppley NYC. Maybe she'd continue with this sales path, after all. She should be first in line for a promotion with her consistent numbers. She contemplated this option while remembering the meeting with Jack and Kai. She had two more days to decide and plenty more time to review the documents again.

But right now, she was the star of the show.

Thirty-five grueling minutes later, she slammed her laptop shut with so much frustration, she worried she'd cracked the screen. She'd never felt more blindsided in her life.

As it turned out, Shawn had been brought on the call, alongside the other teammate, to take the lead and finalize the sale, stealing Christina's client right out from under her. She didn't even get to present her slide deck. After her opening remarks, Shawn and the back-office staff had taken over the conversation. It was instantly clear Shawn had been courting this client at the same time Christina was, and worse—he'd already received permission from the home office to make the sale without notifying Christina ahead of time.

As soon as the conference call ended, she had logged onto her social media accounts and after only a few minutes of scrolling, she found all the proof she needed. Shawn had been golfing with the head of the client's company over the weekend. *What an unprofessional, worthless weasel of a human, not my teammate*, she thought. *I'd like to go golfing with him too.*

She fantasized about all the ways she could thrash Shawn on the golf course, including using his face as a target for practicing her sand wedge, as well as tying him to the golf cart and letting it roll into the pond with the highest probability of snapping turtles.

Heated calls to the home office didn't help. Nor did the extremely tactful but factual emails she sent immediately after the call to express her great displeasure at what just transpired. "It's not even his damn client!" she said too loudly as she walked into an open workspace, drawing a few quizzical stares from the people around her, each working on their own laptops with headphones on.

Her heart rate had skyrocketed during the call and she realized she'd started sweating through her navy-blue silk blouse. As she headed toward the main exit toting her leather workbag with her laptop and folders inside, she sipped her lukewarm coffee and tried to focus on her breathing, watching her heart rate slowly lower on her smartwatch.

She'd heard about Shawn's unsavory tactics before but had never experienced them herself. Somehow he was never reprimanded for taking clients from other salespeople, although it seemed to happen several times a year. She suspected he had an "in" somewhere higher up in the company. Maybe he knew something he shouldn't and leveraged that knowledge to do whatever he wanted. He was, after all, an extreme suck-up—the exact kind of sleezy salesperson portrayed in every movie and comedy skit that made the viewer's blood boil. But right now, all she wanted to do was go home where she could scream into her pillows and regroup.

She texted her group chat as she stepped onto a car on the PATH subway and found a seat.

*Dinner plans anyone? I need a drink.*
*Bad day at work already?* Jane replied.
*Coworker stole a sale ON. THE. CALL.*
*What a tool!* another friend replied.

Thirty-five minutes later, she unlocked the front door of her loft across the river in Weehawken. She'd been able to calm down slightly during the ride. Once she'd worried all she could about this morning's call, she began to replay the conversation on Friday night with her friends when she told them about Jack's offer.

The majority of her friends had given positive feedback, especially after Christina shared what she'd seen online from researching Jack and from the documents he presented at the end of the meeting.[24] Bridget, always the pessimist, had even slightly warmed to the idea, finally admitting that if Christina started the mentoring program and didn't like it, she could always quit and do something else.

Just then, a notification on her phone made her skin crawl. It was an email from corporate. She learned she would be getting a 2 percent finder's fee for making the initial contact with the client, but not the 10 percent fee she should have gotten for closing the deal. On top of that, this wouldn't count toward her bonus since she wasn't given credit for the sale. It was an outright slap in the face. *These people have no idea how to lead a team*, she thought.

She wished she had two margaritas in front of her. She could practically taste the salty rim and feel her anxious thoughts starting to slow.

Right now, Christina was seriously considering quitting Peppley with a scorched-earth email response. But she knew not to make any decisions when she was mad, especially when they concerned finances or big life changes. She then contemplated what *quiet quitting* might look like if she stayed on for another six months or even another year. She'd still be able to make her quota by putting in far less effort than she had been—she was certain of that—but she could slowly pull back from being as present and vocal at work events, as engaged on work chats and inner-office email threads, and as communicative with the other sales team members about daily life. Especially Shawn. *The jerk*.

She pulled up the text chain with Jack and considered sending him a "yes" right now, but hesitated. *Not yet*, she thought, as she clicked back to her home screen and set the phone down. It was only Wednesday afternoon and she had until Friday to decide if she was all in or all out.

Alone in her cozy loft, she stared at her balcony from the couch and took a deep breath as an unexpected tear rolled down her cheek. Life hadn't quite turned out like she thought it would. It wasn't a bad life she'd made for herself, that's for certain. At thirty-four, she had a nice loft in a good part of town, a decent career, good friends, and a winning recreational soccer team. She took one or two vacations a year and enjoyed exploring the big city with her closest friend group, but there was always something missing, a melancholy truth behind the fun-loving, optimistic personality she tried so hard to maintain.

She thought by now she'd be thriving and in control of her career, a soccer mom, chasing a few kids around the field, maybe even coaching a team with her husband, and coming home each night to a rowdy house full of love and a few little faces who considered her to be their whole world. She and her husband would make dinner together, put the kids to bed, and then talk about their day together on the couch, thankful to have found each other and both willing to do the work it takes to create and maintain a solid relationship, something that *hadn't* been modeled for her growing up.

None of her relationships had worked out for one reason or another. Her picker was broken; that's what she told friends when they asked if she'd been on any good dates lately. She consistently chose men who were emotionally unavailable, narcissistic, or who didn't put in the effort that she did. Without fail, a few weeks or a few months into a relationship, the guy would have already started to pull away—about the time she'd just start to notice his behavior—and she felt like she had to constantly remind him she existed.

Texts wouldn't be returned. Date nights didn't happen unless she planned them. She'd drive across town to spend time with a guy, but he wouldn't make the effort to come see her. Again and again, the pattern would repeat—the same guy with a different face and a different name, but the same disappointment and heartache at the end. Just for once, she wanted to be someone's priority instead of feeling like a pretty afterthought.

Every once in a while, someone would ask if she'd considered adopting, or fostering, or choosing to use a donor and raise a child on her own. "You'd be such a fun mom!" they'd say. She knew it was true—she would be an incredible mother—but it was a sore spot. These people were always well-intentioned, of course. But she got tired of explaining that while yes, she *could* do all of those things, she really wanted the solid relationship first. And now, nearing her mid-thirties, she couldn't help but feel jaded by her experiences and frustrated that this huge life goal hinged on whether she met the right man—if she met him at all.

Part of her innate drive in this sales position, and business in general, was directly tied to the vision she held of what she could bring to her future family—joy, stability, and unconditional love—which was the exact opposite of what had been modeled for her growing up. She thought the more money she made now, maybe the easier life would be with a husband and children. More savings. More padding. More options for travel. More date nights. More flexibility for daycare, for school, and everything after "I do."

It had never occurred to her that she was enough, just as she was, without a hefty bank statement attached to her name or a ring on her finger. No amount of money could equate to the joy she found in celebrating the successes of her friends, or in her loyalty and empathy when someone close to her needed advice or wanted someone to patiently listen and hold space for them without judgment. The gifts of true humanity and compassion are priceless. Yet, she made herself a workhorse in the desire to please everyone but herself.

*Maybe if I made more money, if I were more visible with a different career, I might meet the right guy,* she thought as she readied to leave and meet her friends for dinner. This was a recurring thought she'd had for some time, although it was never as loud a voice as right now. *Maybe I should take Jack up on his offer. If I can learn how to buy, scale, and sell a business, my future earnings will be unlimited and I can lead my own team. But what if I'm not smart enough?*

As she passed the mirror in the hallway, she stopped and looked at herself. *Really* looked at herself. She knew she was too hard on herself, too critical of her own accomplishments while she played the role of cheerleader for others. If she really thought about how far she'd come, she couldn't help but feel an inkling of pride, even though it was bittersweet.

Her parents had never been as supportive of her as she hoped. Instead, she more often felt like she was only as good as her performance and was only praised and shown love when she did well. They had even tried to force her to continue playing soccer her junior year in high school when a long bout of untreated pneumonia resulted in a partial lung collapse during a game. Christina thought she might die on the pitch. In the back of the ambulance on the way to the ER, her mother commented to the EMT that she thought Christina was being lazy and trying to get attention.

After a battery of tests proved the severity of her condition, a doctor's note excused Christina for the rest of the season as she recuperated—not at home, but in foster care, having realized she needed space from her parents. She was able to regain her strength and her position for her senior year. She was even recruited to her top pick of schools, but she was never able to rebuild a relationship with her parents, nor did she want to. They'd cared more about their bragging rights based on her performance than about her health. It had always been that way. So now, she kept her distance, avoiding calls and dreading emails, returning home only once or twice a year for holidays, and keeping the conversation light. It was no wonder she had a hard time making herself a priority. She had never been one to others.

With this out-of-the-blue opportunity in the accelerator program, she knew she would experience a lot of changes—both in knowledge and in lifestyle. As a type A person who lived by her daily calendar, she didn't know what the exact outcome would be and that was unsettling. But did she actually need that security to succeed? It was an incredible chance to grow and expand beyond her safe container, and it would have to become her priority. Better yet—*she* would have to become her own priority. And in the process, she'd have to give up her relationship with alcohol.

She contemplated what would happen if she concentrated less on what she *didn't* have right now and more on what she was and could become, for her own sake. After all, her life was good, *really* good, and she knew she had the power to make it greater, if she chose to dig in, take calculated risks, and be open to the possibilities and opportunities ahead.

She read the neon Post-it Notes stuck to the mirror's frame, reminders to herself when she needed a pick-me-up before work, or after a long day. One read, "I can do hard things." Another read, "Life's gifts are abundant. Keep your eyes and heart open." A third, her favorite, read, "I am enough. I am more than enough. I am worthy of every good thing that comes my way."

"That's it," she said out loud, gaining her resolve and straightening her shoulders. "I choose myself. I am worthy of all of the opportunities and successes that come my way. I am ready to live my life for myself. I'm going to be in control. I'm going to be an entrepreneur. That's a full *hell yes.*" She stared into her own eyes, unblinking, until a confident smile appeared. *That's it. She's in there.*

On the walk to the elevator, she remembered seeing a recipe for a sparkling water with cranberry and lime and decided to order that instead of the usual.

A minute later, she stepped onto the sidewalk outside her condo. As she began walking to the restaurant, she pulled out her phone and sent Jack Merrick a text: "I'm in."

## 11

# DESPERATE FOR A NEW BEGINNING

**K**ai got home much later than usual that night after spending several hours at Peter's Pub with a few coworkers to talk through the day's layoffs and the possibility of whether there might be a second round soon. Although Kai was safe, at least this time, it was a wake-up call that he needed to commit to the athlete-entrepreneur program for the sake of his family's security.

He walked in the door just after 10:30 p.m. to a quiet house. He'd messaged Robin earlier and let her know he'd be late. She expressed great frustration for him missing the dinner he'd specifically asked her to make—chicken parmesan ravioli—so he wasn't sure if she'd wait up for him or not. With all the discussion about work, he'd forgotten all about dinner.

Only a table lamp was still on in the living room, and Robin was nowhere to be seen. Kai walked slowly to the master bedroom and saw her outline in the bed.

*Good, she's already asleep,* he thought. He didn't want to have to rehash the day's events this late at night or apologize for ruining their dinner plans. He was already looking forward to leftovers the next day for lunch.

He walked to his daughter's room and saw her asleep in her canopy bed. The outline of her humongous teddy bear sitting in a little rocking chair in the corner had caused him to jump more than a few times until he finally got used to its presence. It was a gift from his mother, Ann. Kai smiled recalling the scene as Mia ripped open the shiny gift paper to uncover a purple teddy bear as tall as she was. She clapped and then immediately dragged the teddy to her little play table for a tea party while the family watched, hearts warmed by the innocence of childhood imagination.

As Kai quietly walked the carpeted hallway back toward the main living space, he thought about getting ready for bed but realized he was so wired, he couldn't turn his brain off. There was no way he was getting a good night's sleep tonight, and there was no reason to wake Robin up with his tossing and turning. He'd been struggling with insomnia off and on for the last several months as his anxiety had increased. He knew he was under too much stress, but he didn't know how to process it other than to keep pushing forward and hoping it would somehow improve on its own. And it needed too soon. Otherwise, his doctor was going to put him on blood pressure medication.

He took a few steps toward the living room, planning to watch TV on the lowest sound setting, when he thought about his games. *I'm not going to get any decent sleep tonight anyway. Might as well enjoy being awake.* He'd been drinking to curb his anxiety and lack of purpose after Robin had gone to bed, unaware that she knew what he was doing. Unfortunately, it did eat into the budget, and their romantic dinner at a steakhouse turned into a far less expensive night at his favorite sports bar. He'd felt remorse about lying so he decided to keep it hidden for a few more weeks until his next paycheck.

He headed into their closet to grab the shooter. He was quietly feeling around on the top shelf for the box when the light flipped on behind him, catching him totally off guard. He stumbled and spun around.

Robin stood with arms crossed. She was visibly upset.

"It's not there," she said in an angry half-whisper, hoping not to wake Mia a few rooms away.

"What are you talking about?" Kai said.

"I found your vodka and I got rid of it. What the hell are you thinking lying to me about your struggles?" She closed the distance between them and pushed her finger into his chest as hard as she could. "We were supposed to use that money for our nice date night that you refused to go on! And why the hell did you ask me to make you dinner tonight if you weren't going to be here to eat it? You know damn well Mia won't eat it and I even made a double batch, cause I know that's your favorite!"

Kai, completely blindsided, couldn't think of a response fast enough so he stayed silent.

"I cannot believe you right now! That you would lie to me. To my face. And then take me to a sports bar and ignore me all night wearing the expensive gift I got you. Couldn't even be bothered to write a heartfelt message in a cheap-ass card. Six years, Kai! You still keep choosing your best friends at work over your wife and child, even though we just had a conversation about you stepping up at home!"

"Hold up, hold up," Kai said, waving his hands. "That card was $11.99 and what do you mean you got rid of the liquor? And you have no idea what I went through today at work! We had layoffs. What do you think about that!?" He spat the words back at his wife in hushed tones, trying to turn the tables and garner sympathy.

"Did you lose your job?!" she practically yelled.

"No, not this time. But I could be next." He shot the words back at her, hoping to garner some sympathy.

"Okay, but did you call that coach about the new opportunity?"

"What?" Kai faltered. "Not yet. I've been dealing with layoffs all day!" With the stress of the day's events, he'd completely forgotten about the Success Coach's offer. He was still marinating in the present, consumed with corporate chaos.

"You promised to call him, Kai. Maybe this is a sign."

"Look! I'll call him when I'm ready. It has to be on my time. My decision!" He stood tall, standing his ground. "Cut me some slack, alright?"

She took a deep breath, not an ounce of pity in her eyes. Only anger and a touch of sadness.

Finally, she spoke. "Kai, you are your own worst enemy," she said, looking at the floor.

"What? What are you talking about?"

She took a deep breath as she looked into her husband's face. "You are not happy. I am *definitely* not happy. You are frustrated at work. You're missing out on spending time with me and Mia and I'm tired of feeling like a single mother. I asked again and again for you to try counseling with me, but you won't, so now it feels like one more thing I'm doing without you." Tears began to fall freely from her eyes. "We talked about this new career opportunity and agreed it was the right thing to do, but you can't even make a phone call. You make promises you don't keep and make excuses to suit your needs. This is not working out."

"What's not working out?" Kai pressed.

"I can't do this anymore. I'm tired of trying. I need some space—and you need to get some help."

"Help? I don't need help. I need people to let me do my job and—"

She cut him off as she turned to walk out of the bathroom. "I need time to think. Tomorrow morning I'll take Mia to Aunt Ginny's for the rest of the week."

"Aunt Ginny" was a sweet older lady they'd met a few years back who had become like extended family, especially to Robin. She only lived twenty minutes away, but to Kai, that felt like Robin was taking Mia and moving overseas.

"Can we talk? Baby, don't leave! Let's talk it through," Kai pleaded, but Robin ignored him and went back to bed, pulling the covers over her head, unsuccessfully drowning out the sound of her crying.

Kai never got comfortable on the couch that night. As he predicted, he didn't fall asleep at all. He lay awake all night replaying every recent argument, and wondering when it all went so wrong. He knew he was in the wrong for lying about his struggles and breaking his promise to save money. He knew his monotonous job and lack of a team was weighing on him. He'd own that. But he still didn't understand why she couldn't just appreciate all his hard work.

He still detested the idea of counseling or therapy, even though Derrick had mentioned it too. "We don't need *therapy*," he remembered saying to Robin, the very word taking on the same condescending tone that children often use for broccoli. Now his pride was blinding him to the truth. He needed help. He hadn't been himself for years. And his stress levels and victim mentality were only compounding the damage.

Unwilling to give in or go back to the bedroom and beg his wife to have an uncomfortable conversation, he stayed on the couch thinking and trying to make sense of the situation until 5:30 a.m. when Robin's alarm went off.

An hour and a half later, Mia waved to her dad with one hand while dangling her huge purple teddy bear in the other as Robin carried her to the car and buckled her in. Robin never said a word as she walked back inside the house and returned a few minutes later with two full overnight bags.

Kai held his daughter's hand and tried to play with her as Robin started the car. He continued to wave at his daughter as long as he could still see the car driving down the road. Long after it had vanished, he stood in the driveway, frozen. What was he going to do? His whole life just drove away, and he let it happen.

He looked at his watch. It was 7:05. Time to head to work.

His actions were purely robotic for the rest of the week. Waking up, going to work, staying late, and drinking heavily every night to dull the anxiety and sadness. All this with minimal communication from Robin, despite his multiple efforts each day to get her on the phone or to at least have a video call with Mia.

On Friday morning at 6:00 a.m., his watch buzzed, his alarm to wake up from another drunken stupor. As he glanced at his wrist, he saw a calendar reminder: "Jack Merrick deadline, yes or no."

"Ugh." He let his arm flop back down beside him as a flurry of anxious thoughts filled his mind. With the week from hell, he'd forgotten all about Jack and about the opportunity of a lifetime to become an entrepreneur.

He checked his phone—no texts or missed calls from Robin. He wasn't sure what to think. Would she come back home over the weekend and try to talk things through? Should he show up unannounced at Aunt Ginny's and demand to see Mia and have a conversation with Robin? He'd seen the way Aunt Ginny could maneuver a cast-iron skillet, so showing up without notice was probably not the best approach.

A hot shower brought some clarity when he thought about the very real possibility of Robin eventually leaving for good if things got bad enough. That would mean he would miss out on so many more moments than he already did, and that crushed his soul. This scenario consumed his mind for the entire workday until he finally got home Friday afternoon just before six o'clock.

Still no word from Robin.

"Dammit!" he shouted out loud to an empty house, frustrated and unsure of what to do. "What is going on? Why is everything falling apart?" He slammed his hand down on the coffee table, shifting its contents by several inches. Then he hung his head low in defeat.

He was about to grab his newest trusty bottle of vodka when he looked over at the picture of his parents on the wall. "Thirty-three years," he said out loud. "How have you made it work that long?" He shook his head. His and Robin's marriage had started out strong, but he wasn't sure they'd ever recover this time. He hadn't told his parents what was going on, and like everyone else who asked, he deflected questions and said they were fine. Always fine. That's what football taught him. Be tough, be stoic, be fine. But they weren't anywhere close to fine.

He knew his parents would just be sitting down to eat dinner on the couch, like clockwork, no doubt watching one of their favorite shows. *Might as well get this over with*, he thought. As much as he hated to admit it to himself, as an only child, he needed his parents' wisdom and guidance now more than ever.

The phone rang a few times before Joe Stafford picked up. "Hey son! Good to hear from you. Your mama made the finest honey-glazed ribs tonight and I wish you were here to taste 'em . . . but there won't be any left!" he laughed. "Oh, and your mama says hello. So, what's going on? How's Robin and my grandbaby?"

Kai took a deep breath. "I don't know, Dad."

"What? What do you mean, son? What's going on?" Joe's concern was palpable.

After a long pause, Kai responded. "They're not here. Robin left me earlier this week and took Mia. We're not doing well at all."

"Hold on, hold on. I need to put you on speakerphone," Joe said, whispering to his wife, Ann, to turn off the TV.

Two hours later, thanks to some tough parental love and encouragement, Kai felt somewhat relieved to have told his parents the truth about his marriage and his personal struggles, but far more ashamed of himself than he ever had. He was embarrassed to be airing his dirty laundry to his parents, of course, but was glad to have their love and support. Before the family hung up, they all agreed on some action steps for Kai to take, and to have weekly check-ins for accountability and continued progress, no matter what the outcome.

One, Kai would find a counselor. He would go even if Robin refused to go with him at this point.

Two, he would quit drinking.

Three, he would reduce his bar time and find a hobby to surround himself with others.

And lastly, he would agree to the opportunity to be mentored by Jack Merrick. Joe and Ann understood the risk of quitting a managerial position at a CPA firm, but thought it sounded like a great opportunity for Kai to gain new knowledge, new skills, and a new perspective.

Kai promised he'd send the acceptance message to Jack as soon as he got off the phone with his parents.

After the text to Jack was sent, Kai took a deep breath and let out all the stale air in his lungs. *What a shitty-ass week*, he thought as he checked his text thread with Robin. Still nothing.

He looked at the bottle of vodka on his shelf. He knew every note, every scent of the drink by heart. He even liked how the bottle felt in his hand anytime he poured himself a double, which had been frequently this week. But if he wanted to save his family, and if he wanted to succeed in this new entrepreneurial venture, his vices were no longer an option.

Instead, he grabbed a bottle of water from the fridge and sat down with his laptop to begin researching counselors.

# PART II

# PLAYING AT A HIGHER LEVEL WITH 10 ELEMENTS OF MINDSET MASTERY

# 12

# *GAME TIME!*

**N**estled along the bank of the Hudson River next to Chelsea, the Hudson Yards project is considered to be a city within a city. And at the top of one of the largest of the dozen skyscrapers was where Jack Merrick did his best work, looking out his large windows to the busy city below. Over the last four years, he'd invested heavily into building out a full floor of office space to perfectly match his goal of providing the most state-of-the-art facilities for learning and athletic training. His organization had recruited top-notch coaches from all over the world, becoming a think tank for high achievers with athletic backgrounds who believed in a holistic approach to life and business—acknowledging that the body and mind needed to work at optimal levels for unparalleled success.

It was Monday morning at 7:35 a.m. when the first of the cohort began to file into the Success Company office. One by one, they were welcomed and escorted to an expansive conference room with whiteboards flanking the east and west walls, a huge screen at the front, and comfortable chairs around a large movable table. Having agreed, upon signing, to follow a strict daily schedule for the next three months, each of them had already worked out and had a healthy breakfast before showering and showing up prepared to learn.

As Kai entered, he scanned the faces, looking to see if he recognized anyone. In the corner filling her thermal coffee mug, Christina noticed him enter and offered a small wave in recognition as she walked over to greet him.

"Hey, I'm so glad to see you here! I was wondering if you'd say yes." She patted his arm, then blew on her coffee before taking a sip.

"I almost didn't. These last few weeks have been some of the hardest of my whole life," he admitted, scratching his head. "But telling my CPA firm to kiss my ass—*respectfully*—sure felt nice."

"Oh my gosh. I know what you mean!" she said, giggling at his delivery. "I was honestly nervous to put in my two weeks because I was worried about bonuses and whether I'll get all my paid PTO . . . but after I read through all the paperwork about a hundred times, I told myself I just have to go for it. It'll all work itself out in the end. And look—here we are!"

"Here we are," he smiled back. "Already sore before the day begins." He rubbed his left deltoid and winced.

For the next few minutes, the chosen group of ten mingled and made introductions, swapping brief backgrounds and stories. It was clear that they were all excelling in their industries. Just as fascinating was the multitude of sports represented among the group of six men and four women, including football, soccer, baseball, tennis, swimming, golf, rugby, lacrosse, and even one Junior Olympic track-and-field star. There was a visceral buzz in the room, a mix of nerves, excitement, and uncertainty. The one thing they all had in common was that they'd each taken a huge chance and left lucrative positions in the hopes of transforming their futures.

At 7:50, Success Coach Jack Merrick walked into the room and placed his leather binder atop a desk. The cohort quickly found their seats and pulled out their laptops, paper, and various writing utensils, ready to take notes.

"Who are you?" he began, pointing toward the mentees as he stood at the front of the class. His energy was impassioned and palpable.

"Ask yourself . . . I'll wait." He stood like a pillar of success, eyes wild with vision and drive.

A full two minutes of silence went by as Jack gazed deep into the eyes of the mentees. They could feel the fire in his soul and their knuckles were white with excitement.

Now he began to walk confidently through the room, his tone lowered. "This question is essential to your life. It is the cornerstone of everything you do. Without knowing who you are, you're nothing. You're lost. You have no identity.

"Finding our identity is not a mere act of self-discovery; it is an act of liberation. It is about having the courage to embrace our past, our failures, and our wins. We are the architects of our own identities, capable of crafting a narrative that resonates with our true essence." He hit his chest with his palm to the rhythm of the words he spoke.

"Each and every one of us is a kaleidoscope of experiences, passions, and talents. We are what we believe we are.

"Close your eyes and take a journey through your life. Focus on your thoughts, your feelings. And focus on your days as a college athlete."

The mentees closed their eyes and accessed their not-too-distant memories of athletic greatness. Some smiled, recalling their best moments. The camaraderie. The coaches. The game. Some furrowed their brows as if pushing through their hardest challenges.

"The 6:00 a.m. workouts you didn't want to get up for.

"But you did." The Success Coach pounded his fist into his hand for emphasis.

"Practice after class all day and you didn't want to go.

"But you did." He pounded his first into his hand again, this time louder.

"The conditioning at the end of practice you didn't think you could do.

"But you did." Another hit.

"Study hall on Thursdays when the rest of the students were out having fun. You didn't want to study.

"But you did." And another.

"The final hour of practice when you wanted to simply go through the motions.

"But you didn't." A hit.

"The coach in your face because you made a mental mistake. You wanted to give up.

"But you didn't." A hit.

"Remember those days?" As his voice escalated, the mentees relived their experiences as if they were in real time.

"It's who you were. You had passion, perseverance, pride, and an identity. You didn't accept excuses! Instead, you kept going. For your team. For your coaches. For yourself."

His tone softened. "Remember when it all ended? When you felt lost? When you thought your best days were behind you? Now open your eyes."

They did. Frustration, sadness, and pain registered on their faces, having grappled with their identities after sports.

"I'm here to tell you that you never lost that identity. That the identity as an athlete is a pillar of your life. It's who you are, and you should be damn proud of it.

"When I left the game of football, I was lost. I felt like I didn't have an identity. That my days as an athlete were my best days and I was a nobody. My anxiety peaked. My passions were gone. No season, no championship. I was going through the motions in life. And at the depths, I tried to take my own life."

Eyes watering with pain but shoulders tall with valor, his bluntness was shocking, yet necessary. The message connected with more than would openly admit.

"A coach saved me. Made me believe in myself, my athletic past, and my new journey in life. He worked on my mindset. Then inspired me to study the game of business. Made me believe I had a greater purpose."

His voice raised and eyes lasered in, he pointed at his heart, his soul. He had survived, transformed. They would too.

"I grew, bought and sold three businesses, and I didn't know a darn thing about business. I used what I'd learned as an athlete: my resiliency, my drive, my passion, my pursuit of excellence, my unwavering ability to keep going, my desire to be on a winning team.

"My life was saved. My identity was resurrected.

"I was an entrepreneur. But, not just any entrepreneur, I was an athlete-entrepreneur."

Again he looked into the eyes of the transfixed cohort. In the faces before him, he saw a renewed pride and determination.

"You're a unique breed, fellow athletes. You're a breed of individuals that keeps pushing when times get hard, jumps with excitement when a teammate wins, and sees the game of business like a sport.

"You have it within you, and you will thrive in this new identity."

The distantly familiar tone of a pregame speech brought an invigorating energy into the room. The mentees' blood was boiling with excitement.

"Mark my words. You will thrive in business and create the life of your dreams.

"As we embark on this journey, all I ask is this: Focus on the process, feel it, sense it, taste it. Day by day. Hour by hour. Nothing more. Nothing less. The Game of Business is built for champions. And you have it in you to be a champion again. You were born for this."

He regained his place at the front of the room. "You are athletes, entrepreneurs, and soon, you'll be athlete-entrepreneurs—the Champions of Business. This is your time. And now, it's game time. Let's get to work."

The ten students erupted into applause, some whistling and cheering as though they'd witnessed the most impactful locker-room speech.

Jack held up a hand, palm out. "Before I share anything else, I want you to know how lucky you are to be here. Each of you has been hand-picked for this program because I saw the soft skills in you that are needed to play at a higher level. In the face of uncertainty, you chose to step up.

"It's not easy to upend your life for a new opportunity, especially when you're in the running for a promotion. Or feel like you're just hitting your stride. Some of you have a family to consider. Some of you walked away from what seemed to be a dream position. But each one of you has made a stand for yourselves. For your futures. You are to be congratulated." The Success Coach applauded his students, who joined in for themselves and their classmates.

"I know one of your top thoughts right now might be how quickly you can become a millionaire. Not an incorrect thought. But not a complete thought. Think *bigger* than money." An intentional pause allowed his words to sink in.

"I want you to consistently expand your mind and your perspectives in search of new ideas, new relationships and partnerships, new solutions, industries, and technologies.

"Think about your *why* and what makes you unique. Why do you think you were selected for this opportunity when we turned down nearly *ninety* others?" He paced the front of the room again, making eye contact with each person. From the surprise that registered on some of the faces, it was clear not everyone realized how few people were offered this opportunity.

"What drives you internally? Again, money can be a driver, but money in itself is not the goal. The ultimate goal is *freedom*, not just money. What type of freedom does money make possible for you? All of you should want to attain financial independence."

He swept his pointer finger across the room.

"Some of you want to start foundations that impact millions and give back to your communities. That's great. Some of you might want to provide a different kind of life experience for your family and create a sustainable pattern of generational wealth. That's great too. There are no wrong answers here, especially when we take the right actions. And the right actions, while not always easy to make, are far easier to live with at the end of the day. That I can promise."

He grabbed his teaching notes from the desk. "You've all reviewed the daily schedule, the coursework, the reading assignments, and the timeline." His statement was less of a question than an expectation. Heads nodded around the room as the Success Coach pointed to a large timeline on the east wall that outlined the entire two-year program.

## TIMELINE & RESPONSIBILITY MATRIX

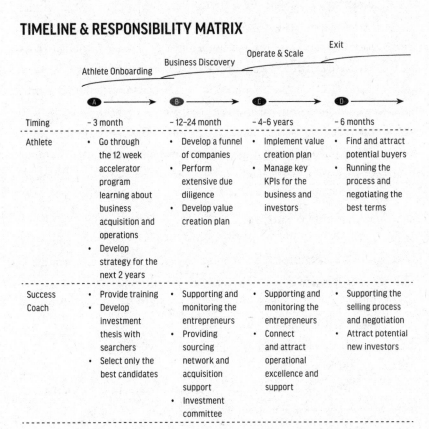

| Timing | A – 3 month | B – 12-24 month | C – 4-6 years | D – 6 months |
|---|---|---|---|---|
| | | Business Discovery | Operate & Scale | Exit |
| | Athlete Onboarding | | | |
| Athlete | • Go through the 12 week accelerator program learning about business acquisition and operations<br>• Develop strategy for the next 2 years | • Develop a funnel of companies<br>• Perform extensive due diligence<br>• Develop value creation plan | • Implement value creation plan<br>• Manage key KPIs for the business and investors | • Find and attract potential buyers<br>• Running the process and negotiating the best terms |
| Success Coach | • Provide training<br>• Develop investment thesis with searchers<br>• Select only the best candidates | • Supporting and monitoring the entrepreneurs<br>• Providing sourcing network and acquisition support<br>• Investment committee | • Supporting and monitoring the entrepreneurs<br>• Connect and attract operational excellence and support | • Supporting the selling process and negotiation<br>• Attract potential new investors |

"This accelerator program is specifically for athletes who are seeking to successfully transition from sport to ownership roles of business, by leveraging the skills developed in athletics. This first three-month course covers five modules of learning. Module 1 includes the ten mindset principles you must learn to hone your mental game. The mind is the most powerful tool you have, and we must perfect our thinking. Modules 2–7 cover topics like finding your niche acquisition target, how to source deals, how to assess a deal, due diligence, and negotiation. We'll rely heavily on the case method, and each of you will be expected to bring practical and current experience to the classroom and to the discussions and interactions."

The mentees looked ready, eager to learn.

"The reason you are in this room is because you possess characteristics that allow you to perform at a higher level over those without an athletic background. Athletes lead businesses and are great CEOs because of the education they learned in athletics, not the classrooms of their youth. The technical skills you learn in the classroom get you the job; the soft skills you learn in sports get you the CEO role. The Game of Business is in the mind; it's your most important muscle, and you've been training your mind as an athlete to win in business—you just didn't know it, until now.

"I am not only going to inspire you to win in business, I'm going to teach you how to use your skills to think like a CEO, buy a business, and transition successfully; I am going to teach you how to operate the business and become a champion again. The ultimate championship is selling that business down the line. My team and I will be walking with you for that entire journey. Showing you the training, the season, the team to win. But for now, I'm going to put everything you know and think you know to the test.

"First thing. You *must* be able to control your mind and not let *it* control *you*. Any questions so far before we begin the Mindset Module?"

Heads shook no.

"Perfect. Let's get started."

## 13

# MODULE 1:
# MINDSET MASTERY

The Success Coach surveyed the group of exceptional students before him. "The view you hold of yourself profoundly affects the way you lead your life. As an athlete transitioning to the energizing adventure of becoming an entrepreneur, your mindset is crucial. Where your thoughts go, your energy flows, so you'll begin this journey to success by rooting your mind in positive thoughts, behaviors, and outcomes."

He walked to the west board and wrote the word MINDSET in all caps, underlining it. "*Mindset* refers to the way you think about and approach the challenges in your life. It is your personal set of beliefs, attitudes, and assumptions that shape how you act, the decisions you make, and the actions you take. And no matter how long you've held a specific mindset, you can still change it and strengthen it.

"This journey requires a strong foundation to succeed. And that foundation starts here." He tapped his head. "In your mind. No doubt you learned about the mental game firsthand throughout your many years of sports. If you can visualize and embody your decisions, your beliefs, your actions, and your goals, you can achieve them far easier and faster than trying to *force* an action that is not aligned with your mindset. In this accelerator, you'll learn how to supercharge your mindset to achieve what few people can."

One of the students spoke up from the back of the room. *"Visualize then materialize.* That's what we always heard in the locker room and on the court."

"Yes. Exactly," the Success Coach said, pointing at her. "That's part of the reason why you spent hours studying videos and rehearsing plays before and after games. Your coach wanted you to review your performance and study the pros and cons, so you could visualize what you should do next.

"By a show of hands, how many of you have tried to force yourself to do something you didn't really want to do?"

A few hands raised. The coach pointed to the golfer, a young man with tightly cropped auburn hair.

"Coach, I've been wanting to learn Spanish for the last two years, and I'm using a language app every day, but I don't seem to be making a lot of progress with my lessons. Does that mean I don't really want to learn?" the golfer asked.

"What's your *why*? Why do you want to learn Spanish?"

"To be able to communicate better with people in the community and people in my industry."

"You might try maintaining the same goal but adding an exciting milestone to motivate you. What if you challenge yourself four months from now to take a vacation in a Spanish-speaking country and only speak Spanish? Would that be more exciting and motivating to you?"

The golfer smiled at that idea. "Yeah, I like that! Thanks, Coach."

The coach nodded at him in thanks and scanned the room to another hand, pointing at a young man wearing a polo and khakis.

"I've been meaning to clean out my storage closet for the last six months, but I always find other things to do that seem to be more important," the lacrosse player said.

"Shoot, my wife has been trying to make me eat better but you see how that's going," said the rugby player. As the short and stocky man rubbed his belly, the classroom laughed at his admission.

"Man, I know how you feel," Kai said, patting his own stomach as he elbowed the rugby player seated next to him.

The coach regained the attention of the class. "As several of you have expressed, desire isn't always enough to evoke the action you seek. By the end of this mindset module, I can promise you that you will be able to align your highest desires and goals with your actions, and be able to *think yourself* into the right mindset to achieve more in less time.

"You are fortunate. So much of what you need to be a masterful business operator has already been *subconsciously* acquired through your athletic training, as you will see in each section. In this program, you're going to see how those skills translate into real life and then leverage them in a way to increase your learning and success." He continued reading the room. "Know that I am here to guide you along the way.

"One last thing I'll say before we dive into today's topic. A healthy mind is *integrated*, influencing not only the multiple vital systems inside your body, but also your actions out in the world. Think of your mind as the coach, or the CEO, of *you*. And think of all your attributes as team members. All team members need to be on the same page to arrive at the correct destination. And don't forget, before you leave this classroom in a few hours for lunch, each of you needs to sign up online for your one-on-one weekly meeting with me."

The Success Coach then walked around the room, handing a thick workbook titled *Module 1: Mindset Mastery* to each person. "Every lesson going forward in this program *will* bring you closer to success, but only if you first dedicate time and attention to the ten principles of this Mindset Module. Please take a few moments to read over each principle as defined on the first page. We will be reviewing one principle a day in depth for the first two weeks of class."

## THE 10 ELEMENTS OF MINDSET MASTERY

1. *Growth Mindset:* Developing the belief that one's abilities can be improved with effort and practice.

2. *Self-awareness & Identity:* Understanding one's own strengths, weaknesses, and beliefs. This is the foundation for closing the identity gap.

3. *Health Mastery:* Prioritizing one's physical, emotional, and mental well-being.

4. *Success Mapping:* Setting specific, achievable goals (goal stacking) and creating a plan to reach them.

5. *Time and Energy Optimization:* Effectively managing one's time to maximize productivity and achieve goals.

6. *Focus through Liberating Restraints:* Turning constraints into opportunities to inspire creativity and drive innovation.

7. *Mindfulness:* Practicing being present in the moment and cultivating a nonjudgmental attitude. Deep dive into the neurochemistry of being present vs. a wandering mind.

8. *Gratitude:* Focusing on and appreciating the positive aspects of one's life.

9. *Emotional Intelligence:* Developing the ability to recognize and manage one's own emotions and understand others' emotions.

10. *Communication Excellence:* Developing the ability to understand your communication partner, paired with the art of being understood, getting what you want, and working with agreements vs. expectations.

"Will there be a test?" one student playfully asked. At that, a few of the students protested with groans as though they were in high school all over again.

The Success Coach didn't miss a beat. "Every day you're lucky enough to wake up is a test. An opportunity to win the game of life and maybe even get ahead. Let's see if you have what it takes."

Each of the students began to read the workbook, flipping through the material, flagging pages with Post-its, and making notes. And with that, the learning had officially begun.

## 14

# THE 10 MINDSET ELEMENTS FOR SUCCESS

## MINDSET ELEMENT 1 | **GROWTH MINDSET**

Most of the students had flipped to the first principle, "Growth Mindset," when the Success Coach invited the class to take a quick trip down memory lane.

"I want you to think back on your very first day of team practice. Picture yourself in your uniform, your gear. Maybe you were four, or seven, or twelve years old. Try to imagine how excited you were to be active while learning something new."

"Boy, I was fly as hell in my little football uniform and shoulder pads," Kai said as he recalled his first day on the field. Several others laughed, offering similar memories of their earliest years of sports.

The Success Coach chuckled, pleased with the class participation. "From day one, your coach began developing the belief within you that with effort, attention, and repetition, you would become skillful—be a good team player. Well, this is the theory of *Growth Mindset*. A growth mindset refers to the belief that individuals can improve their abilities and intelligence with hard work, practice, and dedication. And each one of you is living proof that a growth mindset works.

"On the other end of the spectrum, a *fixed mindset* is the belief that your talents and abilities are predetermined and cannot be changed, no matter how hard you work. And that belief creates a limited ability to learn and grow."

A hand went up. The Success Coach pointed to Christina, who was seated in front.

"Can you have both? I feel like in some areas I have a growth mindset and in others, it's more fixed."

"Great question, Christina. The answer is yes—you can experience both mindsets at varying times, but the goal isn't to achieve a fifty-fifty balance. Equilibrium in this case would cause stagnation. The goal is to continually work toward a growth mindset in all areas, even the ones where you may currently see minimal progress. The fact that you're aware of your growth mindset in some areas is a great indication that you're more dominant in growth and should continue to work on areas of stagnation. By the end of this quarter, you'll be seeing immense growth in all areas of life."

Then another hand raised. "Coach, do you think each person has natural, even genetic limitations regarding growth? For example, even though I won plenty of awards during my athletic career, no matter how hard I train now, I'll never be a world-record marathoner, let's say." The former Junior Olympic track-and-field star spoke confidently, and with a touch of cockiness. "So how do I know how much growth is even possible, and how much effort to expend on any given task or venture? At some point, reserving energy becomes important."

*Challenge accepted*, Jack thought. "You're not going to hold a world record in anything if you believe you can't. You have to start by asking the right questions, always looking for the possibilities and opportunities, instead of looking for loopholes that will excuse your lack of effort," the Success Coach offered. "You have to be curious each day, despite genetics and circumstances, instead of holding on to a fixed mindset."

The track athlete sat still, clicking his pen repeatedly, a nervous twitch.

The Success Coach wasn't finished making his point. "How old were you the very first time you walked out onto the track to practice the 200-meter hurdles?"

"Thirteen."

"Did you have any idea how fast you'd be able to run the event that day?"

"No."

"Did you still give it your best?"

"I did."

"And over the next few years, with consistent practice, did you steadily improve your times?"

"Absolutely."

"Even without knowing in advance how fast you'd be able to become one day?"

The man smiled, acknowledging his logic had been bested. "Thirteen-year-old me had no idea how fast I'd be at eighteen or how many medals I'd win."

"And still, you went out every day and gave it your best."

"Every day."

The Success Coach clapped the young man on the shoulder in approval. He smiled as he continued walking around the table of students. "That's all I'm asking each of you now. That you come out every day, give your best, and keep an open mind. Always look for the possibility of success, even when you don't know all the factors at play.

"A great example of a growth mindset is Michael Strahan, the former NFL player and current television personality. Strahan faced lots of setbacks throughout his football career, including injuries, criticism from coaches, and being cut from the team early in his career. However, he persevered and focused on developing his skills and abilities. In his autobiography,[25] Strahan discussed how he developed a growth mindset by focusing on his strengths *and* weaknesses, constantly setting goals for improvement. He learned to embrace failures and mistakes as opportunities for growth and learning, which is key.

"From your athletic training, you've already begun the journey. You've embraced challenges, learned from mistakes, sought feedback, and exhibited both resilience and persistence. These qualities not only made you successful in sports, but also prepared you for other areas of your life, including entrepreneurship."

The coach was on a roll. "It should be obvious to you that adopting a growth mindset can lead to a range of benefits, including improved physical performance, increased business success, and having greater engagement in all areas of life. A growth mindset naturally causes an optimistic outlook. You'll be more motivated and have less anxiety because you'll see, day after day, how your consistency pays off. And you'll be more resilient to any setbacks you encounter because you already know how to bounce back from those obstacles.

"Now look toward the bottom of page 2. You'll see a study published in the *Sustainability* journal that explores the relationship between physical activity, psychological well-being, academic performance, and growth mindset, specifically in college athletes, examining how growth mindset can potentially mediate the relationship between physical activity, well-being, and academic performance.[26] Studies have also found that students—athletes or not—who adopt a growth mindset perform better academically than those with a fixed mindset. That's because students with a growth mindset are more likely to embrace challenges, persist through difficulties, and view mistakes as opportunities for learning. A growth mindset is necessary in order to find success in this program!"

He paused a moment, allowing for the group to reflect. "Why do you think that is? Why do college athletes have a higher occurrence of a growth mindset?"

Several hands went up, including Kai's. "Kai Stafford, what are your thoughts?"

"My guess is that by college, we've grown accustomed to various learning styles, being coached and taught by multiple people. And we have concrete expectations of growth, both as a student and an athlete. We're basically getting a double dose of coaching and teaching where students who aren't involved in any sports or extracurricular activities are only familiar with teaching."

"Well said. Any other ideas?"

"Perhaps it's because we are used to a more structured regimen, especially if we began our sports as a little kid," said the swimmer. "I had to practice six days a week, even as a five-year-old, to make the local swim team. That ingrained the importance of continual improvement in me, even as young as I was. And I continued to build on it every year."

"Growth was simply a natural part of the process, as long as you continued practicing regularly?" the Success Coach prompted.

"Yes, that was certainly the goal. Quite a few kids dropped out each year, but I stuck with it because I loved the competitive nature. Well, to be honest . . . I really just loved collecting the colorful ribbons and medals." She laughed, diffusing any remaining wisps of tension in the room from the track-and-field star's challenge.

"So, what I'm hearing you say is that you'd like another ribbon to add to your collection at the completion of this accelerator program."

"Yes!" the lady quickly shrieked in response, startling even herself, causing the whole classroom to erupt in laughter.

After several minutes, the class was finally calm again and ready for the first exercise.

The Success Coach wrote the word DOSE on the whiteboard in all caps, underlining it twice for emphasis. "There are four hormones activated and released when we look at life through the growth mindset lens. An acronym to remember for this is DOSE.

"First, *Dopamine* is a 'reward hormone.' It sparks and enables motivation, learning, and pleasure. The effects of dopamine are short and sweet, due to its instant gratification feeling, which leaves you wanting more of it.

"Next, *Oxytocin* is a 'love hormone.' It enables bonding and care. Oxytocin gives you a long-lasting feeling of calm and safety. It can help fight stress, improve relationships, and promote positive emotions that endure.

"Third, we have *Serotonin*, the 'happiness hormone.' It blankets us with a feeling that everything is going well.

"And finally, *Endorphins* are our own naturally released opioids. They alleviate pain, stress, and depression.

"What I want you to remember is that a growth mindset is your secret play for overcoming any challenge or setback. Shirzad Chamine, author of the book *Positive Intelligence*, says that any challenge can be viewed as an opportunity if we ask ourselves an important question: 'What *three gifts or opportunities* might come our way because of our roadblock?'[27] This kind of questioning pivots our brain and body away from the common stress responses of fight-flight-freeze-fawn and allows us to focus on the solutions.

"One of the key researchers in the field of growth mindset is Dr. Carol Dweck. In her book *Mindset: The New Psychology of Success*, she explains how people with a growth mindset are more likely to achieve success in various aspects of life, and this includes sports—as we've discussed earlier—relationships, and entrepreneurship. She believes that when you've got a growth mindset, you're better equipped to handle your challenges because you view them as opportunities for growth and learning.[28]

"Today's exercise is all about celebrating your own success story, as well as celebrating the many stories in this room. You'll have ten minutes to write down your own success story, using pen or pencil—no computers or smartphones—including the specific actions you took, the challenges you faced, and the mindset you had throughout the process. It can be a story about when you achieved a significant goal, overcame a challenge, or learned a valuable lesson. Then you'll each have five minutes to share with the class while the rest of us actively listen.

"This is an easy first activity. The goal is to help you recognize the effort, perseverance, and mindset that led to your success by saying it out loud. I know each of you will be inspired and encouraged by hearing how your classmates and teammates have found success as well. After everyone has shared, we'll discuss the common themes and mindset strategies that are naturally present in these stories."

"Coach, should we focus on our professional achievements for this exercise?" the golfer asked.

"Great question. You can write about either a personal or professional achievement. Challenges are truly what makes life interesting, and using the power of your mind to overcome them is what will bring meaning and purpose to your life."

As the coach clicked the timer, the students began writing their stories. The only sound that filled the room was the rhythmic scratching of memories being transferred onto paper.

For the rest of the first day of class, the ten accelerator students shared their goals, their successes, their dreams, laughter, cheers, and a few tears. An emotional intimacy began to form in the small setting, creating a foundation for how the students would continue to show up for themselves and for each other over the next three months.

## MINDSET ELEMENT 2 | **SELF-AWARENESS AND IDENTITY**

On Tuesday morning, the accelerator students congregated a little longer outside the entrance to the classroom, having experienced a deeper level of connectedness the day before in class during the exercise. As the Success Coach stood to the side, having conversation with one of the cohort, he quickly scanned the room, reading the body language of his mentees. Shoulders were more relaxed. Classmates stood closer during conversation than the day before.

*Good.* He smiled to himself. *They're going to really love today's content.*

A few minutes later he walked to the front of the room as the students took their seats, ready for another day of learning and connecting.

"You've likely heard the old Greek aphorism, 'Know thyself.'"

Several heads nodded yes.

"How well do you think *you* know yourself? Since you now under-stand growth mindset, you're ready to dive into your own identity. As a self-aware entrepreneur, you'll be better able to recognize whether you have certain biases or limiting beliefs, and then take steps to overcome them. You'll also become more attuned to the needs and perspectives of others, making you better able to build strong relationships with your future customers, investors, and team members. You got a taste of con-nection yesterday by sharing your success stories with each other. Today, you'll learn that by understanding more about your own identity, you can harness the power of self-awareness, and unlock new levels of success and fulfillment in both your personal and professional life.

"When you think of your own identity now, what words come to mind?"

"A boy mom to twin toddlers," the swimmer smiled proudly. "Almost two-and-a-half years old."

"T-ball coach, baseball player, brother, son, and *former* VP of my family's business." The baseball player had stepped away from his fami-ly's freight operation to embrace this opportunity.

"First-generation immigrant, athlete, American dreamer." The ten-nis player had shared his success story the day before, having immigrated to the US with his family as a teenager, eventually competing all around the country before becoming a tennis pro at a country club in New York.

"Kai, what about you?" The Success Coach noticed early on that Kai wasn't as focused or talkative this morning and wanted to bring him back into the space.

He cleared his throat. "An Aggie, a proud man, a loving son, a loyal friend, and a damn good father," he said with the slightest touch of anger in his voice.

The Success Coach nodded, thanking Kai for his answer. "All of your answers are great. Your identity includes the characteristics, beliefs, values, and experiences that make you who you are. I believe exploring your identity *now*, once your participation in a higher level of sports has either ended or lessened, can have a significant positive impact on your well-being.

"The majority of you have experienced what is called an *identity gap* since leaving your sport. The last time you walked off the field of play or participated in your last competition, there was a feeling of loss, of grief, and for some of you, that experience of finality left a hole or a gap in your identity.

"How many of you have experienced that identity gap after sport?"

All ten mentees raised their hands.

"I tore my rotator cuff halfway through my senior year in college and wasn't able to heal in time to play our last game," the lacrosse player shared. "I'm still mad about it, honestly. I mean, we all know there's going to be a last game, right? But hopefully that last game is the last scheduled game, not one where you're sidelined from a bad injury."

"Absolutely," the coach said. "When an athlete's career is cut short due to injury or other circumstances, it can feel incredibly unfair, along with the normal feelings of loss.

"There are three components that contribute to your sense of self. A *personal* identity, a *social* identity, and a *collective* identity. Your personal identity refers to the unique characteristics that define you, such as your physical appearance, your personality traits, and your interests. Your social identity is shaped by your social environment, like race, gender, sexual orientation, religion, and cultural background. Finally, your collective identity refers to the parts of you that are shared with a group or community, such as a shared culture, a language, or a history.

"Think about your family of origin and where you grew up. You are also shaped by your cultural background, which includes cultural traditions, beliefs, and values that have been passed down through the generations and can influence your sense of self. Think about the values you adopted through your cultural upbringings. Some of these values may still serve you today. And some of these values may no longer serve you. You get to decide.

"Your family upbringing and other influences can also play a big role. Your parents, caregivers, and coaches instilled values and beliefs that likely shaped who you are today. They may have also had expectations around who they wanted you to become, even what college to attend, which degree to pursue, and what career to choose. Anyone experience that?"

A woman raised her hand. "My family told me from a young age that I was going to be a doctor or a lawyer. That's it. Those were my only two options. My father even refused to help me with college if I chose differently."

"What did you choose?" the former swimmer asked.

"Art History."

The class laughed.

"It's all good though. My dad is actually proud to have a daughter who is—or was—a museum docent."

The Success Coach continued. "Your personal experiences such as trauma, relationships, and accomplishments can also shape an individual's identity, just as she's shared. These experiences influence beliefs, values, and perceptions of your own world.

"What I want you to take away from today's lesson is that your identity is 100 percent unique, and is shaped by a wide range of factors. Understanding and exploring it is essential for personal growth, solid relationships, and business success, because it gives you a better understanding of your sense of self and the momentum to evolve. And we are always evolving. Being engaged and clear about your identity is one of life's greatest gifts.

"For today's exercise, I'd like you to get out your journals. I want you to reflect on your values and beliefs. What is important to you? What do you stand for? Who are you and what factors have influenced you along the way? Reflecting on these questions can help you to better understand your sense of self.

"And for those of you that are more visual learners, you can draw out an identity map, sort of like a mind map, but with different aspects and threads of your identity, both private and public. It's a good exercise to help you know yourself better and to better understand others.

"To begin your own identity map, draw a circle in the center of a page. That represents you. Then draw several spokes coming from the center circle that represent work and family roles, as well as social groups you identify with, such as your religion, social class, race, ethnicity, and gender. These facets can also include more personal characteristics such as your skills, accomplishments, physical traits, personality, and goals. You can continue making associations as many times as you need to fully represent a picture of your identity.

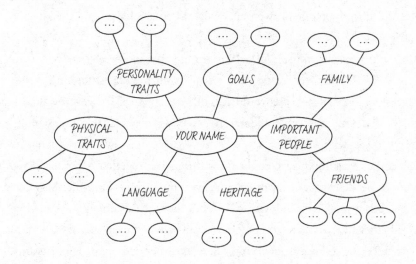

"Your homework is to take two online assessments: a Strengths Assessment, and the 6 Human Needs Narrative Exercise.[29] The Values Assessment you completed in the onboarding process of this program will help you understand the top two values and beliefs that shape your worldview. The Strengths Assessment will discover your top five natural talents and allow you to capitalize on them for growth. And the 6 Human Needs exercise will highlight what you need for a successful and fulfilled life. All of those are linked in your coursework. I also want you to complete your identity map before tomorrow's class. But for now, dig into who you really are. Journal silently for the next hour. No phones, no technology. Let your mind wander in this exercise, but not wander off."

As the majority of the students got to work writing about their identities, Kai was still distracted and unable to focus. After watching him for a few minutes, the Success Coach quietly approached and tapped Kai on the shoulder.

"Come with me," the coach said. Kai followed Jack down the hallway to his personal office. Spacious with floor-to-ceiling windows and a comfortable seating area with a personal library, this was where the Success Coach did his best thinking when he wasn't at home. He motioned for Kai to sit on one of two plush emerald-green chairs. And then he cut right to the chase.

"You're not yourself today. Anything you'd like to discuss?"

Kai folded over, resting his forearms on his knees, looking at the multicolored carpet. He wouldn't make eye contact. The coach waited.

"Last night my wife told me she's moving to Florida with our daughter to live with her parents *indefinitely*. I . . . I don't even know what to think. I was hoping we could work things out together. Robin said we both needed space to work on ourselves, but a thousand miles between us feels unnecessary. It hurts so bad, but the worst feeling is not knowing whether I'll be able to come home to my baby girl every night." He sniffled, trying to keep from crying. "She needs her dad, man. This is gonna break her heart. It's breaking mine."

Jack remained silent.

Kai finally looked up, tears on his cheeks. "I feel like a failure. I made this big jump for them, so I could provide a better life. A different life. Make sure they were always taken care of. The playbook, right? And I think it was too late. A lot of it is my fault. I've been lost . . . for many years. I was so unfulfilled in my work life and it bled into the home. And now . . . now that house is empty!"

"Kai, there are no magical words or advice I can offer you to make it hurt less. But you will survive. And children are resilient."

"Man, I don't know. I got to see Mia over the weekend. Took her to the park and to lunch and then for some ice cream. We had the best time." He smiled through tears, still staring into the carpet as if it was a movie screen replaying their dad-daughter date. "And when it was time to bring her back, she wrapped her arms around my neck so tight and said she didn't want me to go. Killed me, man. I can't do that for the next few months or the next sixteen years. I don't know how people do it."

Jack leaned back, thinking about his own experience. After a few moments, he decided to offer a rare peek into his personal life. "Twenty years ago, I lost myself."

Kai looked up, caught off guard by Jack's admission.

"I thought I had everything. I married my high school sweetheart, we had a baby, a home, and I was with a great company. The playbook of life, I thought. And when you give an athlete a playbook, you know what happens—we consume it, pursue it, and attack it with a drive no one else can match. I was wrapped up in the playbook, but it wasn't for me. I began to lose myself, my passion, my fire, my soul. I wasn't who I wanted to be. It affected every part of me, and I didn't even know it. I treated everyone like competition. My transition from sports into the real world was filled with pain, a misunderstanding of how to succeed in the business world, the real world, and who I was. I neglected myself, gained weight. And I continued to work too many hours on other people's dreams, not mine. But it didn't work."

"What did work? You're successful now, and you seem happy," Kai said.

Jack showed him the background on his phone. It was a picture of Steve Jobs with the quote: *Your time is limited, so don't waste it living someone else's life.*

"*This* work. The work you're doing now in the class with the group. This playbook. The playbook that gives you control over your destiny. All of what I'm teaching is what I had to learn to pull myself out of the funk. I had to unlearn all of my poor habits and learn how to be a more balanced person. To lean into my identity as an athlete and transition it into healthy business and life success. Growth mindset. And in control of my thoughts and my career, versus the other way around while learning from many entrepreneurs.

"It took time, several years in fact, until I finally felt like I knew who I was and I actually liked the guy. And while I wouldn't wish that on anyone, I can honestly say it was the tipping point I needed to become who I am today."

"What about your life now?" Kai asked.

"I am an athlete." Jack smiled with pride. "An entrepreneur. I want you to remember one thing: I am an athlete first, an athlete-entrepreneur: I pursue championships in business. I coach athletes who want to thrive in the game of business. I'm Success Coach Jack Merrick. Enhancing the lives of athletes after sport."

"I'm glad you found yourself. I'm sick of living like my best days are behind me."

"Kai, this may sound insensitive, but I mean it in the best possible way. This may be the very best outcome. This is how it's supposed to happen—there are no coincidences in life."

"What?" Kai recoiled at the statement.

"You cannot change the past. But you can mark this as the tipping point that changes your whole future for the better. You can create an abundant future. And you can finally be the best version of yourself. But you need to be happy with who you are, and the work you pursue. You need to write your own playbook. Find fulfillment and chase greatness again. Be the champion I know you are—*you* know you are."

Kai's shoulders slumped.

The coach read his mentee's body language. "It sucks. No doubt about it. But it doesn't have to break you." Jack placed his hand on Kai's shoulder in support. For the next few minutes, both men sat in silence. Finally, Kai sat up and wiped his face, erasing any trace of sadness.

"You still with me?" Jack asked.

Kai took a deep breath and straightened his shoulders. "Let's go! Win or go home, Coach."

With that, Jack put his arm around Kai just like his college coaches used to do. The two men stood and walked back toward the classroom.

———

After the journaling exercise was complete, the cohort freely shared some of their aha moments gained while brainstorming about their identity. Once more, it was a bonding experience, expanding on communication and trust.

"I'm glad you all found that exercise to be a positive experience. My hope is that you are all a little more self-aware than when you woke up this morning." Kai, along with a few others, nodded in agreement.

The coach picked up a wireless presentation pointer and clicked a button. Instantly an image of the brain filled one of the white-boards. "The concept of 'self-awareness' has intrigued neuroscientists for decades, and several regions of your brain play a critical role in this cognitive process. The prefrontal cortex, for example"—the coach pointed to the image on the board, then to his forehead and the top of his head—"is a region at the front of the brain associated with decision-making and introspection and with self-awareness. Next, there's the anterior cingulate cortex, a part of the brain involved in emotional control, empathy, decision-making, and our thoughts. When this is engaged, neurotransmitters like dopamine and serotonin fire up. Remember, these molecules are involved in regulating mood and motivation.

"Now that we have a better understanding of identity, I am giving you two challenges I want you to complete today."

"In addition to the homework?" the baseball player asked.

"Yes, in addition to the online assessments. And these are fun. First, I want you to seek out new experiences. Try new things that will help you explore different aspects of your identity. This can include trying new foods, traveling to new places, watching documentaries, or learning a new skill. It can even be as simple as listening to new music or going home on a different route. Since we're almost to lunch break, I suggest checking that off quickly by trying a new type of food. We have every type of cuisine you can imagine in the city!

"Second, it's important to connect with others who have different backgrounds and experiences than your own. Over lunch, I want you to get to know each other better, and go deeper than the typical surface-level conversation. You've all come from different backgrounds and faced many challenges to get to where you are. So, share some of that story today over lunch. A bonus activity in this area is to think about joining a group, attending events, or volunteering in your community in a way you never have before. Got it?"

"Got it!" the class echoed in response.

"Class dismissed. I want to hear all about your new favorite foods tomorrow."

---

As the students began pulling up different restaurants on their phones and getting into groups, Kai stood on the periphery, checking his text messages. He'd been messaging with his parents and his best friend, Derrick, since last night when he received the news from Robin about relocating to Florida. He was completely distracted when he got a tap on the shoulder and turned to see Christina and four other classmates.

"Hey! We're going to check out an Ethiopian restaurant in midtown. Would you like to join us?"

"Yeah! I've never tried Ethiopian before." Kai had been so distracted all day, he'd forgotten to eat breakfast. Now, as he tuned in to his body for the first time since waking up, he realized he was incredibly hungry. "Man, I'm starving!" He laughed and patted his stomach.

"Eating good food is one easy thing to check off your list today!" She nudged his arm with her elbow.

"Yeah, and I want to hear all about your football experience in Texas," the tennis player said to Kai. "I always wanted to play football but I wasn't big enough."

"I could talk all day about football, so be careful what you ask for! But seriously, I want to hear more about your background too. It must have been really hard to leave behind everything you ever knew and start over."

Minutes later, the group walked out of the building and headed to the restaurant. Sounds and smells filled the air as the busy streets of New York honked and hummed with life.

The basketball player was in front, walking with Christina and talking about her favorite museum tour moments, but Kai was ruminating on something the tennis player said in the elevator on the way down. Something so simple yet so profound.

The man had been talking about moving from place to place with his family when he was a young teenager, being under duress daily, being hungry, and struggling with uncertainty. But still, he was determined to remain positive every day.

"Even when there was no food, we were thankful for water. Even when there was no water, we were thankful for air. When it felt like there was no air, we had each other. And even if we lost each other, we still had ourselves. Since we were connected by blood, by experience, and by our faith, we knew we would never truly be alone. I chose every day to believe there was a plan for me and my family to survive. It was my job to wake up every day and discover it."

By the time the group walked into the restaurant, Kai had decided that although he had no idea how things would turn out with the divorce, it was his job to wake up every day, ready to discover what life had in store, and to focus on the positives as best he could.

## MINDSET ELEMENT 3 | **HEALTH MASTERY**

On Wednesday morning, the classroom atmosphere was electric with story sharing and energy. The cohort had done their homework and completed their online assessments. From shared conversations, some of the results were no surprise, while others were enlightening and cause for deeper contemplation and self-discovery.

"Did you learn anything new about yourself?" the lacrosse player asked the baseball player. "I was pretty close on what I expected my top two values to be and the strengths. But my human needs results surprised the heck out of me. I never realized how important it is to me to be able to share my knowledge with others, but apparently it is."

"Oh, that's a great discovery though," the baseball player said with a nod. "I guess that means you can be a better conversationalist now, right?"

"Maybe so! I'll definitely make more of an effort to actually listen to what the person is saying."

"Yeah, I have to say the values exercise was the most surprising to me. We had that huge list of values to choose from and I assumed my top two would be Achievement and Success or Responsibility. Something geared toward making more money." The baseball player looked perplexed, like he was still processing new information.

"What were they?"

"Connection and Making a Difference."

"Hmm. Well, that's not too far off," the lacrosse player offered. "If you think about it, it's the same type of energy, just focused on other people instead of yourself."

"You mean it's not all about me?!" the baseball player joked and slapped his new friend's back as the Success Coach walked in. Everyone soon found their seats, ready for another great day of learning and connecting.

"Good morning, everyone. I trust you have some new favorite places to eat after yesterday's lunch. Care to share any of your discoveries?"

The tennis player raised his hand. "A group of us got Ethiopian and it was incredible. The spices of the vegetables and meat were amazing. Very unique. I could eat that injera bread every day."

"You ate almost all the bread they had in the place!" the basketball player joked. She'd only managed to score one piece of bread to dip into the meats and vegetables on her plate while the tennis player went through three pieces, proclaiming it to be one of the best textures he'd ever experienced.

"And I have leftovers for dinner tonight!" he smiled.

"I tried sushi for the first time," the rugby player said as a few in the room gasped in disbelief. "I know, I know . . . I'm the last human in New York to try it. But some of it was pretty good. I ate the heck out of that crunchy shrimp roll." He shook his head, thinking about the three separate orders he placed for the same dish, one after the other.

"Oh, that's not real sushi," the golfer quipped. "You need some raw tuna."

"Hey, I'm baby-stepping here! My wife is just thrilled I'll touch seaweed now if it's swimming around in my soup."

The Success Coach laughed at the dialogue playing out. "And did you learn as much about your peers as you did about your taste buds?"

Most students nodded yes.

"I learned that more people are kind and genuine than I realize," the swimmer said, "and it's okay to be vulnerable. I won't die if I cry in front of people." Christina put her arm around her in a consoling hug. The swimmer's father had been recently diagnosed with ALS, and she'd shared about her family and her fears over lunch with a few of the classmates.

"It's nice to be able to have real conversation without a filter and without having to defend yourself," the baseball player said. "A few of us got together again last night to shoot the breeze. I was telling the guys about how hard it's been to walk away from my family business. The pressure. The expectations. My father is not even speaking to me right now and my fiancée keeps saying I made a mistake, so that's creating tension with us. I shouldn't have to keep defending my decisions. And I don't know how to manage other people's emotions, especially when they think I'm letting them down. It's been tough."

"Sometimes family doesn't understand," the Success Coach said. "They can't take the journey with us. They can be our biggest supporters, and other times they can be a source of our greatest frustrations." He looked directly at the baseball player, but the whole classroom absorbed the message. "You have to continue to trust yourself to make the best decisions for yourself."

"Anyone else have insight to share?" the coach asked, scanning the room.

Christina raised her hand. "My takeaway is that we're all doing really well in our lives, but at any given time we can feel like we're half crazy, or barely surviving, or failing, or we feel alone. And we keep all of that to ourselves far too often. I know I'm too hard on myself nearly all the time," she admitted. "I bet most of us are. It was nice to talk about how I really feel and hear that other people understand it because they feel that way too."

"Half crazy doesn't sound so bad," the Success Coach joked. "Sometimes the chaos we experience can turn into times of increased growth and creativity, if we intentionally direct our energies in that direction."

"Instead of into a bag of peanut-butter M&Ms?" the swimmer mumbled as she grabbed a handful of her favorite treats out of her large leather satchel.

"Hey!" the golfer next to her said, holding out his hand for an M&M. Then another classmate. And another, as the Success Coach watched, amused at the camaraderie developing among the cohort.

"Good Lord. I'm glad I bought the party-sized bag!" she laughed, as eventually every classmate was handed a few pieces of chocolate.

"Now that you're on a sugar high," the coach joked, "we're going to dive into today's lesson, which is self-care. And don't worry—sometimes chocolate can be considered self-care."

"Thank goodness," the basketball player smiled, still savoring her last piece.

"Leaving your sport and your competitive edge can be challenging, as we know, both physically and emotionally. For many formerly competitive athletes, that transition to a more sedentary lifestyle can lead to weight gain, loss of muscle mass, and a decreased overall health and well-being."

The swimmer crunched into her final M&M, intentionally making eye contact with the coach, her unspoken defiance in one bite.

"And, as we discussed earlier, the loss of identity and sense of purpose that often comes with retirement from competition often adds to feelings of depression and anxiety. So today, we will explore the importance of your personal self-care and provide strategies for maintaining your physical and mental health during your journey to entrepreneurship and beyond. For you as an athlete-entrepreneur, this is called your *health mastery.*

"There are five main challenges you face during and after this transition." The coach wrote "5 Challenges" on the whiteboard and underlined it, making a numbered list below. "The first are your physical challenges, which is when you may experience a significant decrease in your physical fitness."

A few rumbles from the class indicated some had already experienced this shift.

"Now, this is a judgment-free zone." He opened his arms to indicate the space of the classroom. "When you signed up for this accelerator, you agreed to live a healthy lifestyle, to have an emphasis on your nutrition, your time, and your physical fitness."

A few of the cohort looked a bit uneasy, the coach thought. While most of them worked out somewhat regularly, a few had walked away from keeping an emphasis on movement and healthy nutrition.

"But I do not expect you to get down to a 12 percent BMI. There are no weigh-ins. You are not required to drop a specific amount of weight or gain a certain percentage of muscle. Wherever you are right now is where you are. My only request is that you focus on being the best version of yourself for your own sake, and for your families. Because when you feel better and have more energy and focus, you can accomplish more and get it done faster. To be at the top of your game in business means your health and mental clarity are at peak performance. Staying active and engaging in regular exercise will increase blood flow and creativity in your brain. So, find something you enjoy and stick with it.

"The next challenge is mental. As you all know, the transition from sports can be mentally and emotionally challenging, especially if you've experienced a gap in your identity. In a synthesis of studies that focused on the post-sport transition of over eleven thousand athletes, the results were overwhelming—former athletes reported anxiety, depression, and feeling lost as a result of no longer having the training and competition they were used to. I think you can all relate to this . . . am I right? Well, today is the start of a new era, my friends. Going forward, to promote mental health, I want you to engage in self-care practices like mindfulness and meditation. Mindfulness is simply being aware of the present moment—what you think, how you feel, any sensations or thoughts.[30] And meditation, in simple terms, is being still and focusing on your breath, connecting with your mind and your body.[31] These practices work hand in hand and can help you process your emotions and develop a new sense of purpose and identity.

"Any questions so far?"

"Coach, is meditation the same as prayer?" the track star asked. "And do you have to sit still and be quiet when you meditate or pray? My ADHD kicks on in full force when I try to sit still and be quiet for too long."

"Good questions. Meditation and prayer can be the same. The term you use isn't important. It's the act of silencing the monkey mind and tuning in to your body. Some people consider that *prayer* and will seek guidance from their higher power. Some people prefer the term *meditation* and like to listen for internal cues from their body and intuition. And to your second question, no, you do not have to be still to meditate, although silence is helpful because you can listen without distraction."

"I like to go hiking in the parks on the weekends when I can and tune in to nature," the lacrosse player offered. "I'll be outside for hours but never speak once. I get really solid downloads in nature. That's my church."

The swimmer raised a hand. "I don't know if this counts, but before I wake my boys up, I like to sit for about five minutes and journal about what I'm thankful for and capture things I remember from the day before, and sometimes write out what I hope to accomplish that day. That helps me get rid of anxiety."

"That absolutely counts," said the coach. "Meditation can be whatever you need it to be. The more important thing is that you make it a consistent practice to have a time of silence to reflect on your inner thoughts and check in with yourself."

He wrote the next point on the board. "Number three is nutrition. This is a critical component of self-care and ties in closely with our physical health. Proper nutrition can help to maintain muscle mass, prevent weight gain, and reduce the risk of chronic conditions. You should aim to eat a balanced diet that includes lean protein, healthy fats, complex carbohydrates, and plenty of water. Dehydration can be sneaky and it will drain your vital energy. So, stay hydrated. Whatever amount you're drinking now daily, I challenge you to add twelve more ounces."

"Challenge accepted!" the golfer chimed in, raising the half-gallon water container he carried everywhere. A few others raised their mugs and bottles in playful solidarity.

"Number four is sleep, which is essential for physical and mental health. Athletes should prioritize getting enough restorative sleep each night. We're all wired differently, and each of you has a particular *chronotype*. A chronotype is your natural inclination to sleep at a certain time. You've heard of people who are an early bird versus a night owl?"

A few nodded.

"I'm definitely an early bird," the basketball player offered.

"Oh no. Not me." Kai shook his head.

"That's all based on chronotypes," the coach said, pointing at the basketball player to acknowledge her answer. "In addition to regulating your sleep and wake times, your chronotype has an influence on your appetite, exercise, and even your core body temperature. Understanding your chronotype can help to reduce stress and promote recovery from both physical and mental activities—and you're doing a lot of both right now.

"Your homework for tonight is to take a Chronotype Assessment[32] to learn more about your style of sleep so you can work with it, versus against it. This is also the time to create healthy sleep habits and establish a consistent sleep schedule. Avoid caffeine and alcohol before bed. And create a relaxing sleep environment."

"Do you recommend we skip alcohol with any dinner meetings?" the baseball player asked.

"That's up to you. Tune in to your body. Do you get a great night of sleep after one drink? Do you feel sluggish in the morning or less than optimal? Your body will always give you clues."

"Wait, I thought we had to give up alcohol," Christina whispered to the mentee next to her, who shrugged.

"What's the question?" the Success Coach asked, hearing a hushed voice.

"Oh, I thought we needed to quit drinking for the duration of the program."

The coach smiled. "You're asked to give up any vices. It's not specifically a mandate to stop drinking all alcohol. Only if you know you are using it as a crutch."

Christina nodded in understanding, wishing she could vanish.

"In many business networking circles, alcohol is involved," the Success Coach expounded. "The key is to use it to your advantage and socialize, but don't ever drink more than your network in these settings. I'll have one and I'll sip on it all night while the other person may have four. Alcohol can be seen as a socially acceptable connection point for conversation, especially in business. But I never cross the boundary to where it's influencing my personality, my decisions, or my conversation. That, to me, becomes a vice. Understood?"

Several people nodded, better understanding the distinction.

"The last piece of self-care is often the most neglected, as some of you have already shared this morning," the Success Coach continued. "Social support is key. Life after sports can be isolating, and it is important for athletes to maintain their social connections for mental health and well-being. This can include staying in touch with former teammates and coaches." He pointed to Kai, who nodded.

"It also includes participating in social activities and volunteering in the community. It's important that you seek out support from family, friends, or a mental health professional if you are struggling. There is no shame in speaking with a counselor, a therapist, your pastor, or a life coach. I have a coach and have worked with many others in a coaching or counseling role over the years. I hope you all know you can come to me with anything during our one-on-ones or anytime. I'm always here to listen and to help in any way I can."

The coach scanned the room for a brief moment, looking out at the people who were entrusting him with so much. He knew this work was difficult at times but also life-changing. He hoped he'd see all of the same faces at the end of three months.

"And now for a quick dose of science!" He pointed to the same picture of the brain from the day before on an adjacent whiteboard.

"When it comes to taking care of yourself, there are several brain regions and hormones that play a critical role in the process. Your amygdala," he pointed at the location, "a small almond-shaped structure in your brain, is involved in emotional processing and helps regulate your stress and anxiety, even during self-care activities. Your prefrontal cortex, a region associated with decision-making and impulse control, helps with planning and completing self-care activities, like journaling or hiking.

"Hormones like cortisol, oxytocin, and endorphins are also involved in the process of self-care. Oxytocin is known as the *love hormone*, and it is released during happy and quiet moments. It can help you feel calm and relaxed."

"Self-care and chill—that's my new slogan," the basketball player smirked as she slid down in her chair, pretending to be completely zoned out.

"I love it!" the coach laughed. "Now, on the other hand, when you're feeling stressed, your cortisol levels may rise, which can lead to chocolate cravings." He glanced at the swimmer in jest as a few classmates laughed. "But you can use self-care practices like mindfulness or relaxation techniques to reduce them.

"Lastly, endorphins are released during any times of self-care that involve physical activity, like exercising or getting a massage. They can boost your mood and promote feelings of pleasure. By understanding the brain regions and hormones, you can develop more effective health mastery strategies and experience greater physical and emotional health for your entrepreneurial journey ahead.

"Of all five main challenges we've discussed today"—he held up his hand and counted off *physical, mental, nutrition, sleep,* and *social support*—"which do you currently struggle with the most?"

"Sleep," the swimmer said. "The twins never want to sleep at the same time!"

"Nutrition," the rugby player said. "And my lack of physical activity."

"Ditto," Kai said, smiling at the rugby player.

"I'd say the social aspect," the golfer spoke up. "I'm a pretty social person but I don't talk about important things to most people. I'm a little guarded in what information I share."

"I definitely feel that way too," shared the baseball player.

"Sleep for me," said the tennis player. "I like to stay up late into the night. It's when I feel most alive. So, this has been a challenge for me. Getting up early every day and coming here to learn. I love it though. Maybe I can be an early bird one day." He smiled.

The coach nodded toward the track star for his answer. "I don't know, Coach. I'm pretty solid on all of these things."

"Is a lack of humility included in mental challenges?" the lacrosse player said from the back, causing the classroom to erupt into laughter at the track star's expense.

"I'm sorry, buddy. It was a perfect set up. I had to!" The lacrosse player got up and high-fived the track star, who acknowledged he'd been had.

"Okay, okay. I guess if I have to pick one, I'd say my nutrition could be better."

"My mental game could be better," the basketball player added. "I've definitely struggled with depression at times and with my emotions. But I'm thankful I do have a great support system."

"Glad to hear it," Coach offered.

"I'm gonna say social," the lacrosse player said. "When I tore my rotator cuff my senior year I didn't feel like I was part of the team anymore, even though I really was. They never made me feel that way—I made myself feel that way. And honestly, I've struggled to stay connected to a friend group or any kind of community since. I always feel a little like an outsider."

"Well, you're stuck with us now!" the tennis player said. "So, you have to deal with it."

Christina was the last to answer, still gun-shy from her earlier question. "Can I say I've struggled with all of them at different times?"

"Yes, you can."

"Then that's my answer. I've struggled in all of those areas at one time or another based on whatever is going on in my life and the fact that I didn't really *need* to have a strict schedule for my work."

"That's a very good point, Christina," the Success Coach responded. "Sometimes life allows leniency where structure could benefit us more. It's up to us to create a structure that supports our best self, our ideal life. Not just a good one.

"More than likely, all of you will have experienced most, if not all, of these factors at some point since stepping away from competitive sports. Life happens. Each day is different. Kids are fussy. Relationships change. Expectations change. Our bodies change. The constant in all of this is that we have the power to *choose* how to approach each day and how we *choose* to react to the world around us. We *get to* choose. The more often we make the same choices, the faster it becomes a habit.

"Who remembers the homework for tonight?"

"Chronotype Assessment," the golfer said.

"Right. And for your second homework assignment, I want you to practice mastering your health. Get used to the idea of self-care. Do something nice for yourself. It doesn't have to look like a massage or a long bath, although it absolutely can if that makes you happy. I want you to think outside of the box here."

"That sounds like heaven!" the swimmer said.

"Then make that a part of your self-care," the Success Coach said. "No one else can do your self-care for you. You need to intentionally block time out and be proactive in order to create consistency here. It's not selfish. It's a requirement. If you owned a million-dollar sports car, would you neglect your oil changes or the check-engine light?"

"Hell no," the rugby player chuckled.

"Think of yourself like a priceless sports car. Your self-care is your regular oil changes, except that you need them on a daily basis. Daily health mastery is essential for personal growth and development."

"Can types of health mastery include golf or working out or fishing? Or does it have to be more of a quiet or relaxed thing?" the track star asked.

"Do those things bring you joy? Do you feel refreshed and rejuvenated afterward?"

"Absolutely."

"Then yes. Your self-care will be unique to you. It should include practicing mindfulness, getting enough sleep, exercising regularly, and engaging in activities that bring you joy.

"Before we break for lunch, I have one last exercise for you to complete. In your journals, I want each of you to create a Self-Care Checklist of at least twenty items, containing both big and small acts of self-care. A big item might be a two-hour hike, a ninety-minute massage, or cooking a healthy meal at home. A smaller item might be ten minutes of morning meditation, five minutes of journaling, or even reading a chapter in a book. Every single day of the week, including weekends, I want you to do at least *two of the things* on your self-care list. You can always change it up as you discover more things you enjoy. But I want you to check them off as you complete them. This will help you identify and prioritize self-care practices in your daily life and track the progress over time."

As the students began making their lists, the coach focused on Christina. She'd mentioned alcohol a few times during classroom discussions and other conversations. He suspected she used drinking as a distraction or a coping mechanism. For what, he wasn't sure. But he'd wait for her to bring it up. After his own unhealthy dance with alcohol decades before, he knew it was only a matter of time before things started falling apart.

He also knew that the athlete-entrepreneur accelerator program was a perfectly good place to begin rebuilding a different life.

## MINDSET ELEMENT 4 | **SUCCESS MAPPING**

It was a chilly Thursday morning when the students filed back into the classroom, ready to learn. The Success Coach was fired up about the topic of goal setting. He was also curious to hear about the self-care lists the mentees had created the day before.

"Good morning, everyone."

"Good morning, Coach," came the echo.

"Who'd like to share a self-care item that you were able to complete yesterday?"

The tennis player was the first to raise a hand. "I took a long bath and slept soooo well."

A few in the class laughed as he continued. "Women always talk about baths but I don't hear men talking about them. They should! It was so nice. I even had my cold water and a little music."

"You just need a few candles and cucumbers on your eyes and you'd be set!" Kai joked, remembering Robin's bath-time routine.

"I'd eat the cucumbers with hummus," he laughed.

"I journaled and then went out to eat with friends," Christina offered.

"Went on a thirty-minute walk with my wife," said the rugby player. "Then had sushi. She loved it!"

The classroom laughed at the new convert.

"Listen, I'm a changed man . . . as long as it's fried!"

"One more example," the coach prompted, pointing a finger at the basketball player.

"I got my watercolor paint set out last night and played around with a landscape I never finished. I forgot how much I enjoy it. It can be so frustrating at times, but I love it."

"I'm so glad each of you were able to do something for yourselves yesterday that you enjoy. Even if there are times where it seems like self-care is one more thing to add on to your busy day, remember that it's a gift you're giving yourself, not a punishment. You are learning to make your time and your needs a priority.

"That leads right into today's topic, otherwise known as goal setting or success mapping. I know each of you have plenty of ideas about what goal setting looks like, as well as the benefits. But today we're going to dive deeper into the science and why it is an essential tool for your success. It's critical that you become excellent goal setters *before* you become business owners.

"As athletes, you are very familiar with setting and achieving goals in the context of sports. Those same principles can be applied to other areas of your life. In fact, research has shown that athletes exhibit higher levels of mental toughness, which includes resilience, perseverance, and optimism; all of which are essential to success mapping.[33] By setting clear, specific, and measurable goals for your life and business, you can stay focused, motivated, and on track toward your goals.

"There are four main points we're talking about today with goal setting." The coach walked to the clean board and made a numbered list.

"The first point is to understand why goal setting is so important for entrepreneurs, specifically. Any ideas as to why it's so important for them?" The coach opened the floor for feedback.

"You won't get to where you're wanting to go without a clear plan, and if you're running businesses, you need to know what you're doing each step of the way," the golfer offered.

"Well said. Setting clear goals will help you define your vision, and then focus your efforts toward achieving that vision. Goal setting also provides a sense of direction and purpose, which will increase your motivation and productivity. Setting and achieving those goals will help you to build confidence and momentum, leading to further success. It all creates positive momentum.

"The second point to make here is that to set clear and achievable goals, we follow the SMART criteria, which stands for Specific, Measurable, Achievable, Relevant, and Time-bound. You may have heard of SMART before in business courses. This means that goals should be specific and well-defined, measurable and quantifiable, achievable within a realistic timeframe, relevant to your vision as the entrepreneur, and time-bound with a clear deadline. Break larger goals down into smaller, manageable tasks to increase their chances of success."

A hand went up from the back of the room. "Coach, that's a lot of criteria to remember. Is there a format that's easier to use to keep all the goals in check?" the basketball player asked.

"Absolutely. In fact, that's your homework for tonight. Gold star for you!" the coach joked. He remembered how much his daughter had loved getting gold star stickers on her weekly chore chart.

"Next, it's important to learn techniques for staying motivated and accountable. Goal setting is incredibly helpful but if there's no accountability, it's far too easy to keep moving deadlines out. We need accountability and motivation from visual cues. One effective technique is to create a visual representation of your goals, like as a vision board or progress chart, to track your progress and stay motivated. We'll talk about that in a little bit. But just know that a visual and tangible list or representation of goals helps make your path clear.

"Starting tomorrow, we will begin a regular weekly review process to evaluate your progress and adjust as needed. I reserve an hour of my time every Friday afternoon to look back on the week, see what went well and what didn't, and make any necessary changes for the next week. I also review the upcoming week in detail and the following six weeks for any possible schedule changes. So, find what works for you and keep doing it."

"Coach?" the track star raised a hand. The coach nodded for him to continue. "How do you get over the feelings of dread at the end of the weekend? Some weeks I start dreading the next week on Saturday night and that can ruin the whole weekend. Sundays sometimes feel like one big stopwatch counting down the hours until Monday. I don't know if that has anything to do with goal setting, but you said *Friday* and it jogged my memory."

"Great question. And yes, goal setting can absolutely help with this. There are a lot of reasons people may start to feel low on weekends as the workweek approaches. But one that I've seen often in high-performing business executives is the anxiety of uncertainty, and that almost always comes down to being unprepared. We'll talk more about keeping an updated calendar tomorrow, but for now, I want you to imagine a scenario with me.

"Imagine that it's Sunday afternoon. This is the time you normally pull up your calendar and review your meetings for next week, looking specifically at Monday's schedule to see if any deliverables are due in the morning that you can prepare for now. But this week, you've lost access to your calendar. If it's a paper calendar, you've misplaced it somewhere. If it's electronic, there's a glitch in the matrix. You are unable to see your future meetings and you know several are crucial. How does that make you feel?"

"God, I think I have hives from just thinking about that!" the swimmer said, rubbing her arms and shuddering at the thought, to the amusement of several classmates.

"I'd probably panic a bit," said the lacrosse player with a hint of sarcasm.

The baseball player added, "I don't know, it might be nice to have a clear calendar!"

That warranted a few laughs while the coach waited for another answer.

The tennis star smiled, thinking he'd discovered the cheat code. "I'd already know everything on it because I always screenshot my calendar and keep it in my photo album in case something like that happens."

"But what if you lost your phone?" the coach responded.

"Vacation week, I guess," the tennis player shrugged and smiled.

The Success Coach smiled in return and made eye contact with the track star. "Does that exercise bring up the same kind of anxiety that you feel over the weekend?" The mentee nodded yes.

"I can guarantee you that once you start a routine of goal setting and reviewing progress, that will decrease the anxiety you feel. I also suspect that sometimes that feeling of dread is because you don't really love your career or the tasks that are filling your week." The coach scanned the room and saw a few nods in agreement.

"Let's quickly review some science before we get into today's exercise." He walked to a board with an illustration of the brain. "As we've talked about, the prefrontal cortex, that region at the front of your brain, is responsible for planning, decision-making, and impulse control. The hippocampus, a part of your brain involved in memory and learning, will help you remember your goals and develop strategies to achieve them.

"Your hormones, dopamine and serotonin, play a huge role in the goal-setting process. Dopamine is released when you experience a reward or sense of accomplishment. And as we learned earlier, that provides motivation and encouragement for you to keep working toward your goals.

"Lower levels of serotonin are linked to depression and feelings of low motivation. But you can boost your serotonin levels through exercise and exposure to sunlight. Remember, that's part of self-care—to get outside, even if it's standing on the sidewalk in the sun for a few minutes each day. By understanding how to regulate your hormones, you can set and achieve goals more effectively and efficiently, leading to greater success and fulfillment in your personal and professional life.

"So, who remembers what SMART stands for?"

Christina answered while reading her notes. "SMART stands for specific, measurable, achievable, relevant, and time-bound."

"Perfect," the coach smiled. "And what are some techniques for staying motivated and accountable when it comes to achieving goals? What techniques have *you* successfully used?"

"I like to give myself challenges and rewards," Christina said. "Like, this past Saturday, I wanted to get done with all my housework early so I could go watch a friend's soccer match before mine."

"What was the specific challenge and how did you accomplish it?"

"The game started at 9:15 so I needed to be out the door by 8:30. I gave myself two hours to do laundry, dishes, trash, recycling, and order groceries online. I set my alarm for 5:45 so I'd have time for a shower and breakfast. And the night before, I laid all my soccer gear out."

"Well done! So, you have a dual reward—you saw your friend play and you came home to a clean house."

"Exactly!" she smiled.

"Anyone else have a technique to share?" the coach asked.

"I'm running a 5K in a few weeks and I want to beat my previous best time," the golfer said. "I'm tracking my time and mileage on a calendar so I can see progress. And if I'm able to beat my time—"

"When," the coach corrected him. "*When* you beat your time. Not if."

The golfer smiled at the helpful yet subtle correction. "*When* I beat my time, I'm getting a new smartwatch."

"That's an excellent reward and I love that you're already using SMART goals to track your progress. What I want you all to do for today's exercise is to create a Goal Map." The coach grabbed a stack of handouts and delivered them to the mentees.

"I want you to create a visual representation of your goals and identify the steps you need to take to achieve them. These could include career aspirations, personal achievements, or lifestyle changes. And once you have your goals and steps identified, you'll give them dates and times for completion.

The Success Coach walked to a whiteboard and drew a large circle.

"Draw a circle in the center of your piece of paper and write your ultimate goal inside. Then, draw spokes radiating out from the circle and on each spoke, write smaller goals that lead up to the ultimate goal. A great example is running a half-marathon." He wrote *half-marathon* in the center and pointed to the golfer to acknowledge his upcoming race. "If my goal is to run a half-marathon, one of my smaller goals can be to run a 5K. And in order to run my best time at a 5K, I need to start running several times a week so I can practice my pacing and increase my endurance. I might also need to purchase new shoes. New running shoes sound great but they won't magically appear at your house. Or, start drinking more water daily. Whatever your goal is, break it down into specific action steps and smaller goals that you need to take in order to achieve the ultimate goal.

"I also want you to identify any potential obstacles or challenges that you may face, and brainstorm ways to overcome them. Once you've written out the main goal and all of the smaller goals to help you get there, turn them into tasks with dates and put them on your calendar. Each of these goals and steps need a date and time of completion, so they can be daily, weekly, bi-weekly, and monthly tasks to make progress. Some might even require you to set hourly reminders on your watch or phone.

"You have five pages to fill with your Goal Map, so please choose five separate goals, personal or professional. Any questions?" the coach asked.

As the classroom began working on their Goal Map the coach walked down the hall to his office to review paperwork and his own daily calendar. Every weekday, he had check-in meetings with two of the ten mentees—one timeslot in the morning before class, and one after—ensuring he was able to spend forty-five minutes with each mentee to discuss the program, the coursework, or anything else they desired.

This afternoon would be his first one-on-one with Christina. While he had no agenda for these meetings, he was genuinely curious about each mentee's story and wanted to help each one succeed in the program. The ten mentees all had very different backgrounds and experiences; he'd learned that from the personal essays on their intake applications. They were each exceptionally gifted in athletics and in their previous career roles, some succeeding seemingly in spite of their circumstances.

The tennis player was certainly one of those students. He'd made the very best out of an uncertain start in a new country and excelled in something he deeply loved.

The coach suspected Christina was another. While running routine background checks on each mentee, he'd discovered an interesting detail in her case, which led him to dig a little deeper. She'd spent half of her junior year and the start of her senior year in foster care. He found two newspaper articles—one about her collapsing on the field during a soccer match, and the second an announcement of her college soccer scholarship with a picture.

At first glance, it was a typical photograph of a bright-eyed teenager signing paperwork at a table, a proud parent on each side. Except, Christina didn't look happy. She looked like she might be trapped—her mother's hands were wrapped around her right forearm, and her father stood over her, big hands clamped down on each shoulder. He recalled that she never once mentioned her parents in her intro essay, or any family connection at all. There was definitely more to the story. But it was hers to tell, if she wanted to.

The Success Coach stared at the black-and-white picture for a few seconds, remembering the faces of so many young athletes he'd coached before, kids and teens who were desperate for a better life but felt unjustly trapped by life's circumstances. While some kids saw sports as a fun thing to do, others saw it as their only lifeline to a different future, or a reason to spend more time away from home.

Years before, he'd spent two years as an assistant football coach at a private school before taking over the same position at a low-income high school across town. Some of the kids at his new school skipped classes almost daily but would always show up at the football field, even if they hadn't been able to afford lunch that day. The team became family, the field a home. The lessons on the turf were tough love and hard work, but also determination, personal accountability, and resilience.

These were the same lessons he hoped to impart in this accelerator.

With ten minutes left in the writing exercise, the coach headed back to class to give final homework and reading assignments and release the cohort for lunch.

## MINDSET ELEMENT 5 | **TIME AND ENERGY OPTIMIZATION**

On Friday morning, the Success Coach could feel the excitement in the room as everyone took their seats. They'd all survived the first week of the accelerator program and had begun to bond during classroom exercises, lunches, and hallway conversations. Although the syllabus included several weekend reading assignments, he'd intentionally minimized the workload to allow for decompression and downtime, at least for this first week.

While most of the students were all in, some were still struggling with the decision they made to step away from their previous roles. As the baseball player had shared with the Success Coach the previous morning during his one-on-one, his father still hadn't talked to him since he'd walked away from the family business. And to add insult to injury, his fiancée told him she no longer trusted he could provide the life they'd talked about, and she needed space.

After thirty years of entrepreneurship and four years of running this accelerator program, the coach knew these breakups and shake-ups happen fairly regularly when making the big leap into a new world. He also suspected it was often for the best when unsupportive people fell away, no matter how unfortunate it may seem at the time.

Standing at the front of the room, the coach surveyed his students. Today would be a fun topic and he expected a lot of participation.

"You've survived the first week! Congratulations!" The coach gave the classroom a round of applause and was quickly joined by cheers and clapping in return from the students. He then looked them sternly in the eyes. "At the end of the day, the only currency we all care about is time."

He put a quote on the board: "*Until we can manage time, we can manage nothing else* —Peter F Drucker."

"Today we're talking about time management because for the next two days, you get to put the principles of time management into practice in real time. The most successful people are selfish with their time. It's important to them. Time management is the process of planning and controlling how much time you spend on various activities to make the most of your day. Effective time management skills can help you prioritize your tasks, reduce stress, and increase your productivity. You can also avoid burnout by owning your time rather than it owning you.

"During the week, you follow a strict daily schedule, but what happens on the weekend? Do you stick with it, do you modify it, or do you throw it out the window completely? That's up to you to discover."

"Coach?" the basketball player spoke up. "What do you do? Do you keep the same schedule all week or do you change it up?"

He smiled, happy to discuss his experiences. "I maintain the exact same schedule every day, even on weekends, even on vacation. I've found that it serves me best to have the same wake/sleep schedule, the same morning routine, and the same wind-down routine so I can maximize my time and the efficiency of my tasks and accomplishments. I'm being proactive instead of reactive.

"If I'm planning to take my car in for an oil change on Saturday, clean the house, meal prep for the week, and I want to meet my daughter for lunch, I still wake up at 4:30 a.m. I work out, eat, clean the house, and meal prep. I'm one of the first customers for an oil change. And I have plenty of time to spend with my daughter. Then I have the rest of the day free to do whatever I want.

"The alternative if I wake up at 8:30 could be that I skip the workout and maybe breakfast too, do a half-assed job at cleaning the house, meet my daughter and feel rushed on time instead of being present with her, wait longer while I get my oil changed because I wasn't there earlier, and then spend the rest of the afternoon doing meal prep when I could have had the whole afternoon free instead. The day is shot. It might initially feel counterintuitive to maintain the same schedule on weekends, but I have more time to relax when I manage my time instead of letting time manage me."

"But even on vacation?" Kai asked. "Don't you ever sleep in?"

"Even on vacation. The only time I veer away from my schedule is if I'm sick and my body needs to recuperate. I honor my body's needs and then as soon as I'm feeling better, I'm back to it. I also know my chronotype and I know I need six-and-a-half hours of sleep each night to feel my best. So, I make sure that's a priority."

Kai was shaking his head in disbelief. "Man, I can't wait to sleep in on the weekends."

"Are you sleeping in because you're sleep-deprived from the week and playing catch-up?"

"Now, that's a possibility," Kai admitted. "I'm a night owl and it's hard to get to bed before eleven."

"Hard but not impossible," the coach responded. "Especially if what we are looking forward to most on the weekends is spending quality time with loved ones."

Kai shook his finger yes to the coach. "You're right. If my daughter wants to wake up at six a.m. and watch a show with me, dad is getting up and watching a show. I see your point, Coach. I'll play around with my schedule this weekend."

"Let me know how it goes. Keeping the same routine can also help reduce feelings of stress and existential dread on the weekends. If you get up at the same time every day, you're fully in control—as much as you can be—of your downtime on the weekends and can more easily avoid distractions.

"Managing your time is a critical skill that can make or break your success. Remember, time is a finite resource, and your most valuable one. Treat it with respect. Today, you will learn the essential skills and strategies that can help you manage your time effectively as an athlete transitioning into the business world. You'll learn how to create a schedule that works for you, the benefits of delegation, and techniques for overcoming procrastination.

"The good news is, you're already a step ahead because of your years of athletic training. Those strict training schedules, goal-setting habits, and discipline will continue to pay off now and for the rest of your life if you embrace the gift of managing time."

The Success Coach walked to the whiteboard where he'd already written the following points:

1.  Strategies for Prioritizing Tasks and Avoiding Distractions
2.  How to Create a Schedule That Works for You
3.  The Benefits of Delegation and Outsourcing
4.  Techniques for Overcoming Procrastination
5.  Your Brain on Time Management

He began to walk through the points as the cohort followed along. "The key principles of time management include prioritization and goal setting, planning, delegation, and overcoming procrastination. Prioritization involves identifying the most important tasks and focusing on them first. Goal setting involves defining your objectives and breaking them down into actionable steps. Planning means creating a schedule that works for you, and delegation involves assigning tasks to others. This requires a clear understanding of your goals and objectives and the ability to separate urgent tasks from nonurgent ones. Finally, organization involves keeping your work environment and your tasks organized so you are less likely to procrastinate.

"Some people joke that procrastination is their superpower. They believe that they magically become more creative right before a deadline and do their best work. But I don't believe it one bit. They have conditioned themselves to believe the lie that they are only creative under stress. What's worse, though, is the time they are wasting by actively refusing to do the task until the last minute. It's always at the forefront of their minds, yet they are expending more energy by allowing it to create more stress. If they completed the task in a timely manner, they'd have more time and a clear headspace to move to the next task."

"Oh man, I procrastinate so much on projects around the apartment," the lacrosse player shared. "I want to do whatever it is, but I can always find a reason to do something else. But I agree, the task is always at the back of my brain, reminding me I still haven't done it."

"How would you feel if one or two of the tasks on your to-do list were completed?"

"Better."

"What if they were *all* done?"

"Whew . . ." The mentee let out a deep breath. "I'd feel relieved and like I could actually relax!"

"This weekend is a perfect opportunity to be proactive and make a different decision," the Success Coach said, smiling at him.

"One of the biggest challenges in time management is avoiding distractions and staying focused on the task at hand. We all know how easy it is to check our phones and then an hour later realize we're completely off task. So, some strategies for avoiding distractions include turning off notifications, setting specific times for checking emails and social media, and using apps to block distracting websites.

"What are some of your biggest distractions and time-sucks?" the Success Coach asked his students.

"Social media for sure," Christina said. "Some days I easily spend four to five hours online scrolling without realizing it."

"TV and any sports channel really," the baseball player responded. "ESPN is my guilty pleasure. I like to have it on in the background when I'm at home, even if I'm not paying attention to it."

"Candy Crush," the swimmer all but whispered under her breath. "When the boys are napping I like to play Candy Crush. It's a mindless game but it's addictive and I feel so accomplished when I get a new high score."

"Ahh, yes. The dopamine hit of online gaming," the coach said.

"It's the reward hormone, right?" she recalled from earlier in the week. "Well, it's true! I look forward to playing almost every day. Does that make me weird?"

Her classmates laughed.

"No, it doesn't make you weird," the coach responded. "It does give you the feeling of instant gratification, but in order to keep feeling that way, you have to keep playing. A fun exercise could be to find something else that would give you that same dopamine hit, but while marking something off your to-do list."

"I'll see what I can find," she replied with a confident nod.

"My biggest time-suck is email," said the track star. "I have four email addresses for personal and business, and I check them constantly."

"This will be a great experiment for you, then," the Success Coach said. "We often think that a quick response is necessary, but it's not healthy or realistic to be accessible 24-7. There's not just one correct technique for time management—it's whatever works best for you. Like many of these mindset elements, there's not a one-size-fits-all answer. But there are some helpful steps to consider.

"First, I want you to think about your personal preferences, your energy levels, and your peak performance times. Are you more focused in the morning or the afternoon? When do you feel most energetic?

"Next, you need to have a clear understanding of your workload or the task at hand to divide your time effectively. Some helpful tools include electronic calendars, to-do lists, and time-tracking apps. It's also important to schedule breaks and downtime to avoid burnout. Yes, you can do focused work for two to three hours. But a ten-to-fifteen-minute break in the middle to walk around and drink some water can help maintain mental clarity, while adding more movement to your day.

"Any questions so far?" the coach asked.

"I have one." The basketball player raised her hand. "So, I've toyed around with online calendars and tools to help with productivity. But from what I've experienced, they can easily feel like they're just adding to the online clutter of apps and tasks rather than helping me streamline and save time. Do you have any thoughts about how to best utilize the tools so they don't become distractions themselves?"

"Absolutely. Great question. We'll talk about this more in-depth next week, but yes, at the start of this process when you're trying out tools to see which ones you like and which ones will actually help, it can feel like you're spending more time than anticipated in the search to streamline your life. That can feel counterintuitive and frustrating. But hopefully temporary.

"From personal experience, I can tell you that learning how to use your chosen tools in line with your daily schedule can help to streamline tasks so you won't feel overwhelmed with the technology. I check my calendar, my email, review social media and online news, and my texts only three times a day at the same time every day. When I incorporate these tools into my normal daily routine, I train myself—and more specifically my brain—to expect consistency. That lessens any feelings of anxiety. I have a plan and I stick to it. And others in my life understand and respect those boundaries too."

"Coach, what if there's an emergency or someone needs to get in touch with you sooner?" Christina asked. "I feel like I always have to have my phone on me or next to me in case someone needs to reach me."

"The people on my priority list can still call and get through even if I have my notifications off," he responded. "Since I set boundaries on my notifications and my online time, I've only gotten two urgent calls—one notifying me that a childhood friend had passed away, and one when my daughter went into labor. I understand that feeling of always wanting to be available and connected, but what it is really doing is causing you to always be on alert. Your cortisone levels will remain elevated, causing you to feel stressed. That makes it harder to focus and harder to be fully present in anything you do."

She nodded. "I do feel mild anxiety fairly often. I guess I haven't really slowed down enough or set enough boundaries with tasks and times to know what it would feel like to *not* have that underlying stress."

"My guess is that it would allow you to have more freedom with your time and to discover more about yourself—who you really are, what you really want in life, and how you want to feel each day." He looked around the room. "That goes for each of you. If you are always on high alert, always busy, always distracted, you aren't leaving any space to listen to *yourself*. I think every one of you are extremely talented individuals, capable of incredible things. And you should slow down and get to know the real you." He smiled. "I bet you'll really like who and what you discover. Maybe you'll decide you'd like to make a few changes. With time management and intention, you can bring your best to the table each day.

"And that brings us to delegation!"

"My favorite," the rugby player laughed.

"*Delegation* involves assigning tasks to others, like when I ask my assistant to update my calendar or review travel plans. *Outsourcing* involves hiring professionals to perform specific tasks. Think of all the things you can outsource now—grocery shopping, cooking, cleaning. With the help of AI, we can quickly outsource things like research, assistance with emails, and even business proposals."

"I love getting my hair blow-dried and styled now and then," the swimmer said. "Saves a little time and it's a treat to myself."

"I'm waiting for the ability to outsource my six-pack abs," the rugby player said, which got a rise out of Kai.

"And miss out on the lessons of dedication, hard work, and making your health a priority?" the coach asked in jest.

"Oh, we can't have that now," the rugby player said, slapping his stomach. "I'm already down six pounds this week. Gimme six months and I'll blow all you suckers out of the water in a wet T-shirt contest."

Once the class regained composure, the coach touched on the brain science of time management and then discussed tips for overcoming procrastination, including different ways to utilize lists to break tasks into smaller, more manageable steps; setting deadlines; and using rewards to motivate actions. As they started the day's written exercise, centered on learning how to set rules and boundaries around tasks, the coach made eye contact with Christina and nodded for her to follow.

During their one-on-one the previous afternoon, she had expressed excitement about the classwork and getting to know her fellow students. He'd asked a few direct questions about various mindset elements and what she'd gained from group discussions, and she'd answered with ease and confidence. But she always deflected the conversation away from herself and her abilities. In fact, at least twice during their talk, she'd demeaned herself, one time insinuating that she wasn't as intelligent as her classmates. The second time she made an offhand comment, it was about her enjoying learning more about her classmates' stories but not sharing much of her own because she didn't think her story was that important or interesting.

It struck the Success Coach that the reason Christina was so open in dismissing herself was likely because she'd been doing it for a long time. Worse, she believed she wasn't worth getting to know.

"So, are you excited for the weekend?" the Success Coach asked as he sat down in one of the comfortable plush chairs in his office.

"Yes! I'm going to dinner with my teammates tonight and I'm going to do some research on time-blocking apps. And I'm going to stick with my daily schedule over the weekend." She offered "the right answer" with a smile. The same smile she always offered in class. The same guarded smile he remembered seeing the first time they talked in the coffee shop.

He sat for a few moments before deciding on a direct approach.

"Christina, I'll just be blunt."

She stiffened like a child in the principal's office.

"I don't think you feel like you deserve to be here."

She blinked, looking confused. "Are you kicking me out of the program?"

The coach sat back in his chair, waiting.

"I do want to be here. Very much. I'm doing all of the assignments on time and—"

He cut her off as her voice was starting to sound panicked. "You're not in trouble." He leaned in. His face softened.

"It's my job to observe, to mentor, to lead from the front of the room. I pay attention to the conversations and to the words people use. And I can't help but notice that in classroom exercises and even in our one-on-one yesterday, you're very hard on yourself. You use language that leads me to believe you don't like yourself very much."

"That's sometimes true." Her left eye started to water. She blinked to keep a tear at bay. "I have my faults but I'm a nice person."

"You are undoubtedly a very nice person. You're also a very smart person. A talented person. A person who has been through a lot. I suspect you aren't nice to yourself because you learned that at a young age."

She sucked in a breath.

"During the onboarding process, I came across the newspaper articles of your soccer accident, and the picture of you signing your scholarship papers with your parents. I also saw that you spent some time in foster care."

"Yes." She sat motionless, a robot in human form.

"I don't know your backstory and it's none of my business unless you feel comfortable sharing. And you never have to. But it's important that *you know* that you deserve to be here. You belong here, just as much as every other student in the class."

He handed her a Kleenex to wipe the tears away.

"You have incredible potential. I'm just not sure you see it. And you'll need to get there to be completely successful in this accelerator—and in life. You can work your way through any content. You can network like nobody's business. And you can close a deal with ease. But when you go home at the end of the day—are you proud? Do you know who you are, and do you like that person?"

A deep sob escaped her throat, then silence as she shook, holding the tissues to her face, trying to muffle her pain. After a while, she regained her composure enough to speak.

"They told me they wished I had died during the game so they could have sued the school and won enough money to never work again."

The coach didn't have to ask what she meant. The dots connected themselves.

"They only said they loved me or that they were proud when I won matches, when I scored, and when I did well in school. So, I always tried my best. I thought if I could score one more goal or get one more A on a test, they'd decide I was lovable enough. It never happened.

"When I was in the hospital recovering, I finally told a nurse what was going on and she got children's services involved. Six months of good behavior and pretending to be concerned about me later . . . I went back home. But things only got worse because my parents said I'd turned on them.

"By the middle of my freshman college season, I had to tell my coach what was really going on because I was having panic attacks before home games, when they'd visit. Thankfully, he alerted campus security, and they were never allowed back on campus again. Not even during graduation, although they threatened to sue.

"I found a great therapist and went no-contact my sophomore year. I've gone back home for Christmas twice since then, but I always get physically sick. We pretend to be civil but they hate me because I took away their identity and the spotlight for being the perfect soccer parents. They still email me asking for money and I ignore them most of the time, but it really hurts."

"So, you became a high achiever, a perfectionist, a chameleon of sorts, and a person who gives her time and efforts to others but neglects herself because she doesn't feel worthy of love or genuine connection, although you desperately crave it," he said.

"Have you been reading my journal, Coach?" she joked, finally making eye contact again.

"It's okay to struggle with impostor syndrome now and then. But it's vital to know who you are and the innate value you hold so you know that those thoughts are fleeting lies and not the real you."

She nodded in understanding. "I think that's why I look forward to spending time with my soccer teammates. I don't have to think about anything in my life. I can just listen to other people's stories for hours. And alcohol helped." She sniffled. "Maybe a little too much. I gave up alcohol before the program started because I thought we had to. That's why I was confused the other day when the guy asked about drinking with dinner. But I sure miss my margaritas."

"I'm glad you brought that up. I know from my own experiences that I never, ever found my best self at the bottom of a bottle. Sometimes when I drank, I was the life of the party. Sometimes I was mean and belligerent and said terrible things I regretted later. I knew I couldn't build the life I wanted and continue to add value to the relationships that meant the most to me, if I was using alcohol to numb myself to the pain in my life."

"I get that. The version of me after two or three drinks is super fun and talkative and confident. It's how I wish I felt in real life."

"I'm certain you can be those exact same things without a couple of margaritas, if you choose to be. Look, I'm in no way suggesting that you need to live a completely sober lifestyle. I think in social settings and celebrations and business meetings over lunch or dinner, it's great to have your favorite drink if you choose to because you enjoy the experience and the company around you. The key is to realize when you're using it as a crutch, a distraction, or a coping mechanism."

"I've definitely used it for all of those things," she laughed in admission, feeling a little better now that the metaphorical elephant had left the room. "And I'll stick with the no-alcohol decision. It's a lot cheaper!"

"That's very true," he agreed, smiling. "Remember, you always have a choice in what you do and how you spend your time. I hope you choose to spend time making friends with the real you. She's worth getting to know."

"Thanks, Coach."

After a few moments, the two walked back to the classroom to continue the day's exercise.

## MINDSET ELEMENT 6 | **FOCUS THROUGH LIBERATING RESULTS**

The second Monday of the program, the mentees showed up to class looking far more relaxed than they had a week earlier. As they shared what they'd tried in terms of time management hacks and daily schedules, the bond between them grew. They'd survived a full week of learning, homework, balancing responsibilities and personal lives, and were ready to learn more.

Kai stood with the baseball player, who had officially ended his engagement over the weekend. "It was a hard decision to make, but I know it's the right one. We met for dinner on Saturday night and when I told her I needed someone to be all in and supportive of my career instead of mad that I couldn't continue to pay for shopping trips for a while, she threw her ring at me in the middle of the restaurant and walked out."

"What? That's like reality TV!" Kai said, stifling a laugh for his friend's sake.

"You're telling me. Three hours later, she called wanting the ring back. I just hung up on her and blocked her on everything. I can't believe our relationship came down to the money and material things, but I guess it did and I'm an idiot for not seeing it sooner."

"Hey man, don't beat yourself up over that. Relationships are hard work. Believe me. I'm going through it right now with Robin moving," Kai said. "As long as I get to see my daughter as often as I can, that's all I care about right now."

"How was the fair this weekend?" the baseball player asked Kai, who proceeded to pull up a whole folder of pictures of Mia with a painted face from their trip to a local craft fair.

Across the room, Christina sat at a table with the basketball player and the swimmer, sharing stories of the worst bloopers of their dating experiences.

"The very first date my husband and I went on, he accidentally put a picnic blanket down over a doggy pile and I sat on it," the swimmer said. "Didn't know it until I felt something wet, and it had already ruined my white pants through the blanket. He was horrified and offered to dry clean them. Still married him." She shrugged with a hearty laugh.

"Oh my gosh!" the basketball player laughed. "My worst date blooper was hands down accidentally doing the splits in the middle of the road. I was wearing new shoes and it started to lightly rain and I slipped on the pavement. I looked like a giraffe on ice skates."

"I'd pay to watch that show!" Christina laughed. She then shared a few of her favorites, feeling much more relaxed this week to share pieces, funny though they were, of her personal life.

"Class is in session," said the coach, walking to the front of the room. "You all look refreshed and accomplished. That's a great way to start every week. And today, we're piggybacking on Friday's lessons, since you've had all weekend to test out time management techniques.

"We are going to talk about achieving ultimate focus by using *liberating constraints*. It might sound like an oxymoron at first, since constraints are often viewed as barriers to success, but they can also be a powerful tool for innovation and creativity. You can even think of liberating constraints as using parameters or boundaries to give you more freedom—not less. Instead of limiting you, they actually help you focus your time and energy on what's most important. They act as a guide, helping you to make decisions and prioritize your tasks. Just like maintaining the same daily schedule frees up more time over the weekend, you can use constraints or parameters to inspire creativity and drive innovation, which you, as an entrepreneur, can use to your advantage.

"We have three main goals to review today," he said, as he created a numbered list on the whiteboard next to him. "One, to understand the concept of liberating constraints and the benefits for entrepreneurs. Two, to learn strategies for identifying and using these constraints to inspire more creativity. And three, to identify techniques for reframing constraints and turning them into opportunities.

"As you work to accomplish your goals, it can be easy to become overwhelmed by the sheer number of tasks you need to complete. You probably saw that last week when you completed your Goal Map, the wagon wheel with all of the spokes. We can always add more tasks, right? But it's so easy to get bogged down in the details that you may find yourself losing focus on your ultimate goal. One way to combat this feeling is to use liberating constraints. You'll see they work hand in hand with your time management techniques.

"Here's how to use them." He wrote a five-point list next to the first one. "First, define your goal. What are you trying to accomplish? Next, identify your constraints. What limitations are there on your time, energy, and resources? For example, you might have a limited budget to purchase that smartwatch, or you might only have a certain amount of time each day to work on your goal of practicing for the half-marathon.

"Instead of feeling defeated before you begin, turn these constraints into opportunities. Partner with them to make progress instead of seeing them as obstacles. How can you use your limited time, energy, and resources to your advantage? For example, if you only have a limited amount of time to work on your goal each day, you can use that time to focus on the most important tasks first.

"Next, prioritize your tasks. Once you've identified your constraints and turned them into opportunities, it's time to focus on the details. What tasks are the most important to achieving your goal? Focus your time and energy on those tasks first and let the rest fall into place.

"Finally, you'll want to reassess regularly. As you make progress toward your goal, you may find that your constraints shift or change. You may have more or less time or resources in any given week. Stay flexible, and adjust your approach as needed.

"Who can share an example of a liberating constraint and a way to work with it instead of against it?"

"I guess one could be the colors of paint I use on a painting," offered the basketball player. "If I had fifty different colors, I could feel overwhelmed at the decisions to only use a few. But if I only have five, I can get creative with blending and see it as a fun challenge."

The tennis player's hand shot up. "The syllabus is one. If you told us every week we needed to pick a book we thought would be helpful to read, I wouldn't know where to start. But having a list of homework and specific reading assignments allows me to plan my days and my reading time. It takes the stress out of the process so I can enjoy the reading."

"Excellent. Who else? One more."

"My waistband," joked the rugby player. "Or even the scale. But not for long!"

The Success Coach laughed. He admired the rugby player's dedication to becoming healthier and for bringing humor to the topics. "Very true. Using liberating constraints can be a powerful way to focus your time and energy on what's most important. By turning your constraints into opportunities and prioritizing your tasks, you can stay on track and make progress toward your goals, even when faced with limited resources. So, the next time you feel overwhelmed, try using liberating constraints to help guide your way forward.

"One of the most powerful liberating constraints we have is technology, specifically our calendars and our ability to electronically track time and time block. We only have twenty-four hours a day, seven days each week. We can proactively structure our time, like we discussed on Friday. Or we can fail to make the best use of time and become reactive to the many demands that our lifestyle, our families, and our careers place on us.

"Our exercise today pairs time management with liberating constraints in the form of a technology detox."

A few of the mentees looked curious. After all, the Success Coach had just touted the benefits of technology to help track time.

"I want each of you to take out your cell phones and place them on the table in front of you."

"You're not going to make us smash them, are you?" the swimmer quipped.

"No. Better. I'm offering you a challenge. I believe this exercise is important, but it also requires your participation and agreement. I want you to open your home screen and tell me how many apps just on the front screen are time wasters.

"Oh man," the golfer said, reviewing his sports-betting apps and his social media. "I have five for sure."

"Well, you all know what my favorite is," said the swimmer, fighting the urge to open the game in the middle of class.

"Coach, does all social media count as a distraction?" asked the track star. "It can be incredibly helpful for work."

"That depends on how you primarily use it. Do you use it to post about your career or to follow related topics? Or do you most often scroll through for entertainment purposes?"

"A little of both, but probably more for entertainment."

"I 100 percent rely on funny memes or cute posts about dogs and cats at the end of my day for a good laugh," Christina said.

"Me too," Kai said. "I have six different text threads going at the same time with different groups of friends. The stuff we send each other cracks me up, but it can eat up a lot of time. I had to put all of them on mute so I don't get distracted."

"That's a good first step, Kai—turning off notifications. So, here's the first challenge. Who has a smartwatch?"

Eight of the ten raised their hands.

"Your first challenge is to turn off notifications on your watch for calls or texts."

"Ooh," the lacrosse player said. "I see where this is going."

All eight students did as instructed.

"Good. Your next challenge is to turn off notifications for texts, emails, shopping, and news on your phone. You're not stopping anyone from contacting you. You're merely deciding on when you choose to see their messages."

"What am I going to do if I can't see every single text as it comes in?" the swimmer jokingly lamented.

"More time for Candy Crush?" the tennis player offered, then quickly winced from a playful slap on the arm.

This took a little more time, since the students had to go into their settings for each app and turn off notifications, but a few minutes later, all eyes had refocused to the front of the room.

"Now, here's a big one. Delete at least one app from your phone that you know is a big time-waster." He grinned at the swimmer.

"Do I have to?!"

"No." He laughed at her response. "You don't have to. But I'd hon-estly give some thought to the time you're spending on the app, versus the time you could be doing something else more meaningful."

"Okay. I'll at least move it off of the home screen to another folder."

"That's great progress!" he encouraged.

Among the shared deletions were dating apps, gaming apps, news apps, online shopping apps, and Pinterest.

"Now, who has either a laptop or a desktop computer?"

All students raised a hand.

"Can you access your social media from your computers if you needed or wanted to?"

"Sure can," said the basketball player. "Although the usability isn't the same for all of them."

"Understood," the coach nodded. "For the social media apps on your phone that have the same accessibility on your computers, I chal-lenge you to delete the apps on your phone."

He leaned against his desk, amused at the expressions on a few of the mentees' faces as they grappled with which apps to remove, if any.

"Dammit!" Christina said, flipping her phone face down after delet-ing two of her social media apps. "I love my memes, but I know I spend too many hours a week online."

"You're not getting rid of the access," the coach clarified. "You still have all of your same accounts, and you can log in online or even add back the apps to your phones if you choose to. What I want you to pay attention to are the feelings of loss, of dread, of uncertainty, of missing out that might be circling through your minds right now as you are doing these challenges. Everything about social media is geared toward drawing you in and creating an addictive behavior so you'll keep using it. Remember, we're working on being in control of your time. This will be crucial when you are running a company."

"I'm reclaiming my time," the basketball player said with a smile after deleting a few apps.

"Okay. I have one last challenge for you today in class. There are a few other suggestions in the homework, if you choose to go all in. But for now, your last challenge is . . . to turn your cell phone off for the rest of class today. That's only two more hours."

"Like *off* off?" Kai asked. "Or just on silent?"

"Off."

While a few students had zero hesitation completing the task, several looked stunned as they wrestled with the idea.

"What if someone needs me? What if my sons get sick and I have to pick them up from daycare? What if someone dies?" the swimmer asked with concern.

"Do the daycare and your husband and family have the main phone number here?"

"Yes," she gulped.

He remained silent, allowing her to process her emotions in real time.

"I don't remember the last time I turned my phone off, to be honest."

The coach took his phone out of his pocket, turned it off, and placed it face down on the desk. "You may not remember what life was like before cell phones and laptops, but it was glorious," he said. "Back in my day, in the summers, we'd leave the house in the morning for hours and come home for lunch and then go out again until dinner. We played together. We had neighborhood adventures. I'm not saying it was perfect, of course. But we weren't connected to technology 24-7. It felt like we had more time and headspace in those formative years. You had a similar mental and emotional freedom before you had your first social media accounts or bought your first electronic devices."

"I worry about my boys growing up too fast and especially using technology," the swimmer mused. "One of the little girls at their preschool has a cell phone at five years old to text her parents. *Five!* What in the world does a five-year-old have to say?"

"Kids grow up fast for sure," the coach replied. "It's our job as parents to set a good example of boundaries for them, and that means setting them for ourselves first."

The swimmer hesitated for a few seconds, then held the button down on the phone until the screen went black. She placed her phone inside her purse.

"Challenge accepted."

## MINDSET ELEMENT 7 | **MINDFULNESS**

On Tuesday morning, the topic of discussion was mindfulness, a favorite of the Success Coach.

Instead of walking into a well-lit, orderly classroom like they'd come to expect, the mentees hesitantly entered the dimly lit room and discovered it had been decorated like a relaxing spa, with flickering candles throughout, plush furniture, and oversized, cozy throws. On one side, a bubbling water feature gently poured water over a rock wall, cascading down into a clear pool below. Lush plants and ferns were placed throughout. A table to the left had several glass pitchers of cold water with either lemon, cucumber, or orange slices floating inside. The slightest fragrances of lavender and eucalyptus diffused into the air. The two large conference tables had been replaced with ten comfortable seats, complete with a movable desk that rotated up from the side of each chair.

As the students slowly walked around admiring their new classroom, the coach entered from the hallway. "Welcome to a morning of mindfulness and meditation," he said.

"This is gorgeous!" the swimmer said, plopping down in her seat of choice and draping a blanket over her lap. "Can we book a massage too?"

"A massage of the mind," he said with a smile as the rest of the students selected their seats for the day and got settled in.

"We'll get started soon enough, but what I'd like you all to do is to silence your phones, put away all technology, and get comfortable. Bill Gates, Russell Simmons, Ray Dalio, Oprah Winfrey, Joe Rogan, Marc Benioff, and Ariana Huffington. Besides leading incredible enterprises, they all have something in common: mindfulness and meditation.

"Mindfulness and meditation are two practices that are often used interchangeably, since they can be done at the same time. But they are distinct techniques with different focuses and applications.

"*Mindfulness* involves paying attention to the present moment and observing thoughts and feelings without judgment. *Meditation*, on the other hand, involves intentionally focusing the mind on a specific object, like the breath or a special mantra or phrase, with the goal of achieving a state of calm and clarity. It's usually practiced in a quiet, dedicated space and requires a specific time commitment, even just a few minutes.

"This morning, we're going to begin by meditating for seven minutes. If the word *meditation* doesn't sit well with you, feel free to replace it with prayer, or simply a period of silence. This is your time to relax, decompress, and simply focus on your breathing. I'll guide you for the first thirty seconds and then you'll continue on your own, breathing, focusing, listening to your body. When the time is up, you'll hear a bell chime."

The students wiggled and crossed or uncrossed legs, leaning back into their chairs to get comfortable.

"Feel free to close your eyes," the coach guided. "Take a deep breath and hold it in for 10 . . . 9 . . . 8 . . . 7 . . . 6 . . . 5 . . . 4 . . . 3 . . . 2 . . . 1 . . . and exhale."

The students offered a collective breath out.

"Inhale again for 1 . . . 2 . . . 3 . . . 4 . . . 5 . . . 6 . . . 7 . . . 8 . . . 9 . . . 10 . . . and hold it." He paused a few additional seconds. "Then out," as he repeated the countdown to 1. He instructed their inhaling and exhaling two more times and then prompted them to go back to breathing normally, focusing on their breath. For the next six minutes, the only sound in the room was of deeply relaxed breathing.

"Take one last deep breath and exhale," he instructed as a gentle bell chimed in the background. "And when you're ready, open your eyes."

One by one, the mentees began to open their eyes until the swimmer was the only one with eyes still closed. "You can open your eyes," he prompted again, thinking she might have fallen asleep.

"I don't want to," she said with a giggle, then opened her eyes to focus on the Success Coach.

"How do you feel? What did you notice?" he asked the students.

"I know my heart rate slowed down," said the basketball player, confirming her suspicions on her smartwatch. "I feel super relaxed."

"I want to start every class like this. I almost fell asleep!" the tennis player shared.

"I noticed my left hip muscles are a little sore," Christina said. "I hadn't noticed that before. I guess I need to stretch more before and after matches."

"It was hard to shut my thoughts down. But maybe I just need practice," said the baseball player.

"Those are all great observations," the coach said. "You may have heard that in order to meditate you have to completely quiet your mind. But that's not true. With practice, it is easier to still your thoughts because you're creating a habit and your brain understands this is a time it can relax. But your mind doesn't have to be quiet or still for you to get the benefits of meditating.

"As you focus on your breath and the sensations in your body, you will begin to notice things you hadn't noticed before, like a sore hip muscle or a crick in your neck that's causing a mild headache. When you close your eyes, you can focus on your other senses. What do you smell? What do you hear? How does your body feel in the chair?"

"I definitely smell lavender," Kai said. "My mother has grown it in every garden she's had. It always reminds me of her." He smiled, making a mental note to call his parents later.

"I've done yoga a few times and at the very end when we're relaxing like we did just now, I've gotten a little emotional," Christina said.

The coach nodded. "That's perfectly normal. You're slowing down and quieting the noise, allowing your body and your mind to be heard, instead of ignoring signals and stuffing down emotions, like we so often do. It's a very healthy response to feel emotion during meditation."

"Coach, can you explain the difference again between meditation and mindfulness? I'm not sure I understand," the rugby player asked.

"Sure. Think of meditation as an activity that most often requires you to sit still for a period of time, to focus on your breathing and your connection with your body, and relax. Many people close their eyes during meditation so they can focus without the distraction of the visual world around them.

"Mindfulness is when you're aware of the present moment, allowing thoughts to come in and out of your mind, observing the world around you without judgment or distraction. You can practice mindfulness while driving, or while hiking, even while watching a movie or in conversation with friends. Think of mindfulness as you being an acute observer of life. It's an awareness of the present moment, without worrying about what you have to do later in the day or something embarrassing you said fifteen years ago."

"That sounds like what I experience when I hike on the weekends," said the lacrosse player. "I'm there with my thoughts and the trees and wildlife. I do think about things as I walk but mostly I try to pay attention to my surroundings and take it all in."

"That's exactly right.

"Over the last several years, many NBA, NFL, and college teams have embraced mindfulness and meditation practices to enhance their players' focus, manage stress, and optimize performance.[34] Even Naomi Osaka, the pro tennis player who has won four Grand Slam singles titles, has been open about her use of mindfulness in her training and personal life. She practices mindfulness as a way to manage the intense pressure and anxiety she experienced during tournaments."

"Oh, I get that," the tennis player said. "Mindfulness is huge in tennis, although I'd call it extreme concentration. You have to make so many calculations with each point, you can't help but be present at all times."

"Great example. Entrepreneurship can be a stressful and demanding endeavor, with lots of competing demands and pressures. Mindfulness and meditation can both help you manage stress, feel content, and increase focus and productivity, especially when you incorporate them into your daily routines. And it doesn't have to take a lot of extra time. In just seven minutes, it can lower your heart rate and help you feel relaxed, as we saw.

"Think of a time when you were so engaged in what you were doing that you lost all sense of time and space. How did that feel?"

"I often feel that way while painting," the basketball player said.

"I've felt that way on some of my runs," the golfer said.

"Yes, you got into the zone, the runner's high," the coach affirmed.

"I don't know if this counts but when my twins were born, it was such an emotional moment, I was fully present because I didn't want to miss a single breath," the swimmer said. "I wanted to remember exactly what they looked like in every moment."

"That's a beautiful example," Christina said, smiling at her friend and classmate.

"I felt the same way when I proposed to my wife," the rugby player added. "I don't even remember exactly what I said, I was so focused on not dropping the ring and praying she would say yes." He showed the slightest hint of emotion, earning an encouraging pat on the back from the baseball player seated behind him.

"So, why are meditation and mindfulness so important to you as entrepreneurs?"

"We're implementing self-care practices regularly?" Christina offered.

"That's a great way to look at it. When you're under pressure—and you will be—these practices will help to reduce stress and anxiety by promoting relaxation and calmness. You make better decisions with a calm mind. Hands down. Next, mindfulness can increase focus and productivity by improving concentration and mental clarity. Imagine combining what you learned about goal setting and focus last week with mindfulness. You'll be on fire! Finally, mindfulness can enhance your emotional intelligence and improve your relationships by promoting empathy and compassion. As you become more aware of your surroundings, you become more in tune with the people around you and naturally develop deeper connections."

Kai spoke up. "Coach, all of these mindset elements we're learning, do you have them all memorized and scheduled into your day? Or have you done them so long they're automatic now?" A man who loved keeping his calendar updated, he was starting to wonder how much time these elements would take up in his schedule every day.

"A little of both. Anything that can be included in my morning routine, such as reviewing my calendar and any other time management tasks, mindfulness, meditation, stretching, working out, mindful movement practices such as yoga or tai chi, or journaling—I always have that time blocked out on my daily calendar. Even though I don't need a reminder, the blocked-off time creates a boundary and prevents anything else from being scheduled at that time.

"And remember, you can also practice informal mindfulness throughout the day, by focusing on the present moment, using all your senses, during regular activities like eating, walking, or even checking email. I personally like to schedule fifteen minutes in the middle of the afternoon to check in with how I'm feeling. That helps me overcome the afternoon slump when I have less energy and focus.

"Now, I want you to take three minutes and list as many ways as you can think of to incorporate mindfulness and meditation into your daily schedule." The coach slowly brought the lights back up and clicked off the flickering candles with a remote. At the end of three minutes, he walked over to a whiteboard, marker in hand. "Rapid fire, tell me your ideas." As they were called out, he bulleted each one until over thirty-five ideas were written on the board.

"With this many options, you will never become bored with how and where you choose to meditate and practice mindfulness. And now we're going to talk about your brain on mindfulness and meditation.

"Studies have shown that regular meditation can increase gray matter volume in regions associated with attention, sensory processing, and emotional regulation, meaning meditation can increase our physical capacity to do these tasks.[35] It can also increase the production of gamma-aminobutyric acid (GABA), a neurotransmitter that can reduce anxiety and promote feelings of calm." He pointed to the image of the brain on the right side of the board. "Meditation has also been shown to *decrease* the size and activity of the amygdala, a region associated with fear and stress, leading to greater emotional stability and resilience. What's more, meditation can *increase* the activity of the prefrontal cortex, the region we've talked about that is involved in attention, decision-making, and impulse control. All of this means that by practicing meditation regularly, you can harness the power of your brain to promote greater mental and emotional well-being.

"Can you see how both mindfulness and meditation could influence your other mindset elements, like time management, focus, and self-care?"

The mentees nodded.

"It's all connected," said the tennis player, staring at the drawing of the brain.

For the next two hours, the mentees finished their in-class reading assignments along with a journal prompt on how they felt before they walked into the classroom earlier in the day, and after the meditation exercise, drawing on all of their senses.

Just before the end of class, the coach made his final point of the day. "As you can see, meditation and mindfulness are powerful tools to manage stress, increase focus, and improve overall well-being. By incorporating them both into your daily routine, you can reap the many benefits of a calm mind and achieve greater success in your life and business endeavors.

"I'd hate to not make the most out of this space today, so for the last ten minutes of class, I'm going to turn the lights down again if you'd like to practice meditation before you head to your lunch meetings."

Soon all of the mentees were relaxed and taking deep breaths, enjoying the extra time to unwind.

With only two minutes left, a loud snore punctuated the silence, then another, causing several to laugh and look around. The tennis player was out cold, having fallen fast asleep.

"See, it really works!" the rugby player said to the lacrosse player as the rest of the students quietly gathered their things and snuck out of the room, stopping at the doorway to see how long it would take the tennis player to wake up.

Two minutes later, the Success Coach graciously woke him up to the applause of the rest of his classmates.

"C'mon, sleeping beauty!" the baseball player said as he held the door to the elevator. "We've got lunch plans."

## MINDSET ELEMENT 8 | GRATITUDE

On Wednesday morning, Kai arrived a few minutes late—a first for someone who took pride in always being a little early to any event. He was clearly aggravated. Everything had gone wrong from the moment he got home the night before when he'd opened his front door and stepped in a puddle of water that covered the foyer and the entire kitchen floor. A pipe had busted under the kitchen sink, and although a plumber had come out on an emergency call and fixed the issue, Kai spent the next few hours sopping up water and setting up fans to minimize damage. He hadn't gotten to bed until 1 a.m. And when he woke up at 6 a.m., he had three missed texts from his father. He'd forgotten to call his parents during dinner, their new weekly Wednesday night routine.

As he stepped onto the subway and took a seat, he opened today's online syllabus and laughed at the topic of gratitude. "That's some irony for you," he said under his breath. Clicking over to check his emails, he saw a credit card receipt for Robin and Mia's flight to Florida that was the same amount as he'd paid the emergency plumber last night. "Ain't that some bullshit!" he mumbled before riding in silence the rest of the way, annoyed at how his day was starting, knowing he'd be late.

"Sorry, Coach." Kai walked in and quickly found a seat at one of the long tables. He didn't even notice that the spa setting had been removed and replaced with their normal classroom layout.

"Everything okay?" the Success Coach asked.

"Emergency plumbing issue at home," Kai said. "Got it all cleaned up but wasn't on my schedule." He took a deep breath, trying to slow his pulse.

"I'm sorry to hear that. Things like that happen now and then and they throw a wrench into our plans and our finances."

"You've got that right," Kai said, mentally debating which credit card to pay down first.

"But it's a perfect example of why gratitude is so important."

Only the Success Coach noticed Kai rolling his eyes as he glanced down at his phone, then put it away.

The coach put a quote on the board: "When you are grateful fear disappears and abundance appears. —Tony Robbins"

He was impassioned as he continued. "Gratitude is a positive emotion that arises when we recognize and appreciate the good things in our lives. It's an essential aspect of well-being and happiness, and research shows that cultivating gratitude can have numerous psychological and physical benefits. Today, we'll explore the neurological benefits of gratitude. We will also discuss some strategies for cultivating gratitude in our daily lives.

"Before we get started, by a show of hands, who has something to be grateful for this morning."

Nine hands went up. Kai was still fuming.

"What are you most grateful for today?" the coach asked.

The first hand he saw was the baseball player's.

"I talked to my dad last night for the first time in almost three weeks."

While the rest of the class congratulated him on his news, Kai was still self-absorbed. He shook his head, guilty that he'd forgotten to call his parents.

"I'm thankful for my sweet next-door neighbor," Christina said. "She left me a bag of homemade cookies and a note on my door yesterday because she knew I'd started this program. It was so kind of her and completely unexpected."

"Psst, did you bring any of those cookies?" the swimmer whispered as Christina took the bag out of her tote and started to pass it around. "Ooh, I'm thankful for this sugary treat!"

"Honestly, I'm thankful to be here with all of you," offered the basketball player. "I've really enjoyed getting to know each of you a little better and to challenge myself to learn new things every day."

A few more students had finished sharing when the rugby player cleared his throat. "Well . . . I've got some news to share." The rest of his classmates turned at what sounded to be an important announcement.

After a pause to gather his emotions, he spoke. "I found out last night I'm gonna be a dad!" His classmates cheered and stood to hug him. "We took three tests to make sure. We've been trying for seven years now."

Kai couldn't help but soften as he congratulated his classmate. He flashed back to when he and Robin had experienced the highs of positive pregnancy tests. "That's amazing, man. You're gonna be a great dad," he said. Instantly, he realized how grateful he was for Mia, and for his parents, and for his house, even with plumbing issues. He remembered the lesson from the day before about mindfulness and decided to put it into practice in real time.

"I'm thankful for my daughter, Mia, and for the time we spend together," he said as he relaxed into his chair, setting aside the outside world.

"There are several ways to cultivate gratitude in our daily lives," the Success Coach said, walking around the room. "One effective strategy is to keep a gratitude journal, which some of you already do. Starting today, each day, I want all of you to write down three things you're grateful for. This exercise helps to train your brain to focus on the positive aspects of your life.

"Another strategy is to practice gratitude during meditation, building on what we learned yesterday. During this meditation, focus on the things you are grateful for, such as your lifetime of good health, your pet, your children, your significant other, or your home. As you focus on each item, you can notice the physical sensation of the gratitude in your body and mind.

"Expressing gratitude to others is another powerful way to cultivate it. This could look like writing a thank-you note or expressing your gratitude in person or over the phone. This not only makes the recipient feel good but also reinforces your own feelings of gratitude. It's a win-win."

Kai decided to call his parents during the first break in class. Just to say hello. He'd call them for a longer conversation later.

"One awesome example of an athlete who practices gratitude is NBA great LeBron James," the coach was saying. "'King James' is known for his skill and his ability to maintain a positive mindset, even in challenging situations. When you see him in interviews and even on social media posts, he often expresses gratitude for his teammates, his coaches, and his fans. He also frequently speaks about the importance of practicing gratitude in his daily life, and says that it helps him maintain perspective and stay focused on his goals."

"If it's good enough for LeBron, it's good enough for me," the basketball player said.

"Then you'll be happy to learn that practicing gratitude is a powerful way to boost your mood and increase your overall sense of well-being. The part of your brain associated with emotion and empathy is activated when you feel gratitude toward others. Additionally, once again, the region involved in regulating stress and the release of hormones is activated when you experience gratitude. Oxytocin, the love hormone, is released during positive thoughts about others and during social interactions, which sparks feelings of trust and generosity. Similarly, serotonin, which regulates our mood and contributes to feelings of happiness, is also released during expressions of gratitude. When we experience something that makes us feel good, we feel so good that we want to continue the positive thoughts. If you give gratitude a try, you can trigger your own pleasure and reward state.

"For today's exercise, I want you to journal for thirty minutes about who and what you are grateful for."

"That's a long time," the tennis player responded. "I don't know if I have enough things to write about for thirty minutes."

"Sure you do," the coach said. "Think about all of the steps you've taken to get to where you are now. And all of the people along the way who have played significant parts in your story. That could be family, friends, teammates—"

The tennis player jumped in. "The attorney who helped my family file for asylum. The families who let us stay with them in California and gave us clothes and food for months. The manager who gave me my first job." He shook his pen toward the sky as he looked up. "Yes, I do have much to be grateful for."

For the next thirty minutes, the mentees wrote about family, friends, coaches, and teachers—people who believed in them and called out their potential.

"If you want to go even further," the Success Coach said at the half-hour mark, "I have a stack of stamped envelopes and paper up here if you'd like to write and mail letters to those who have made a significant and positive impact on your life. Express your gratitude and appreciation to this person. Be specific and detailed, and describe how this person has made a difference in your life."

One by one, the mentees grabbed a few envelopes apiece and sat down to write their heartfelt thanks.

The rugby player began writing a sweet letter to his wife.

Christina decided to write a thank-you note to her neighbor for the cookies and kindness.

Kai grabbed his pen and started to write a letter to his parents. Just before he put pen to paper, he had a change of plans. Instead, he wrote, "To Robin, my wife, and incredible mother to our daughter, Mia . . ."

## MINDSET ELEMENT 9 | **EMOTIONAL INTELLIGENCE**

Kai was much more relaxed on Thursday morning as he arrived early to the athlete-entrepreneur offices. In a long, much-needed talk with his parents the night before, sharing the latest on the divorce process and the plumbing snafu, he told them he'd written Robin a letter of gratitude.

"Son, do you think she'll even read it? Or will she throw it away?" his father asked on their video call.

"I don't know, Dad," Kai sighed. "I hope she reads it. I honestly don't think it will change anything, but I decided to do it for myself and for Robin, and Mia too."

"For Mia?" his mother asked. "Did you write a letter to her too?"

"No, but that's a great idea. I'll make her a little card tonight with a drawing." He wrote a reminder on a notepad next to where he sat on the couch.

"With everything I've been learning about mindset and positivity and mindfulness, I'm realizing that most of it is a choice. It's a decision to choose positivity or gratefulness, even when I don't feel like it. It's a decision to manage my time instead of letting time manage me and then having to react and play defense. It's a choice to continue to show up for my daughter and stay positive, even though I hate having to drop her off and wave goodbye. I want her to see me as a calm, loving father, not a negative one. So, I want to start thinking and acting like a person who is always positive, who isn't fazed by much, who can show emotions and talk about feelings, and be someone she knows she can trust because I'm easy to talk to."

"That's right, son. Model that consistent behavior for her so that you remain accountable to yourself as you continue to grow and evolve," Joe replied. Ann squeezed her husband's arm in agreement.

"We're proud of you, Kai," she said. "This is not easy. We will get through it together."

Kai was making his way to his seat when Christina accidentally bumped into him, splashing her water on herself.

"Oh, Kai! I'm so sorry." She wiped water off her clothes and Kai's sleeve.

"All good," he said, completely unbothered by the few drops of water. "Hey, how are you enjoying the program so far?"

"Oh, it's good." She didn't elaborate and didn't look up. She appeared incredibly distracted.

"Are you okay? You seem a little off this morning."

"Yeah," she quickly replied, looking away. "Well, no. Not really. I got a crappy email yesterday and I'm having a hard time shaking it." She finally looked up to see a concerned friend looking back at her.

"Do I need to go whup someone's ass? Because I will." He postured and puffed his chest up.

She laughed, thankful for his big-brother protection mode and humor. "No, but I wish you could."

"I mean it," he said, eyebrows raised in sincerity. "Want to talk about it over lunch?"

For a few moments, she contemplated doing what she'd always done in similar situations, which was to downplay the issue and then go home and cry while she punched her pillows. This time, she made a conscious choice—a different choice.

"Yes. I'd really like that."

As the Success Coach walked into the classroom, the students found their seats.

"How many of you mailed letters out yesterday?"

Six students raised their hands.

"I'm mailing several today," the baseball player said.

"I made a few calls and sent some texts and emails yesterday," said the rugby player. "It was a great time to share my good news too."

"Did anyone practice gratitude meditation?"

"I did." The swimmer raised her hand. "I already make a gratitude list when I journal in the mornings. It was easy to add in a few minutes of meditation."

"What about aha moments or breakthroughs?" the coach asked.

Kai raised his hand. "I mailed a letter to Robin, thanking her for being a great mother to our child and for being there for me, for making our house a home. I told her that she deserved to be made more of a priority when it came to my time and that I was sorry for not doing my part."

The class was silent for a few moments. Kai had shared bits and pieces of his marital struggles in conversations with classmates.

"It was a hard letter to write. I've never said any of those things to her in person. Should have. But didn't. She might throw it away without reading it. But I felt like it was important to say those things anyway."

"Well done," the Success Coach nodded. "You've displayed great emotional intelligence, which is what we're discussing today.

"Emotional intelligence is the ability to identify, understand, and manage our own emotions, and recognize the emotions of others. It is a crucial aspect of personal and professional success. Today, we'll explore the neurological benefits of emotional intelligence. We will also discuss how emotional intelligence relates to your earlier life in athletics.

"One great example of emotional intelligence was embodied in another NBA legend, Kobe Bryant, who tragically passed away in 2020. Bryant had an extraordinary way of connecting with his teammates and coaches. He was known for his ability to regulate his emotions and maintain a positive mindset, even in high-pressure situations. He often spoke about the importance of emotional intelligence in his interviews and even wrote a book called *The Mamba Mentality*, where he discussed his approach to basketball and life. If you haven't read it, I highly recommend it.[36]

"When you're a CEO, it's crucial to display emotional intelligence and to understand how it relates to performance and team dynamics. It is a critical skill in personal and professional relationships, helping to improve communication, build trust, and resolve conflicts. And no matter how well your organization operates, there will always be conflicts and unexpected circumstances. Comes with the territory. So, you must be skilled at managing your own emotions before you are in a position of elevated leadership, being called upon to manage others."

"That's so true," the swimmer said. "I've seen that play out in the work environment a few times where a manager or team lead had a really negative reaction in front of other workers. That can sour relationships and productivity in a hurry and then it takes even more time and effort to build back the trust that was lost."

"Exactly," the coach said. "As an athlete-entrepreneur and a CEO, it's your responsibility to keep a level head at all times because people are looking to you to lead, and your team, your organization is feeding off of your energy.

"The first key here is to practice self-awareness. This goes back to the mindfulness exercises we did on Tuesday. Start by becoming more aware of your own emotions, both positive and negative. Pay attention to how you feel in different situations and identify the triggers that can cause you to have emotional reactions. This can help you better understand your own emotional patterns and develop greater control over your responses.

"Next, improve your empathy. Empathy is the ability to understand and feel the emotions of others. To improve your empathy, try to imagine yourself in someone else's shoes, having the same life experiences, and imagine how they might be feeling. Practice active listening and be open to other people's perspectives and emotions.

"Then, develop your social skills. Social skills are the ability to communicate effectively, build relationships, and resolve conflicts. To improve your social skills, practice clear communication, active listening, and assertiveness in asking for what you need and want. Learn how to give and receive feedback in a constructive way, and practice resolving conflicts in a respectful and collaborative manner. The scorched-earth method rarely works in business. If you botch a situation because you're not in control of your emotions, you erode the trust of the team and it's less likely they'll come to you in the future with issues."

Christina smiled to herself, remembering how she daydreamed about taking that approach when she was burned at Peppley NYC, but had resisted. Since her departure, the company had reached out to her repeatedly, asking if she'd be interested in part-time consulting work to teach new hires how to effectively close deals, but she declined each time. She knew she'd made the right decision to join the accelerator.

"And finally, you want to practice emotional regulation, which is the ability to manage and control your own emotions in different situations like Kobe Bryant. To improve your emotional regulation, practice the techniques you've learned like deep breathing, meditation, or mindfulness to help you stay calm and focused during stressful situations. Learn how to express your emotions in a healthy way, without letting them take control of your actions.

"I'd like you to pair up with a partner for this next exercise and spread out throughout the room. Decide which person will speak first while the other listens."

The mentees each chose a partner and a location, and waited for further instructions.

"This is a perspective-taking activity, and it might involve some vulnerability and risk. I want you to practice open and honest communication, active listening, putting yourself in your partner's shoes, and seeing things from their perspective. This activity helps develop empathy and compassion, and a greater understanding of your own emotions and the emotions of others.

"If you're the person who speaks first, raise your hand."

Five hands shot up.

"You have seven minutes to tell a story about the person you admire most and why. Don't make it short and sweet; dig deep to convey the emotions and the memories and details of that relationship and how this person has made an impact. The second person will practice active listening."

The coach clicked a timer and the conversation in the room filled every corner as the mentees divulged memories and experiences that had shaped them. When the time was up, the pair swapped roles—the active listener now became the speaker, sharing a story of the person they admired most and why, while their partner listened.

When that exercise was complete, the Success Coach instructed the class to switch partners and repeat the exercise with a different question: What was the most significant play or moment of your athletic career, and why?

Conversation became lively and the decibel rose as mentees shared their impassioned memories of the plays they'll never forget. When roles reversed, the second partner became the speaker, sharing their most memorable stories.

Once the exercise was complete, the coach regained control of the room. "Of those two different exercises—the two topics—which one did you enjoy talking about more? The person you most admire or the most significant play of your career?"

Unsurprisingly, most of the students chose the most significant play of their careers.

"Why do you think that is?" asked the Success Coach.

"For me, it's the emotions involved," said the baseball player. "I can talk about sports all day because that gets me fired up and happy. The person I admire most is my grandmother, and she's in hospice. I get sad every time I think about it. I don't know how much longer she has." He rubbed his eyes to stop the tears.

"How often do you let others know when you're sad?"

"Never, really. The way I grew up, men don't really express emotions other than happiness and anger—and they sure don't cry in public."

The coach remained silent, allowing the student to process his beliefs.

"I mean, I do cry. I get sad. I guess I just don't feel comfortable showing that side of me because I don't want people to think differently of me."

"You don't want people to think you're human?" the coach prodded.

"Uh . . . well . . . yeah, I guess."

"And how is that working for you?"

"It could be better."

The coach walked to his desk and sat on the front edge. "We all come from different backgrounds. We've had different experiences. Different family structures. As adults, you have the opportunity to reflect on your family, how you grew up, what you were taught to believe as the truth. And you get to decide if you actually believe those things. Maybe you do. Maybe you don't. If you realize there are some patterns you are repeating that no longer serve you—then you get to be the one to break those patterns. And I'm not just picking on you." He pointed to the baseball player. "This applies to all of us.

"As competitive athletes, you were no doubt told to toughen up, suck it up, or some version of that. You learned to play through the pain—physical, emotional, and mental. You learned to shield your emotions when they might be perceived as weak. You learned to stuff your problems down until an emotional trigger brought everything to the surface.

"Part of developing emotional intelligence includes working through those areas, those emotions that are blocked, that you've not allowed yourself to express."

The baseball player nodded.

"You are all driven leaders who are used to winning. You are used to hard work. You are comfortable with long hours, late nights, deadlines, tough decisions, demanding excellence from yourself and expecting it from others. But if you are unable to show a range of emotions as a CEO, what does that convey to your team?"

"Maybe that you're unapproachable or unrelatable," said the rugby player.

"Maybe you're cold and don't really care about anyone else?" the basketball player asked.

"That it's not acceptable to have many emotions at all," the baseball player said. "And if that's the case, I imagine the employees wouldn't want to communicate freely for fear of getting in trouble."

The coach looked around the room. "We must allow ourselves the gift of a healthy range of emotions. To allow ourselves to fully feel our experiences: happiness, sadness, fear, hope, anger—all of it. Emotions don't make you weak, like society would have us believe. Being able to process and express your emotions is a strength. As you practice emotional intelligence and emotional regulation, you will develop a greater understanding of your own emotions and the emotions of others.

"The greatest leaders aren't unyielding, unreasonable dictators. And they aren't sappy pushovers, either. The best leaders have a backbone and a heartbeat, and they use both to keep a level head. With emotional intelligence, you'll be better equipped to handle stress, manage conflicts, and make thoughtful decisions."

For the next two hours, the mentees worked through reading and journaling assignments until it was time for lunch.

A few minutes later, the students were exiting the elevators, paired up for lunch conversations. Kai and Christina walked south. Her mouth was made up for Chinese food but the fluttering anxiety building in her stomach threatened to ruin the impending conversation.

Kai sensed her hesitancy and broke the ice first. "So, you got a bad email?"

"Yes," she gulped. "From my parents."

As she began to tell him the whole story, she held nothing back. Not for the sake of shock factor but because she was tired of being ashamed of her past, hiding behind the façade of being so well put together. Although by the time they were seated at a booth, he *was* shocked.

"They said what?!" He leaned across the table, eyes wide, as she told him the nasty things her parents said about wishing she'd died on the soccer field. To her, it was just another ding to her confidence, as normal and frequent in their house as washing her hair.

"They keep emailing me for money and just saying really terrible things . . . like I owe them because they supported me through high school and I got my soccer scholarship because of them, so it's my duty to repay the favor," she said in between slurps of wonton soup.

"But that's their job as parents!" he replied. "They're *supposed* to feed you and clothe you and give you a place to live."

She shrugged.

"Unbelievable," he said between big bites of orange chicken. "Look, you're a better person than I am. If someone treated my daughter *half* as bad as they treated you, I'd be lifting weights for the next fifty years in prison." He shook his head.

She sighed deeply. No one had ever known the severity of her situation until she had some space to process and confide in someone neutral while in the hospital. She was scared to let on to the atrocities in her home.

"But look," he said, tapping the table for emphasis. "You not only survived that hellhole, you made a way out on your own terms. And look at you now. In this accelerator program. You've got friends, you got handpicked for this opportunity. You've got the whole world in front of you!" He smiled.

"Thanks, I know. Coach said I was too hard on myself, and I really am. I'm working on it. I just can't figure out why I don't completely cut ties. I feel awful every time I see an email from them. I feel like I'm in trouble all over again!"

"You said you've blocked the phone numbers, social media, and you have a PO Box so they don't have your address, right?"

"Right."

"You know you can create a filter for their emails that goes right to trash? You'll never even see them."

She'd contemplated this exact scenario a hundred times but could never make a permanent break. "Part of me still hopes they'll apologize. Say something nice like they're really proud of me, they love me, or that they'd like to somehow start over."

Kai raised an eyebrow. "If you had a daughter, would you leave her with your parents for the weekend?"

She physically recoiled at the thought. "God no!"

"Then why are you trying to force yourself to have a relationship with them?" He looked her in the eye as tears formed in hers. "They failed. They failed you as parents. They don't get to dictate your life anymore. They don't deserve your presence, your response, or your money."

She wiped her face with her napkin, nodding in agreement.

"And look, I get the fact that you still have hope. I think that's beautiful, honestly, that you could even think about a new beginning after what you went through. But, Christina, they can't give you what they don't have."

She repeated his line, testing how the words sounded out of her own mouth. "They can't give me what they don't have."

"They don't have love, respect, or common sense. You gotta learn how to love yourself. Parent yourself. Respect yourself. Give yourself what they couldn't or wouldn't."

"That's really wise, Kai."

His big laugh lightened the mood. "You can thank my counselor."

———

Later that night, as Christina was getting ready for bed, she opened her email and paused, eyes focused on the latest cause of so much pain. The subject of the email from her father read: "Send $1,200 asap for your mother's appointment."

She took a deep breath and opened the email again. By now, she'd practically memorized the whole message, which ended with her father calling her a "greedy brat" for not sending money regularly, which meant anytime he demanded it. But instead of reading it again, she clicked a few buttons, making a rule that any further emails would go straight to the trash without landing in her inbox. The last option to check before the deed was done read: "Apply this rule to 206 additional emails." If she clicked the box and hit save, all of the emails her parents had sent would vanish. Forever.

For a brief moment, several reasons crossed her mind for keeping them. What if there was ever a lawsuit and she needed to prove the things they'd said? What if one of them died and she had no way of being notified? What if? What if? What if?

She removed her hands from her keyboard and shook them, increasing blood flow and giving her time to breathe through her feelings.

Then she clicked the box.

## MINDSET ELEMENT 10 | **COMMUNICATION EXCELLENCE**

On Friday morning, Christina walked into the accelerator classroom feeling emotionally lighter than she had in years. She nodded to Kai and smiled. He understood, giving a thumbs-up as the Success Coach walked to his typical spot at the front of the room.

"Today we're going to start out with a game from childhood," the coach said, rubbing his hands together. "Everyone deserves to feel like a kid again sometimes, right?"

"I hope it's not Twister. I don't want to throw my back out before the weekend," said the rugby player.

"I hope it *is* Twister!" the swimmer laughed.

"It's not Twister, but I'll make a mental note to bring that in the last day of classes. Instead, we're going to play the telephone game. Do you remember that game?"

The tennis player raised his hand. "I don't know that one, Coach. Can you explain?"

"Yes. Students sit or stand around in a circle and one person whispers a phrase to the next person, and that person repeats it to the next person, and so on, until the last person has to say out loud what the message was. But you don't get to repeat the sentence or phrase. You have to be a good listener. It's usually completely wrong but funny."

"Oh, okay! We had a game like that as kids and we called it 'pass the message.'"

"Yes. Same thing," the coach said. "So, everyone stand up and form a circle up here next to me. I'll start by whispering a message, and the last person has to say it out loud. Again, you only get one chance."

As soon as the mentees had formed a circle, the Success Coach whispered, "Dogs dig holes for big bones," into the swimmer's ear.

She laughed and repeated it by whispering to the lacrosse player, and so forth. About four people in, confusion set in as words became jumbled and uncertain. Once the last person, the track star, had received the whispered message, he cocked his head to the side and laughed, certain that it had changed dramatically from the original message.

"I heard 'ducks and dogs like big butts.'" He covered his face laughing as the rest of the class joined in, including the Success Coach.

"I like big butts and I cannot lie!" said the tennis player, doing a little dance. "That's a good song."

"What did you really say, Coach?" the baseball player asked.

"Dogs dig holes for big bones," he repeated, motioning for everyone to find their seats again. "Can anyone guess the point of this exercise?"

"To make sure my mascara is truly waterproof?" Christina said, dabbing her eyes with a tissue from laughter.

"Close. It's to show the importance of active listening and good communication. You all got a dose of this yesterday during the emotional intelligence exercise where one person was speaking and one was listening. While one was using transparent communication, the other was an active listener. Today, we're going to take that up a notch.

"In your sport, you used active listening to really hear your coaches, teammates, and support staff, which led to improved performance on the field and a stronger team dynamic. The same is true for your career. Entrepreneurs who practice active listening are better able to understand the needs and desires of their customers, clients, and team members. This means better decision-making, improved relationships, and increased profitability.

"Active listening is a communication skill that involves engaging with the person speaking, focusing on their message, understanding their perspective and feelings, and then providing feedback to demonstrate understanding.

"The 1992 Olympic men's basketball final between the United States and Croatia shows a great example of active listening. Has anyone seen that video?"

A few raised their hands, including the basketball player, who said, "It's an iconic performance."

The coach nodded. "During the game, the American team was struggling to defend against the Croatian offense, and head coach Chuck Daly was stuck—he couldn't think of a solution. At one point, Michael Jordan suggested a defensive adjustment that he believed would help the team, but Daly didn't want to listen to him. However, Coach Daly finally took Jordan's advice, and it worked! The US team won the game and the gold medal. Afterward, Daly credited Jordan with the idea and praised him for his active listening and communication skills.

"This lesson is extremely important for athletes and entrepreneurs, because it will help you make better decisions, build stronger relationships, improve your communication skills, and become a better leader."

The Success Coach asked for a volunteer and moments later, Kai stood face-to-face with him.

"To demonstrate first what we are trying to avoid, Kai is going to tell me about the last time he was caught in traffic." Kai began to share his memory and only six seconds in, the Success Coach interrupted him.

"I know what you mean," he said. "Traffic is so terrible. In fact, I got stuck on I-95 a few days ago for two hours! I missed my dinner plans. Ruined my whole night. Don't you hate it when that happens?"

As Kai stood silent, the coach smiled, acknowledging his intentional faux pas of interrupting someone mid-sentence and then dominating the conversation. "You see how annoying that is?"

The class agreed.

"Would you want to keep talking with me?"

"No," the mentees echoed in response.

"Unfortunately, we do this all too often when we're trying to make a connection and find common ground. We want the person to know we understand and empathize with them, but by cutting them off and flipping the conversation back to ourselves, we're showing them that we aren't truly interested in hearing what they have to say. Nothing will kill a conversation quicker than interrupting, one-upping, and being rude.

"Now, Kai, would you tell me again about the last time you were stuck in traffic."

As Kai began to speak, the Success Coach made sure to maintain eye contact and leaned in slightly, nodding in understanding, his face mirroring the frustration in Kai's voice.

"That's awful," the Success Coach commented only once, shaking his head in frustrated solidarity as Kai explained the scene. Then, only after Kai had finished his story, the Success Coach paraphrased it back to him, complete with the emotions he'd expressed.

Turning to the class, he said, "The difference here is that while I can absolutely understand how Kai feels, since I've had a similar experience before, my goal is not to one-up him and immediately share my own experience. Instead, it's to ensure I'm actively listening so I hear what he says. As he's talking, I might empathize with short declarations that mirror his emotions. I'm empathizing with his situation by paying attention and using nonverbal cues. I want him to know that I'm 100 percent present. Once he's finished talking, I can ask clarifying questions to get a better understanding of his story. And then, if I feel it will add value to the conversation, I can share my own experience."

And with that, the Success Coach asked the students to partner up and take turns sharing the story of how they were recruited into the athlete-entrepreneur accelerator.

"You each have ten minutes to share. Then the listener will ask any clarifying questions and paraphrase the story back to the first speaker. Then, we'll switch. And we'll swap partners a few times, so get comfortable sharing all of the details."

As the mentees began to share their stories, the coach watched and listened, noting the body language being used. Across the room, Christina was sharing her story with the lacrosse player. She appeared more confident than ever.

At the end of the exercise, the students found their seats for the next lesson.

"We communicate every day, but are we communicating as well as we could be?" the coach asked. "There's always room for improvement.

"Communicating your needs is a critical skill that involves clearly expressing your desires and expectations to others. To make sure you're being heard, it's critical to distinguish between agreements and expectations or assumptions. This will help you and those you're communicating with to avoid misunderstandings.

"Agreements are mutual commitments made between you and other people or groups of people. They involve a clear understanding of what each person is responsible for and what is expected of them. This can be a contract, a relationship, even a conversation about who will make the travel plans for your next vacation with friends. Agreements are important in all relationships because they help establish boundaries and promote effective communication. Both parties have a clear understanding of their responsibilities in the matter.

"Expectations, on the other hand, are assumptions or beliefs about what should or will happen because the need hasn't been clearly communicated—and even if it has been clearly communicated, it's not always clear that the other party has fully agreed to the request. This leads to misunderstandings and resentment when expectations are not met, even though the other party may not even be aware of the expectation. This often leads to disappointment and conflict.

"How many of you have had an argument because of an unmet expectation that you thought was an agreement?"

Most of the mentees raised their hands.

"Who would like to share an example?"

"A few weeks back, my husband and I had a stupid argument because I asked him to pick up dinner on the way home and he didn't," the swimmer said. "I was so annoyed with him."

"And what happened?" the coach asked.

"I sent him a text in the afternoon asking him to bring home dinner. He didn't respond but I assumed he'd see it and take care of it. When he came home empty-handed, I complained and he had no idea why, so that set him off. I pulled up my text thread to prove my point, and I realized I'd accidentally sent the message to my landlord instead. That was awkward. It was my fault for not reaching back out to my husband when I didn't get a response. I would have realized that I sent it to the wrong person."

"Great example. Anyone else?"

"I had something happen right before I joined the accelerator," Christina offered. "I was supposed to get a referral fee for a sale since I'd started the conversation with the lead first, but another salesperson closed the deal even though I was the lead on the call." She rolled her eyes. "I assumed incorrectly that the person who made contact was the one credited with the deal because that's how it had always been, even though it wasn't written policy."

The Success Coach nodded. "Verbal agreements and handshake deals are no good in business. Unless it's clearly written communication that both parties have agreed upon, you can't assume anything. There's too much at stake. An incorrect assumption during a business deal where there should have been an agreement can cost you time, money, and sanity. Maybe even legal issues depending on the severity.

"Today's journal exercise begins with a series of prompts covering different situations and relationships." He handed each mentee two pages with written prompts and plenty of blank space. "Again, to communicate your needs effectively, it is important to be clear and direct about what you want or need. This can involve using 'I' statements to express your feelings and needs; actively listening to the other person's perspective, like we practiced last week; and finding common ground to reach a mutually beneficial solution.

"It is also important to establish clear agreements with others to avoid misunderstandings and assumptions. This requires setting clear expectations, defining roles and responsibilities, and, especially in business, establishing a system for feedback and accountability.

"Start by thinking of a situation that makes you unhappy. It could be real or imagined. Let's say you are going to have a conversation with someone who could help you resolve this issue, typically the person who is causing the needs gap and feelings of unhappiness.

"I want you to spend the next forty-five minutes working through the scenario in the prompts. Remember to use 'I' language—I need, I want, I will, I feel, I am. Your ultimate goal is to be clear and direct about what you want or need for this situation to be resolved. Don't be vague or leave any room for assumption. I'll ask for a few volunteers at the end who want to share their scenarios."

Each mentee chose a scenario and then reviewed the list of prompts:

The issue that I need to resolve is:

1. How long has this been going on?
2. How bad are things? Determine the current impact.
3. How is this issue impacting me and my personal life or work?
4. When I consider the impact on myself and others, what are my emotions?
5. If nothing changes, what's likely to happen? Determine the future implications.
6. What's at stake for me and for others?
7. How have I contributed to the problem? Even if you believe the other person is guilty, find some way you've contributed to the issue.
8. Describe the ideal outcome. When this issue is resolved, what difference will it make in my life?
9. Commit to action. What is the first step I could take to move this issue forward? When will I take this step?
10. What's going to attempt to get in my way, and how will I get past it?

Mentees wrote about health issues, disagreements with loved ones, previous work situations, and other personal matters. Kai chose to write about his struggles with anxiety, depression, purpose, and a loss of identity since walking off the football field. He'd been making good progress with his counselor, and was finally able to acknowledge that he hadn't felt like himself in years. He was able to clearly see how his struggles affected every facet of life, from his work to his relationships.

When the exercise was done, each classmate was better able to understand how wide-reaching miscommunication can be. Christina blinked down at her paper, wiping a few tears off the side of the page. She had journaled through the issues with her parents and said everything she'd always wanted to say but couldn't, advocating for her needs, her health, her goals, her happiness, and her desire to be loved and valued as a child should be. She could see, in black and white, how far she'd come. Now she was finally ready to step into the next chapter of life with a deeper understanding of her abilities, skills, and desires. The past was a closed door. Before her lay endless opportunities to embrace.

At the top of the page, she wrote: "The issue I need to resolve is: Learning to confidently advocate for myself in all areas of life because I am an athlete-entrepreneur and a future CEO!"

When the Success Coach asked for volunteers to share what they'd written, her hand was the first one in the air.

# 15

# MODULE 2: ENTREPRENEURSHIP THROUGH ACQUISITION
## Identifying Acquisition Targets

The following Monday morning, after a long but fulfilling final week of mindset elements and learning exercises, the athlete-entrepreneurs filed into the classroom ready to learn. The ten elements would enable them to manage their time, their emotions, and their relationships more effectively. Mindset was critical to their peak performance as an entrepreneur. As challenging as it had been, this was the easiest part of the program. Now, the learning intensified.

The remaining ten weeks of the three-month boot camp would require immense focus, excellent time management, and sharp critical-thinking skills as the topics shifted to selecting an industry to target, learning how to position themselves as a desirable buyer, and analyzing businesses and market trends.

At the start of the third week of classes, the reading assignments doubled. Outside of class, the mentees would spend hours each week reading case studies of high-profile athletes, CEOs, and startups, as well as doing research on their industry of choice. And today, the coursework would dive into the next module—learning how to identify businesses to acquire in the process of becoming a savvy owner.

"As an owner, you must be at the top of your game day after day. You must rely on your metacognition and resiliency," the Success Coach said, walking to a whiteboard and pointing to a list of thirty-six characteristics.[37] "How many of these characteristics, at a minimum, do you need to embody to position yourself for success as a CEO?"

The students read over the words.

| Intrinsic motivation | grit | focus | effort | confidence | optimism |
|---|---|---|---|---|---|
| need for achievement | resilience | discipline | preparation | accountability | courage |
| self-determination | commitment | self-regulation | challenge | internal locus of control | risk taking |
| passion | mental toughness | metacognition | self-efficacy | need for autonomy | action-orientation |
| competitiveness | goal orientation | work ethics | belief | independence | proactive personality |
| perseverance | long-term orientation | practice | esteem | positivity | self-sufficiency |

"Twenty," said the lacrosse player.

"I'll guess thirty," the basketball player said.

Kai guessed twenty-four.

The tennis player said, "All of them," which was the answer the Success Coach wanted to hear.

"Exactly. You must possess *all* of these characteristics to continue moving forward, regardless of the circumstance. If you're lacking in any area, it will create areas of weakness. You cannot afford to have character gaps and skill deficiencies at this level. I'm not saying you'll always have fruitful conversations, dream partnerships, and close every deal. But you must be able to pivot, to filter information, to continue driving in the face of hearing *no* repeatedly without losing your edge. Again, this is where all your years of athletic training comes into play. In the face of a setback, do you regroup and keep driving forward? Or do you quit right before a victory?"

"We don't quit!" the rugby player shouted from the back of the room. "Mama didn't raise no quitter."

"That's right!" the Success Coach answered. "You put your head down and keep driving. And that's one of the keys to success—your resilience and determination to keep seeking opportunities. Here's a fantastic quote regarding athlete owners:

> In particular, the findings show that athlete-owned firms are more profitable, allocate more capital to long-term projects and to marketing activities, and use less debt as compared to non-athlete-owned firms . . . Bringing in leaders with valuable qualities, revealed and developed through years of practice and participation in sport competitions, such as goal-orientation, intrinsic motivation, need to achieve, discipline, strong work ethics, resourcefulness, and long-term orientation, can make companies more profitable, efficient, financially sustainable, and competitive.[38]

"What that means is athletes run really good businesses. It's data backed. That's why all of you are in this room. I believe in you. And you'll need to make an owner believe in you too."

He walked back to his desk and picked up that day's syllabus. "Now that you've mastered the 10 Mindset Elements, it's time to learn the rules of the game when it comes to identifying your future acquisition targets. There are more targets now than ever before. In fact, retiring business owners will sell $10 trillion worth of assets by 2040.[39] Research says that while 70 percent of these businesses are expected to change hands, 58 percent have no plan in place to make that happen.[40] If their kids or grandkids aren't interested in taking over, they don't know who they are selling to or what to do."

"Wow. That's a huge percentage!" said the basketball player. "But I see how that works in our favor if we can connect with them and show them that we can take their business to the next level."

"Spot on. And before you start reaching out to businesses and networking, you have to have a solid understanding of who you are, what your values are, and your goals, and how to package and position yourself for success. It's your goal in this program to buy a business. But remember, the owner of that business has to buy in *to you* first. They must have confidence that *you* are the right buyer who will help them achieve their vision. They are very cognizant of their legacy.

"Why should someone pick you over another buyer who might have more experience? Give me some reasons."

"An owner should pick me because I'm honest, hardworking, and I'm driven to succeed despite any obstacle," said the tennis player. "My whole life story proves that."

"I'm a great leader, a great listener, and I value connection and team building," said the basketball player. "Three years being chosen as team captain speaks to those qualities."

"I'm the best damn networker out there and I can sell anything to anyone. I can get better results in less time because I'm attentive and prompt," Christina said confidently.

"Those are all great attributes, and you should remember those when you begin crafting your website and personal statements," the coach said. "Everything is relationship based. Business is built on relationships, and to establish a relationship, you have to be honest about your intentions, confident in representing who you are, and genuinely interested in getting to know the other person. Seems obvious enough, but the conversations you'll be having with business owners will be pivotal in deciding whether you move the ball forward together or the door closes on the opportunity. So, this week, you'll learn about the different types of acquisition targets, how to position your story, how to talk about your failures and successes, and how to connect with business owners, brokers, and others for networking."

"Failures?" the track star raised his hand. "What kind of failures?"

"All of them," the Success Coach smiled, confusing the track star further. "All of us have experienced failure. I have. You have. We do everything in our power to avoid screwing up, but no one is immune. Business owners know this. We have to give them credit. A seasoned owner doesn't just want to know about your wins. They want to know how you overcame disappointment, how you bounced back from failures. They want to feel confident that no matter what you face as the new owner of their company, you're in it for the long haul and won't veer off course at the first sign of turbulence. In fact, part of your coursework this week is to craft a failure resume."

"That's a new one," the swimmer said. "Does it look like a traditional resume?"

"Yes. And it's exactly what it sounds like," said the coach. "A well-written resume of all your failures, humiliations, stumbles, and mistakes as it pertains to your business experiences and personal life. You'll include lessons learned, insights, and growth opportunities. You'll find several examples in your coursework, and you can find hundreds more online. It's both a humbling and enlightening exercise."

"Will we be sharing the failure resume with owners?" asked the baseball player.

"Yes. And if they ask questions about how you've overcome failures or obstacles, you'll be prepared to share several well-thought-out instances, as well as your lessons learned. In return, ask them how they would overcome these failures. This creates a connection and bond between you two. How you overcome failures and what you learn in the process is what counts. In fact, some business schools and job postings are requiring applicants to submit failure resumes when they apply. I believe we can learn more about ourselves in times of failure than from the multiple instances of success. I suggest you continue to add to your failure resume long after this one exercise to see how far you've come and how your perspectives have evolved.

"But for now, we're going to shift gears from failure to farming." He clicked his pointer and a fifteen-second video played silently on one of the boards: expansive tracts of American farmland, stitched together like a patchwork quilt from an aerial view. "I want you to think about all the farmland in America—over 893 million acres. That represents all of the businesses that exist in every sector—Manufacturing, Retail, Services, Construction, Wholesale, Agriculture, Information Technology, and Creative Industries. Your job is to find one plot of land to purchase. To find your plot of land, you'll first have to choose your industry. And then within that industry, reach out to one thousand people, planting seeds of possibility to see which of those opportunities will grow into something more.

"Small businesses can be found in a wide range of industries, including those listed in your coursework for today's lesson."

The mentees reviewed the following eight industries:

1. **Manufacturing**: SMEs (small-to-medium-sized enterprises) in the manufacturing sector produce a variety of goods, from consumer products to industrial equipment.

2. **Retail**: SMEs in the retail sector operate stores and online shops that sell a range of products, from clothing and electronics to groceries and household goods.

3. **Services**: SMEs in the services sector provide a range of services, including consulting, accounting, legal services, healthcare, and hospitality.

4. **Construction**: SMEs in the construction sector include general contractors, subcontractors, and specialty trade contractors, such as electricians and plumbers.

5. **Wholesale**: SMEs in the wholesale sector purchase goods from manufacturers and sell them to retailers or other businesses.

6. **Agriculture**: SMEs in the agriculture sector produce crops and livestock for sale or use in food production.

7. **Information technology**: SMEs in the IT sector provide services such as software development, website design, and cybersecurity.

8. **Creative industries**: SMEs in the creative industries include businesses in the fields of art, design, music, film, and advertising.

"Coach, how do we know what type of business to pursue if there are thousands of options, even within each industry?" asked the golfer.

"You narrow your focus by a process of elimination. I suggest you choose something you are familiar with or already interested in. Then spend time evaluating the market trends, the industry attractiveness, and the growth potential. There may also be a geographical advantage or industry advantage to consider, so make sure you do your research.

"Your goal is to purchase a small-to-medium-sized enterprise with one to five million in net income. Once you've determined the industry, you'll want to define your search criteria further. Where do you want the business to be located? You can choose a specific state, a region of the country, or be completely open and see where the opportunity takes you."

"I'd like to be on the California coast," said the tennis player.

"I'd consider moving back to Texas, to be honest," Kai offered.

"We can stay where we are, right?" Christina asked.

"Good question," the swimmer said. "I don't want to uproot my family if I don't have to."

"You can absolutely stay where you are, if you can source a business that fits within the criteria and is one you'll be proud to run. Once you put together your strategy and criteria, you'll begin searching and conducting market analyses. There are several successful ways to source a private business acquisition. Here are some of them." The Success Coach clicked his pointer again and a slide appeared on one of the whiteboards with information about the multiple locations and means to help the athlete-entrepreneurs with the search process.

1. **Networking**: This is a great way to source private business acquisitions. Attend industry conferences, events, and meetings, and talk to people in your network to see if they know of any businesses that are for sale.

2. **Business brokers**: Deals are done through who you know, not what you know. Business brokers specialize in helping buyers find businesses that are for sale. They have access to a large database of businesses and can match buyers with businesses that fit their criteria. Many are regional, so you'll need to develop relationships with these brokers.

3. **Online marketplaces**: There are many online marketplaces where businesses can be listed for sale.

4. **Industry associations**: These can be a good source of information about businesses that are for sale. Many associations have classified sections on their websites where members can list their businesses for sale.

5. **Direct outreach**: The best way to find a business for sale is to reach out directly to business owners. This is our most important method. Look for businesses that are a good fit for your investment criteria and reach out to the owners to see if they are interested in selling. You'll find thirty proven messages in your handout.

6. **Professional advisors**: Lawyers, accountants, consultants, and other advisors may be able to refer you to businesses that are for sale or assist you in the acquisition process.

"Each of these methods has its advantages and disadvantages, and the best approach will depend on your specific circumstances and investment criteria. Working with a team of advisors and doing your due diligence on potential acquisitions is crucial to ensure a successful acquisition. I'll be working with each of you, and you'll be assigned a small team of advisors to help guide the process and offer education and feedback along the way.

"Once you've done the necessary research to choose your industry and location, you'll begin gathering data. I want you to select one thousand businesses to reach out to. As you gather contact information, pay attention to online reviews of the companies as well. Glassdoor is a great site for reading reviews written by employees, as is the Better Business Bureau. Look at what their customers are saying online. Are they satisfied with the service? Would they recommend the company? Customers and employees and their happiness are the lifeblood of a business. If you discover a company has a high rate of turnover, investigate why. It might be a red flag."

"Coach, quick question. Is one thousand overkill? Is it more like hundreds of potential businesses or do you really mean a thousand?" the golfer asked.

"You should have a list of a *minimum* of a thousand businesses. Out of one thousand businesses, there may only be one hundred that are open to a conversation. It sounds daunting. It takes grit and hard work to get to that stage, but you're fully capable of the task. Plus, the use of technology makes it easier to gather and synthesize the information. And you'll be using tools we've developed to rank the opportunities.

"Part of your homework this week is to decide on your specific industry. And whether there's a specific region of the country where you'd like to focus your efforts. I also want you to begin writing your failure resume. Everyone will read theirs out loud on Friday during class."

"Really?" Christina said with a grimace. "That sounds like torture."

"Fair point. We've put such an emphasis on being perfect that we might tend to dismiss or discredit all of the personal growth and new ideas we've experienced as a result of failing. But it's time to let go of the façade of perfection and embrace the power that comes from acknowledging our faults and failures. Our determination to succeed and reinvent ourselves is what resonates most with business owners."

"I get that," the tennis player said. "I don't want to spend time with people who are perfect, who have never made mistakes. I want to be around people who have overcome obstacles in life and became better somehow."

"Exactly," agreed the Success Coach. "Some of my biggest wins have come directly after my worst failures. Success is rarely in a straight diagonal line. But as long as you keep moving forward, you'll achieve your goal.

"You will also craft a target company profile. This will help you focus your search, and help to mold your company profile later on when you have a website and you're actively reaching out to owners."

A hand raised. "Coach, is that the same as our elevator pitch where we talk about our accomplishments and why we're the right choice as a buyer?" asked the lacrosse player.

"Good question and not quite. Do you remember completing the values exercise as part of the accelerator onboarding process?"

"Yes."

"What were your top three values?"

"Growth, independence, and knowledge."

"Good. So, let's say you choose to focus on the pool construction and service industry in the Southwest. You already know your goal is to find a small business with the financial performance of one to five million in net income. Your target company profile might read like this." With that, he walked to the whiteboard, grabbed a marker, and wrote: "My target company is a pool construction business that is operated in the Southwest and has a financial performance of $1M–5M in net income. I value discipline, processes, and teamwork and believe this asset will complement my value system."

The students nodded, understanding the assignment would allow them to easily discern which companies were a match and which were not.

"The next step is to begin market analysis to identify potential niche industries and assess the potential for growth and market positioning of your acquisition targets. Christina, which industry are you leaning toward?"

"Marketing with an emphasis in athletics."

"And where do you want to be within the US?"

"Ideally, I'd love to stay here and travel when needed."

"What are your three values?"

"Freedom, creativity, and purpose."

"Excellent. So, you might search for a marketing services business that is operated remotely with a portfolio of work in the sports industry."

"I agree! That sounds perfect!" she said, beaming.

"When you are analyzing each opportunity, you can easily see if it aligns with your values and your target company profile. Or not. And then, like when buying a house or a car, do your due diligence. If you're looking at marketing agencies, how much have other marketing agencies of the same size and scope sold for recently? How much did other comps sell for over the last three years. Is it an upward trend or downward trend? And why? Research online, talk with business brokers and CPAs who specialize in your target market—your farmland. Business brokers specialize in matching owners and buyers. They represent owners and are the gatekeepers and stewards of many deals. It's important to create a relationship with the business broker community in your farmland. Develop these relationships as you go and continue to gain knowledge and the tools necessary to identify and pursue promising acquisition opportunities."

The Success Coach looked out at the mentees. They all looked ready, eager, and excited about the tasks ahead.

"To recap, this week you will select your specific industry and ideal location. You will craft a target company profile that includes your top three values. And what else?"

"Share our failure resume on Friday," Kai said. "I'm looking forward to it, really. I have plenty of things to reflect on."

"You can go first then," smiled the coach. "Take the lead."

"Remind me to keep my mouth shut," he mumbled under his breath to the swimmer seated next to him as she giggled at his misfortune.

"For now, I want you to spend the next two hours defining your acquisition criteria. What kind of company do you want to lead? And where? At the end of class today, you can each present your initial ideas and receive feedback. You still have time to change your mind, so don't worry that you must keep what you select today. Think through all the details."

The mentees got to work, laying out their values in a statement and selecting their industry and location.

Kai wanted to focus on accounting businesses in the Southern states and really liked the idea of moving back to Texas, where he still had a lot of college friends and connections. His top three values of loyalty, trust, and hard work easily fit that industry.

Christina was truly excited about buying a digital marketing company with a focus on athletics. If she could work remotely, she could keep her home base in NYC and travel as often as needed for meetings, to help promote the company, and for networking. As she brainstormed and conducted online research, she felt more fired up about her career than she ever had.

# 16

# MODULE 3:
# PERSONAL BRANDING FOR ACQUIRING SMALL BUSINESSES
## Positioning Yourself for Success

By the following Monday, all the mentees were feeling a heightened sense of confidence after having read their failure resumes aloud to the class, including how they overcame, pivoted, and learned from those experiences. Being vulnerable was key, and the Success Coach made it clear that this was important when connecting with owners looking to sell. Each person became stronger with each challenge, a testament to their athletic training and determination to keep forging ahead—signs they were becoming true athlete-entrepreneurs.

They had also decided which sector they wanted to pursue. Kai was certain about accounting businesses, but he needed a little advice.

Fifteen minutes before class, he found the Success Coach in his office, knocked on the doorframe, and was welcomed in.

"Coach, I feel confident in focusing on accounting since I already have some knowledge from my analyzing hundreds of financials of other firms. Plus, I get along with many folks in the accounting industry. But . . . I'm concerned about potentially having to move away from my daughter. And Robin. Especially now. I don't know how things are going to play out with our relationship."

The coach understood. The mentees were making tough decisions—and they'd only become tougher. Family and friends wouldn't always be supportive or understand. And sometimes growing pains accompanied big changes, a lesson he'd learned early in his entrepreneurial journey.

"What's your ultimate goal?" asked the Success Coach.

"To own a successful business and be able to sell it for well more than the purchase price. To win the championship in business. Then keep that trend going."

"Your *ultimate* goal," the Success Coach asked again as Kai contemplated the question. "When you're an old man looking back over the last fifty years of your life, what do you want to be most proud of?"

Kai sucked in a breath and nodded. "That I provided a wonderful life for myself and my family. That I loved my wife and daughter unconditionally, and to know we have a great relationship, even through the ups and downs. To know I made a real difference in my community and the world with what I was able to accomplish, create, and give back."

The Success Coach folded his fingers together and rested his hands on his desk. "We have to take calculated risks and make decisions that others may not like and that may cause discomfort. It's all part of our journey, making our own way in the world. I can't predict the future, but I do know you won't get very far if you're living in the past and what might have been."

Kai straightened, realizing it was time to live for himself and his goals. He would work hard so he could create a solid financial future to build on—including being able to provide the life he wanted for his daughter, even if she was several states away.

"We can never know what the future holds," the coach added. "Moving away might be the best decision you could possibly make. You have two mindsets to choose from. Are you playing offense or defense? A promotion and growth mindset, or a prevention and fearful mindset? It's up to you to decide. And let the rest work itself out."

"Thanks, Coach." Kai smiled, then walked back to the classroom.

The Success Coach made a few final notes in his journal, then followed the hallway to the classroom, excited to continue the lessons . . . and to introduce a special guest.

———

"It's important to understand that people want to view their life as a story. For business owners, much of their story is found in their businesses. It's their baby. It's often what they created from scratch—an idea and sheer willpower. The ability to leave a legacy through their business is vital to their story. To speak about the importance of building story, I've invited a guest lecturer to help teach this module. Charles is the founder of a successful marketing agency in Los Angeles, and he helps people create and connect to story every day. Charles—" the Success Coach stepped aside as Charles nodded his thanks and walked to a whiteboard.

"Thank you, Coach." He turned to address the mentees. "There are several reasons why people view their life as a story." He pointed to a whiteboard with four points written out: a sense of coherence, identity formation, emotional connection, and legacy.

"First, seeing our life as a story can help bring a **sense of coherence** and meaning to our experiences. By creating a narrative out of the events and experiences of our lives, we can make sense of them and feel a greater sense of control over our lives.

"The second is **identity formation**. Stories help us form our identity by creating a sense of continuity between our past, present, and future selves. We can see how our choices and experiences have shaped us into the person we are today and how we might continue to evolve.

"Next is an **emotional connection**. Stories can create emotional connections between people, and seeing our own life as a story can help us connect with others by sharing our experiences and finding common ground, and a common connection."

The Success Coach chimed in and addressed the cohort. "You experienced this connection when you shared stories with how you came to be in this program, and also when you shared your failure resume last week.

"Absolutely," Charles nodded. "Finding that same common ground with owners will make a huge difference in their willingness to open up to you.

"And last, viewing our life as a story can help us think about the **legacy** we want to leave behind."

From his seat to the side of the room, the Success Coach made eye contact with Kai, who nodded in understanding. It was time to build a legacy.

Charles continued. "By creating a narrative of our life, we can reflect on our accomplishments, learn from our mistakes, and think about how we want to be remembered.

"Each one of you has a story that you'll be working to refine over the next few weeks, including fine-tuning the failure resumes Coach asked you to complete last week. The buyers have stories, too, of how they built their businesses, what they learned and overcame, and what it means to them as a part of their personal identity.

"Always remember, there are three things that they are super emotional about: their family, their house, and their business. All of that adds up to their legacy, which is a powerful concept. If you are positioning yourself to buy a great company in Ohio and reach that owner, you've got to understand the owner is living a story and you need to position yourself to be the best option. You've got to know what that owner is trying to achieve, and what they are trying to do with their business.

"If I'm a business owner considering selling, I want a buyer who has discipline, self-regulation, and high metacognition. I want someone with a work ethic. And studies say that athletes have these qualities at higher rates than nonathletes. This is where you can bring your former athletic experience and discipline to these conversations, along with your unique skills, strengths, and values.

"Business owners want to feel certain that they are making the best choice by selling to you, that you respect what they've built, and you'll contribute to their legacy when they step away by expanding on their vision. And if you ever find someone who doesn't care what you do with the company or their employees, I can assure you, you don't want to buy that business."

Charles walked around the room, handing out stapled pages. "We'll start by understanding the seven points of a story arc as it relates to positioning yourself as the ideal buyer.

"First we must **identify the business owner's problem**. This should be framed in a way that is relevant and relatable to them.

"Second, as an athlete-entrepreneur, you will **position yourself as the guide** who can help the business owner solve their problem with the messaging: '*My* dream is to help you achieve *your* dream.' This involves communicating your authority and expertise in a way that builds trust. Identify your unique strengths, skills, and values, and think about how you can use these to differentiate yourself from others and align with the business owner." He nodded to the Success Coach to comment.

"Think about the thirty-six attributes and characteristics we reviewed on the whiteboard on Monday. Draw from those," directed the Success Coach.

"Third, you will want to **develop and refine your online presence**. In today's digital age, having a strong online presence is essential for building your personal brand. This includes creating a professional website, optimizing your social media profiles, and regularly sharing content that showcases your expertise."

A hand went up from the back. "How do we convey that we want to buy their business without mentioning the obvious reason that we want to make a lot of money?"

"Of course you want to make money," Charles replied. "They know that. They want to make money too. But you are different because you want to improve yourself in the process of becoming an owner. You want the challenge. You want to lead people. You want to help people just like the business owner has."

"Got it. Thanks, Charles," the rugby player responded.

"For the fourth step, as the guide, you will **offer a clear plan** or process that the buyer can follow to solve their problem. This should be simple and easy to understand. To build a strong personal brand, it's important to be authentic and consistent in your messaging and actions. Your brand should reflect who you are and what you stand for, and you should consistently deliver on your promises to build trust and credibility with your audience.

"In the fifth step, you will **provide a clear call to action** that motivates the buyer to take action. This could be a specific product or service that you offer, or a free resource that you provide. You'll provide empathy by acknowledging the business owner's emotions and showing that you understand their problem. I cannot stress it enough that *owners sell on values and trust*. There's plenty of people out there talking about the money part of the deal. That's secondary; empathy is first."

"That's like the exercise we did last week, Coach, when you cut me off," Kai joked.

The coach smiled. "Being actively engaged in an owner's story is a great way to show that you are taking their legacy seriously, and to build trust in those initial conversations."

"Next," Charles continued, "you will **show social proof** that you are the right person to buy their company: a trustworthy, ethical, credible, and value-based individual. This could be in the form of testimonials or case studies from coaches, colleagues, friends, community members, or influencers. Use other people's reputations to endorse yours.

"And—starting today, if you haven't already, review all of your social media as far back as you can go and clean it up. Being seen as an outgoing, social person is great. Being seen with alcohol in most every picture, and posting unflattering opinions, pictures, or political content can be turnoffs to some buyers. You're not trying to remove your personality, experiences, or accomplishments. I'm not telling you to sanitize your entire life. I am saying that you will be researched heavily, so review your content accordingly. You want to ensure that whatever is online is an accurate representation of who you are now, as a future CEO."

"What if we have our social media set to private? Is it better to delete our accounts entirely?" asked Christina, thinking of the security steps she had taken because of her parents.

"Yeah, good question," the swimmer said. "Most of my pictures are of my boys and my family. And I hardly post on LinkedIn, although I do have a profile. Will that make me look too family-oriented and not serious enough about business?"

"It all depends on your target audience," said Charles.

"And the conversations that you have . . . and how you position your own story to the buyers," said the Success Coach. "Do your posts infer that you're lazy, irresponsible, and self-centered?"

"Absolutely not!" the swimmer responded. "If anything, they show that I'm a loving mother, a caring person, and able to accomplish a lot while still being very involved with my family, friends, and community."

"Then I'd say your social proof is working for you and not against you," Charles responded before continuing.

"Finally, you will **cast the vision**—offer a transformation that the business owner will experience by selling to you. This should be framed in a way that is emotionally compelling and inspiring. For instance, you will be pleasant, respectful, and efficient in buying their business. You understand time is the ultimate currency and will be responsive to their communication. And you genuinely want to enhance their life instead of taking away from it."

"Exactly, Charles," the Success Coach said. "Know that deal fatigue is a real thing and the longer it takes to close a deal, the more likely the seller is to become frustrated. This used to be a strategy—intentionally drawing out deals to wear the owner down. But I don't advocate for it because it's not respectful to my time or their time. I'm not trying to beat them into submission. I want to partner with them toward the same goal."

"Can you talk a little more about the communication?" asked the golfer. "What does being responsive look like when we're also focused on time management? I don't imagine someone would call at two in the morning wanting to talk about the potential deal, but I guess they might call right when we're in the middle of dinner with family or during another meeting. What's the best way to handle communication during the buying process?"

Charles nodded to the Success Coach, who stood and walked back to the front of the room before giving his response.

"I've never seen a successful person put off important communication and still close deals. They might answer a call and explain that they're in the middle of dinner and ask for a good time to call the person back. But they don't let calls, texts, or emails go unanswered for long periods of time. I believe you can create a system that works for you and allows the owner to feel seen and valued, especially if they have to wait a few hours for you to call them back. Remember, it's all about communication, and timely communication creates trust."

"Thanks, Coach."

"You bet. Now, when it comes to reasons to sell a business, what do you think are a few of the most common?"

"Wanting to retire," said the basketball player.

"What if they sense a change in the market and want to take advantage of it?" asked the rugby player.

"Maybe they've decided to move and can't manage the business anymore," said the tennis player.

"Those are great answers," the coach said. "And yes, they're all reasons a person may choose to sell a business. Here are ten of the most common." With that, he clicked his pointer and an image flashed onto a whiteboard with the most common explanations behind why people choose to sell.

1. Retirement: The business owner may want to sell their business to fund their retirement.

2. Burnout: The owner may be feeling overwhelmed and no longer have the energy or motivation to continue running the business.

3. Health issues: The owner may be dealing with health concerns that prevent them from continuing to manage the business effectively.

4. Financial difficulties: The business may be struggling, and the owner may choose to sell in order to avoid bankruptcy or financial ruin.

5. Partnership disputes: If there are multiple owners, disagreements may arise that lead one or more owners to want to sell their stake.

6. Lifestyle changes: The owner may want to make a significant change, such as moving to a new city or country, that makes it difficult to continue managing the business.

7. New opportunities: The owner may have other business opportunities or interests that they want to pursue, and selling would allow them to do so.

8. Family considerations: The owner may need to sell the business in order to provide for their family or to resolve inheritance issues.

9. Market conditions: The owner may be selling the business in response to changes in the market, such as a decline in demand for their product or service.

10. Business growth: The owner may sell to take advantage of an opportunity for significant growth, such as merging with another company or being acquired by a larger one.

After allowing a few minutes for the mentees to read the reasons, the Success Coach continued. "As you can see, the decision to sell can be influenced by a wide range of factors, both personal and business-related. A business owner might share their reasons with you at the start of the conversation, but not always. It's up to you to be a good listener and create trust so the owner feels comfortable sharing their reasons. And part of building trust goes back to what we talked about earlier in the week—sharing our own story. Personal branding is key! So, Charles, tell us more about positioning."

"Defining your own personal brand and creating an online presence takes time and intention, but here are some steps you can take to get started." He clicked the pointer and a slide filled the whiteboard with nine tips.

"Number one, **define your personal brand** through self-reflection. Start by identifying your unique strengths, values, and passions, and use these as the foundation for your personal brand. Think about what drives you, what sets you apart in your field, and what you want to be known for. Were you a team captain? Did you earn your scholarship after walking on? Home in on your experiences and what makes you unique.

"Number two, **identify your target audience**. Conduct thorough research on the values, motivations, and aspirations of the business owners who are looking to sell their businesses. Understand their generational mindset, work ethic, and the factors important to them in a potential buyer. Consider their needs, preferences, and pain points, and tailor your brand messaging accordingly.

"Three, **identify shared values**. Look for the common ground between your own values and the values of the business owners. Identify the areas where your personal brand aligns with their needs and desires. This alignment will form the foundation of your personal brand strategy.

"Four, **craft your personal narrative** with a brand statement. Develop a compelling story that communicates who you are, explains your journey, and tells why you are passionate about acquiring businesses. Highlight the values and strengths that make you an ideal buyer. Make sure your story is authentic, relatable, and inspiring. And for online use and marketing purposes, you'll want to create a clear and concise statement that encapsulates your personal brand and what you have to offer. This statement should be used consistently across all platforms. I hear you're already working on these, so that's great. Let me know if you need any help."

A hand raised. "Charles, what's the difference between our brand strategy and a brand statement?"

"Great question. Think of the brand strategy as the road map to get you to your goals. It includes the body of work you're creating in this accelerator program. All of the data you're collecting by doing research, identifying your own values—these are all part of the long-term plan that will help you be identified as the best option as a buyer. A brand statement is one to three sentences that showcase who you are, what you do, what makes you unique, and why you are the best option for an owner to consider selling to."

"Can you share an example?" came the reply.

"Of course. As a former athlete, I can say my personal brand values revolve around teamwork, loyalty, hard work, and financial security. Leveraging these values, my brand strategy is to position myself as a passionate and dedicated entrepreneur who understands the importance of building strong relationships, creating a supportive community, and achieving long-term financial stability. Does that help?"

"Got it. Yes, thank you."

Charles continued with his list. "Five, **establish your online presence**. This includes creating a professional website. Your website is the foundation of your online presence. Make sure it is professional, visually appealing, and easy to navigate. Include your brand statement, contact information, and links to your social media profiles. Now is also the time to establish a presence on social media if you don't have one, or review and revise the accounts you have so you can align with your goal of buying a business. Choose social media platforms that are relevant to your target audience, and create professional profiles that are consistent with your brand messaging. Engage with your audience by sharing valuable content and participating in online discussions.

"Six, **focus on networking and relationship building**. Actively engage in networking events, conferences, and industry gatherings where you can connect with business owners and key stakeholders. Build genuine relationships by demonstrating your genuine interest, listening attentively, and offering support and value without an immediate expectation of return. This is where active listening goes a long way.

"Seven, you want to **communicate and engage**. Tailor your communication approach to resonate with the values of the business owners. Clearly articulate how your personal brand aligns with their goals and highlight the benefits they can expect by choosing you as the buyer. Be empathetic, transparent, and responsive throughout the communication process. And remember that consistency is key to building a strong personal brand. Make sure your messaging and branding are consistent across all platforms and that you maintain a consistent voice and tone. A bit later, we'll talk through a call script I've created to give you somewhere to begin when you're cold-calling business owners."

"Ugh . . . that's been a part of my roles for years, but I still don't love cold-calling," said Christina.

"What parts don't you like?" Charles asked.

"The hanging-up-in-my-face part!" Several in the class laughed.

"And the name calling," said the basketball player. "I had to cold-call donors at the museum twice a year and although most people were incredibly nice, I always caught one or two people on a really bad day."

"You can't win them all," Charles laughed. "But I do believe that by following a script and being genuine in those conversations, you can get far better results and build trust quickly once you let a business owner know that you can help them solve a big problem and make money at the same time."

"That's a good point," Christina nodded. "Talking to someone about continuing their legacy has to be a lot more inspiring than trying to make office furniture sound sexy."

After a good laugh, Charles continued. "Number eight, **deliver value, build trust, and be consistent** by offering valuable content, whether online or in person. Establish yourself as an authority in your field by publishing high-value content such as blogs, articles, and videos. Make sure your content is well-researched, informative, and relevant to your target audience. Demonstrate your credibility and expertise by providing relevant insights, guidance, and resources to business owners, even before the acquisition process begins. Show your commitment to their success and the legacy of their business. Act with integrity and honesty to build trust and establish a reputation as a reliable buyer.

"And finally, number nine—**monitor, adapt, and evolve**. Continuously evaluate the effectiveness of your personal brand and make adjustments as needed. Seek feedback from business owners and industry professionals to understand how well your personal brand is resonating with the target audience. Stay open to learning and adapting to changing market dynamics and generational shifts."

Wrapping it up, he said, "Remember, building a personal brand aligned with the values of business owners takes time, consistency, and a genuine commitment to understanding and connecting with their needs. By following these steps, you can establish yourself as an authority in your field and create a strong and memorable brand that sets you apart from others and makes you irresistible to owners. As an athlete, you have an advantage when you *knock on the door*, given your solid reputation in the field of play. Use it to your advantage."

Charles took a seat as the Success Coach regained the lead. "Thanks, Charles. You knocked it out of the park. Okay, we'll spend the rest of the week on positioning, so keep fine-tuning your failure resume. Next, review your social media, collect testimonials or other social proof that you can use in conversation or your website, and begin to craft your own story. What makes you the best option as a buyer? Why should a business owner trust you over someone who has more experience?"

"Coach, what kind of testimonials are we going for here?" the rugby player asked. "I've never owned a business, but I know I need some kind of social proof to show I'm a trustworthy person."

"Have you ever gotten accolades in writing from people you work with for going above and beyond or doing great work?"

"I have."

"Ever won any awards or scholarships for your athleticism, team mentality, or intelligence?"

"Absolutely."

"I don't believe the intelligence part," quipped the lacrosse player.

"Hey! My mother says I'm smart and handsome, so zip it."

The Success Coach reminded everyone to pull up their letters of recommendations, and any positive feedback and encouragement from professors, coaches, and former coworkers and bosses.

"We'll provide each of you with a solid and unique endorsement based on your performance in this program, but never underestimate positive recognition, no matter the source."

———

After a break, the mentees returned to work on a call script with Charles and the Success Coach.

"The format of each call will begin with you giving a quick intro on yourself and your values," the coach began. "The owner will also introduce themselves and their business. Then the meeting opens up for a more casual back-and-forth discussion. Remember, you are in sales mode! We want you to exude confidence, stability, and enthusiasm about a potential future together. Which is why we are providing some best practices to preview prior to meetings.

"To put your best foot forward, it's a good idea to prepare brief opening remarks, less than five minutes long, describing both your business and acquisition goals. I'll share a sample script that incorporates key information owners typically want to know."

The Success Coach walked a small stack of handouts around the room so each mentee could follow along.

"This information is a starting point for owners to see what a good fit you could be as a buyer," Charles said. "I recommend a pitch similar to this, tailored to your specific situation, of course. I hope this helps, and remember, we are always available as a resource to answer any questions or address any concerns."

"Let's have two participants to read this aloud," the coach said. Kai and Christina both raised a hand.

"Perfect. Kai, you are the athlete-entrepreneur and your sport is football."

"Naturally," he beamed.

"And Christina, you are the business owner. First we need to add some details, ad-lib style. Let's pick an industry."

"Landscape management," someone said.

"Okay, and a location."

"Newark, New Jersey."

"Name a college or university."

Now everyone shouted their alma maters.

"Hey, I'm the guinea pig so I'm using mine—Texas A&M," Kai said.

"Name an industry that would in some way be related to landscape management."

"A construction firm?"

"That works," said the Success Coach. "Kai, go ahead."

Kai and Christina stood up and he read aloud, "Hi, Miss Christina, the business owner, my name is Kai Stafford. For fifteen years I played football and learned that integrity, hard work, and honesty were the only way to win on the field. My teammates were always number one, and I built a toolbox of characteristics that I know will serve me well in owning and operating a landscape management business in Newark, New Jersey. After graduating as a top student-athlete from Texas A&M, I decided to work in the construction industry so I could hone my business acumen. With the support of my team, I have been diligently looking for a business in the landscape management industry that has the same values as I do, and my goal is to buy and operate the business."

"Okay," said Christina, grinning at her easy line.

"Well, I came across your business and I'm really impressed with what you've built. I'm interested in potentially buying your business, but before we get into that, I wanted to take a moment to share a bit about my values."

"Sure, go ahead."

"So, one of my core values is honesty. I believe in being up-front and transparent, which is why I wanted to be open with you from the start about my interest in your business. Another value that's important to me is integrity. I strive to always do what's right, even when it's not the easiest or most profitable path."

"I appreciate your honesty and integrity, but I have to say, I've had a lot of interest in my business over the years. What makes you different from the others?"

"I understand where you're coming from, and I know there are a lot of buyers out there. What sets me apart is my commitment to building a long-term relationship with the businesses I acquire. I'm not just looking to make a quick profit and move on to the next deal. I want to work with your team to grow and improve your business, and to ensure that it continues to thrive for years to come."

"I have to say, that's refreshing to hear. I've put a lot of time and effort into building this business, and I want to make sure it's in good hands if I decide to sell."

"I completely understand, and I'm here to answer any questions you may have and to work with you every step of the way. If you're interested, I'd love to set up a meeting to discuss the details of a potential sale."

"That sounds good to me. Let's set something up!"

With that, the two took their seats to a playful round of applause.

Charles smiled at each of them. "By expressing his values and emphasizing his commitment to a long-term relationship, Kai, the athlete-entrepreneur, was able to create a connection with Christina, the business owner, and express his interest in buying her business. I know it sounds simple. And it is. But it's also where so many things can go wrong. This straightforward approach can help build trust and establish a foundation for a successful business transaction."

"Now," the Success Coach said, "I want you to pair up, fill in the details, and practice having these conversations. I want you to find four different partners for this exercise. Even if it feels silly or awkward at first, the more often you have the conversation, the easier and more natural it will become. And that's what you want to feel before you begin cold-calling."

"Cool, calm, and collected," Christina said as she turned to pair up with the swimmer.

# 17

# MODULE 4:
# FINANCIAL ANALYSIS FOR
# ACQUIRING SMALL BUSINESSES
## Understanding the Scoreboard

The following Monday, the students arrived and realized there would be another guest speaker, as a woman stood talking with the Success Coach at the front of the room, clicker and notes in hand. After everyone was seated, the coach introduced Sherry, an expert on financial analysis and entrepreneur who had purchased many firms.

"Welcome to the Financial Fitness Training program!" she said with a broad smile. "Just as you trained your bodies to excel in your respective sports, it's time to strengthen your financial muscles."

"Last week you learned how to position yourself for success in early conversations with business owners," the Success Coach said. "Once they express an interest in discussing a sale, it's time to take a look at their business to see if it's worth continuing discussions. Offer the owner a nondisclosure agreement (NDA) so they are comfortable with sending information and discussing the business freely. This week, Sherry will teach you how to perform a ten-minute financial analysis of a small business by reviewing three documents you will request: the balance sheet; the income statement, otherwise known as a profit and loss statement, or P&L; and the cash flow report."

Sherry nodded. "Precisely. These three documents provide a snapshot of a company's financial health. I call it 'Understanding the Scoreboard.' By acquiring this skill, you will understand the importance of financial ratios in assessing performance and stability. And you'll be able to identify and evaluate any financial warning signs and potential risks like declining profitability, excessive debt, or cash flow problems that could impact the success of your acquisition.

"By the end of this week, you'll be able to make informed decisions and quickly pursue acquisition opportunities with confidence, which will be immensely helpful since you will be reaching out to so many business owners.

"Who here has gone through business school or taken business classes before?"

Several hands simultaneously raised.

"Wonderful. And how many of you have some working knowledge of these three documents?"

All hands raised, although a few tentatively so.

"We're off to an excellent start then. My goal will be to make these easy to understand. And to help, I'm going to compare them to the world of team sports."

*This should be interesting*, Kai thought. Coming from the accounting world, he had an excellent understanding of how to read these documents, and the thought of relating them to sports was intriguing.

Sherry clicked the first slide—a balance sheet—onto the screen.

## BALANCE SHEET

"Imagine you're a coach preparing for a big game. The balance sheet is a snapshot of three important factors—your team's *assets*, *liabilities*, and *owner's equity*—giving you a clear picture of your team's financial position at a specific moment, just like a team lineup before a match.

"In this example, think of assets as your team's resources. These are things that your team owns and can use to help win the game. Assets can include cash or money in the bank; equipment like your jerseys, balls, and training gear; and even your team's reputation and brand value.

"The liabilities are like your team's opponents. These are the obligations or challenges that your team needs to overcome. It could be the other team's strong defense or the pressure to perform well. Liabilities can also include debts or financial obligations, just like the challenges you face during a game.

"Last we have owner's equity, which is like the team's overall value or net worth. It represents the difference between your team's assets and liabilities. It's the value that you and your teammates collectively bring to the game. The higher the owner's equity, the more valuable and financially strong your team is considered to be.

"Just as you evaluate your team's lineup to understand its strengths and weaknesses before a game, analyzing the balance sheet helps you understand your team's financial health and resources. It shows you how much cash you have, what equipment you own, and any financial obligations you need to tackle."

Kai's big smile caught Sherry's attention. "Is this making sense?" she asked.

"Oh, absolutely. When you put it in those terms, it's very easy to understand. I've worked in accounting for the last eight years and I wish I'd thought of this analogy. Could have saved my coworkers and clients some frustration."

"Yes, I agree," the tennis player remarked, turning to Kai. "I've always heard of a balance sheet and I've seen several in the office of our tennis center but it looked like Greek to me because all I saw were numbers with no explanation. Now I understand."

"I'm glad it's hitting the mark," Sherry said. "By studying the balance sheet, you can gauge if your team has enough resources to compete effectively, just as you assess if your team has the necessary equipment and financial stability to take on the competition. It also helps you understand if there are any financial challenges or debts that need to be managed.

"Remember, just like in sports, a strong balance sheet with sufficient assets and manageable liabilities is crucial for a team's success. It provides a solid foundation for your team to achieve its goals and win the financial game of business."

## INCOME STATEMENT

"Next, the income statement, also known as the profit and loss or P&L statement, provides a summary of three things: revenues, expenses, and net income (or net loss) over a specific period. Think of the income statement as the scorecard or scoreboard of a game that tracks your team's performance. It shows how well your team has performed in terms of scoring points and making progress, just like tracking your game statistics.

"Revenue is like the points your team scores during a game. It represents the money your team earns from its activities, such as ticket sales, sponsorships, merchandise sales, or any other income sources related to your team's operations.

"Expenses are the costs your team incurs while playing the game. Just like you need to invest in equipment, training, travel, and other expenses to compete effectively, a team has various expenses as well. These can include player salaries, coaching staff, travel costs, equipment purchases, and marketing expenses.

"Net income is like the final score of the game. It represents the result of subtracting your team's expenses from its revenue. If your team's revenue exceeds its expenses, it results in a positive net income, which indicates a profit. However, if your team's expenses are higher than its revenue, it leads to a negative net income, which indicates a loss, and you'll be in the red.

"Analyzing the income statement helps you understand how well your team performed financially during a specific period, just as analyzing game stats helps you assess your team's performance on the field.

"By studying the income statement, you can determine if your team generated enough revenue to cover its expenses, just like you evaluate if your team's scoring points were sufficient to outweigh the opponent's score. Positive net income indicates financial success and profitability, while a negative net income suggests financial challenges that need to be addressed.

"Remember, just as you aim to win games and achieve success on the field, a healthy income statement with consistent revenue growth, controlled expenses, and positive net income is crucial for your team's financial success. It reflects your team's ability to generate income and manage expenses effectively, just as you strive to excel athletically and achieve victory in your sports endeavors."

The lacrosse player raised a hand. "Sherry, what if a business has a bad year or two, but is overall making progress? How do you know whether the bad years are an indication of a warning sign versus growing pains?"

"That's a great question! It depends on all the other factors and documents you'll be reviewing. It is entirely possible for a company to have a negative year or two, or a down quarter or two, but still be a fantastic purchase. Think of it like a football game." Kai perked up. "Your team might play a strong first quarter to take the lead, struggle in the second and third quarters and fall behind, but then rally in the fourth to win the game. You have to look at all of the factors within the game to evaluate progress as you move through each time period.

"In business, those come down to the numbers, the trends, the market forecast, and the transparency of the owner. And I'll talk more about warning signs in a bit."

## CASH FLOW REPORT

She clicked again and a cash flow report replaced the balance sheet. "Think of the cash flow statement as tracking the movement of money in and out of your team's financial 'game.' It's like keeping a record of how money flows through your team's operations, similar to tracking how energy flows during a game. Again, our magic number is three. We're going to be looking at the operating activities, the investing activities, and the financial activities.

"Operating activities are like the actions you take on the field during the game. These are the day-to-day activities that generate cash flow for your team, such as ticket sales, concessions, and merchandise revenue. They also include the expenses directly related to running your team, such as player salaries, coaching fees, and equipment costs.

"Investing activities are like making strategic moves to strengthen your team's capabilities. They involve using money to acquire long-term assets or investments that will benefit your team in the future—such as purchasing new equipment, upgrading facilities, or investing in player development programs.

"Then we have financing activities, which involve managing the team's financial resources and sources of funding. It's like strategizing how to raise funds or support your team financially. This can include obtaining loans or sponsorships, issuing shares, or paying back debts.

"The cash flow statement summarizes the inflows and outflows of cash resulting from these activities, helping you understand how money moves within your team's financial game. By studying the cash flow statement, you can assess whether your team is generating enough cash from operations or operating activities, making wise investments through investing activities, and managing financial resources effectively, which are the financing activities.

"A positive cash flow indicates that your team is bringing in more cash than it's spending, giving you the financial flexibility to grow and invest. Negative cash flow means your team is spending more than it's bringing in, requiring careful management and potential adjustments to ensure financial stability. Any questions at this stage?"

No hands went up as mentees continued to process all of this information.

## SELLER DISCRETIONARY EARNINGS (SDE) AND EBITDA (EARNINGS BEFORE INTEREST, TAXES, DEPRECIATION, AND AMORTIZATION)

"Thank you, Sherry." The Success Coach looked to the mentees. "Who knows what SDE stands for?"

"Seller Discretionary Earnings," Kai answered.

"And what about EBITDA? Someone other than Kai." The Success Coach smiled. "He's got insider knowledge."

"Earnings before Interest, Taxes, Depreciation, and Amortization," said the baseball player.

"He's got insider knowledge too!" Kai joked.

The coach laughed. "Businesses are valued and sold based on a multiple of either of these numbers." He displayed a chart on the board.

"Very true," Sherry chimed in. "Imagine you're assessing the overall performance of a sports team, and you want to understand the team's true value beyond just the scores on the scoreboard. SDE or EBITDA allows you to do just that by considering different aspects of financial performance. For more in-depth explanations, flip to today's coursework and you'll see several definitions listed and explained with our sports terminology.

"Think of SDE or EBITDA as a measure of the team's collective performance, taking into account the overall financial success of the business. It provides a more comprehensive view of the team's earning potential, profitability, and ability to generate cash flow. In athletic terms, EBITDA can be likened to a player's individual performance without factoring in external influences. It shows the team's profitability before considering interest expenses, taxes, depreciation of assets, and amortization of intangible assets.

"Just as you have individual skills and contributions that impact the team's success, SDE takes into account the owner's discretionary earnings. It considers the total financial benefits derived from the business, including the owner's salary, personal expenses, and other perks.

## Median Deal Multiples by EBITDA Size of Company

| EBITDA | Manufacturing | Construction & Engineering | Consumer Goods & Services | Wholesale & Distribution | Business Services | Basic Materials & Energy | Health Care & Biotech | Information Technology | Financial Services | Media & Entertainment | AVERAGE |
|---|---|---|---|---|---|---|---|---|---|---|---|
| $0-$999K | 4.0 | 3.5 | 4.3 | 4.0 | 4.0 | 3.0 | 2.5 | 4.5 | 4.5 | 5.0 | **3.9** |
| $1M-$4.99M | 6.0 | 4.5 | 6.0 | 5.3 | 6.0 | 4.0 | 6.3 | 5.5 | 5.0 | 6.0 | **5.5** |

Source Pepperdine Private Capital Markets Project, 2020 Private Capital Markets Report

"To calculate SDE, you would add back the owner's salary, personal expenses, and nonessential business expenses to the net income. For EBITDA, you would start with the net income and add back interest, taxes, depreciation, and amortization.

"SDE and EBITDA are commonly used in the business world to determine the value and potential of a business. Just as a sports team's performance impacts its market value and potential for growth, these metrics evaluate a business's financial health, profitability, and attractiveness as an investment opportunity.

"By understanding SDE and EBITDA, you can assess the overall financial performance of a small business from an athletic perspective. It allows you to gauge the team's collective performance, profitability, and earning potential, providing valuable insights when evaluating potential acquisition opportunities or making informed financial decisions.

"And now, the fun part!" Sherry said, wrapping it up. "How to identify financial warning signs."

"I was hoping for something really fun, like a box of puppies," said Christina.

"Me too," the basketball player said with a laugh.

"If you become a savvy and financially fluid business owner, you can adopt all the puppies your heart desires."

"Bring on those warning signs, Sherry!" said the swimmer in her best wrestling announcer voice.

Sherry smiled at the fun group of students. "The last lesson before our partner activity will be understanding common financial warning signs that indicate potential issues. You want to be able to identify declining profitability, excessive debt, or cash flow problems, and be able to evaluate potential risks that could impact the success of an acquisition.

"We'll be looking for five things to tip us off: declining revenue, increasing expenses, negative cash flow, excessive debt, and low profit margins. First, let's discuss **declining revenue**. Just as a dip in your team's scoring is a red flag during a game, declining revenue is a warning sign in business financials. It suggests that the business is facing challenges in generating sales and may struggle to cover expenses.

"Next is **increasing expenses**. Imagine your energy levels dropping rapidly during a game due to excessive effort. Similarly, if a small business experiences a significant and continuous increase in expenses, it could indicate inefficiencies or cost management issues, which may lead to financial difficulties.

"Cash flow is like the oxygen that keeps your team running smoothly. If a small business consistently experiences **negative cash flow**, it means they are spending more money than they are bringing in. This can lead to cash shortages, difficulty paying bills, increased debt, and potential insolvency. Understand how they are collecting cash and making payments, or accounts receivable versus accounts payable.

"**Excessive debt** can be compared to carrying a heavy burden during a game, slowing down your performance. If a small business has a high debt-to-equity ratio or struggles to make debt payments, it could signal financial instability and potential difficulty in meeting financial obligations.

"And last, we want to look for **low profit margins**. Profit margins indicate how efficiently a business is converting revenue into profit. Just as optimizing your shooting percentage helps maximize scoring, a small business with consistently low profit margins may struggle to generate sufficient profit, impacting long-term sustainability."

"Sherry, what's a good ratio of growth?" the swimmer asked. "You mentioned earlier that it doesn't necessarily indicate a warning sign if a company has one or two bad years."

"You're looking for positive growth each of the trailing three years. I do want to mention that the growth rate can be dependent on industries. For instance, construction and manufacturing may grow more slowly than a marketing firm."

The Success Coach stood and grabbed a stack of papers to hand out. "You've provided a fantastic explanation, Sherry. There are detailed notes in your curriculum, but the best way to learn how to read these documents is to spend a lot of time reading the documents!

"I want you to partner up for a Financial Analysis Challenge and put your financial analysis skills to the test. You're going be presented with a fictional small business's financial statements, ratios, and metrics. Your task is to analyze the provided information within ten minutes and answer a series of questions to assess the financial health of the business. This assessment will evaluate your ability to apply the knowledge gained from the lessons and make informed decisions based on financial data.

"Remember, just like in sports, practice makes perfect, and we'll spend the next two hours reviewing documents, so don't hesitate to seek clarification if you have any questions at all. Sherry and I will be walking around the room to help."

And with that, the mentees paired up and got to work, feeling a buzz of excitement and confidence.

# 18

# MODULE 5: DEAL STRUCTURING AND VALUATION

By the following week, after reviewing over fifty batches of financial documents from small businesses, each mentee could quickly and easily review the three important financial documents: the balance sheet, the income statement, and the cash flow report. This week would teach the process of valuation, as well as how to write a letter of intent.

"Our first lesson today will be valuation based on those important financial documents and your independent research," the Success Coach said. "And I'm going to use Sherry's comparative approach from last week. Just like assessing the worth of an athlete on the field, we can estimate the value of a business using a simplified approach. This will help you understand the basics in less than ten minutes.

"Let's talk through four methods of valuation." He flashed a slide onto the screen, as the mentees read and took notes.

"First, we have a **revenue multiplier**: Think of the business's performance as its revenue, similar to an athlete's performance on the field. We'll apply a multiplier, which represents the market demand for the business. Just like in sports, different positions or industries may have different multipliers. Multiply the business's annual revenue by the multiplier to estimate its value. For instance, service businesses have been trading for a .9–1.2x revenue multiplier.

"The next is the most common—the **SDE/EBITDA multiplier**. You can find these online as well as in your coursework.

"Then we have the **rule of thumb**. In sports, there are rules of thumb to estimate player value based on specific metrics. It's similar in some industries. Let's say you're in the B2B services industry. We can use the SDE/EBITDA value as a metric and multiply it by a factor like three or five to estimate the business's value. We have a proprietary athlete-entrepreneur Scoring System you'll be using for this.

"And last, you can do a quick **comparable analysis**. In sports, we often look at how similar athletes are valued in the market. Similarly, we can look for recent sales or acquisitions of similar businesses in your industry. You can also think of this like running comps if you want to buy or sell a property so you can see what similar properties have recently sold for. Use these comparable transactions as a reference point to estimate the value of the business you're assessing.

"Remember, these methods provide rough estimates and are not as accurate as a detailed analysis. Just as a quick assessment on the field doesn't reveal the athlete's full skills and potential, a more thorough valuation of a business requires considering factors like profitability, growth potential, assets, and liabilities. It's always a good idea to consult professionals like myself, your CEO mentor partners, brokers, accountants, or other professionals, or use more comprehensive valuation methods for a precise assessment, so you can keep hustling on and off the field.

"Once you have found a business—or several businesses—and your ten-minute analysis is in the ballpark of the seller's expectations of value, it's time for an in-depth review, and you'll submit an LOI—a letter of intent to acquire, similar to putting an offer on a home.[41] It's important to note here that it is often nonbinding. You are not agreeing to buy the business. Instead, an LOI creates an exclusivity where the seller can't go talk to other people while you are reviewing the information. You typically have thirty to sixty days to review the business and decide if you want to deliver a final purchase agreement."

"Coach, do you suggest sending one LOI at a time or can you send out multiple letters at once?" the golfer asked.

"You can submit multiple offers at a time to the owners of the businesses you want to buy, but be careful: you don't want a reputation as a lookie-loo and not a serious buyer. If you connect with the seller, have good communication, and the financials check out, spend time on it. Finding a profitable business with a great owner is the key to success. An LOI doesn't guarantee that you're going to make the purchase. It's just a way to show your interest and start a more in-depth conversation with the owner of the business. Be sure to value their time and yours. If you're really interested, you need to look under the hood. You might tell them why you want to buy their business and what you plan to do with it if you own it.

"When there are millions of dollars on the line, people sometimes make poor decisions or don't disclose everything they should. But rather than be investigative in this process, which can make the owner defensive and suspicious, remember that you are not on opposite sides of the ball. You are on the same side, both trying to get this deal into the end zone. A meeting of the minds can usually find a way to reach each other's goals.

"And if, during the process, something becomes too cumbersome or just doesn't smell or feel right, then it doesn't work out and that's okay. I've had as many as ten LOIs out at the same time and none worked out. On to the next. The one thing we humans can't get back is *time*. We all get older, and the more successful you become, the more you understand that time is all you really have. We will cover Due Diligence in the next module.

"We're only looking to purchase one company anyway, right?" asked the lacrosse player. "So that means the majority of these conversations we have will end without a sale."

"Yes. And when it's not a match, you shake hands and say, 'Good game.' You are still on the same team and support each other in life. You might send other buyers their way or tell them to come back to you once they correct any issues. You never know where those relationships can take you, so never slam the door behind you.

"Just like when you write a letter to a friend, you want to be polite and clear in your letter of intent. The most important terms can vary depending on the specific transaction, but here are some common terms that are often included."

The Success Coach clicked to the next slide where nine important details to include in an LOI were highlighted.

1. Purchase Price: the amount of money the buyer is willing to pay for the business.

2. Payment Terms: how the purchase price will be paid, whether it's in cash or through financing, and over what period of time.

3. Due Diligence: the process by which the buyer will investigate the business to make sure there are no surprises or hidden issues that would make the purchase undesirable.

4. Assets Included: an outline of which assets are included in the sale, such as equipment, inventory, intellectual property, and contracts.

5. Contingencies: conditions that must be met for the sale to go through. For example, the buyer may require that certain licenses or permits be obtained.

6. Closing Date: the date by which the sale must be completed; it's important that both parties agree on this date.

7. Confidentiality: the requirement that both parties keep the details of the sale confidential.

8. Non-compete Agreement: whereby the owner agrees not to compete with the buyer in the same market for a certain period of time.

9. Dispute Resolution: how any disputes or disagreements between the buyer and owner will be resolved.

"These are just a few of the important terms that are typically included in a letter of intent. You'll find a sample LOI in your coursework this week, and we'll be creating several in class so you can get a better feel for what to include and how to communicate your desire to learn more.

"In the LOI, you will need to mention the payment amount and financial deal structuring. Overall, the financing mechanisms can be complex and varied, and there may be opportunities to use a loan program with a bank. The deal structure is important and you need to account for risks, such as one-time revenue. It is important for you, as athlete-entrepreneurs in our fund, to work closely with our team to determine the best financing structure for your specific situation. But let's review the most common mechanisms to structure a deal."

With another click, a chart appeared, explaining the different financing options:

| Mechanism | Summary |
|---|---|
| Cash | The athlete-entrepreneur uses a pool of capital from investors to finance the acquisition. This pool of capital is typically structured as an equity investment, where investors receive an ownership stake in the fund and share in the profits of any acquired company. |
| Debt Financing | In some cases, the athlete-entrepreneur may also use debt financing to finance the acquisition of a company. This can come in the form of traditional bank loans, SBA loans, or other forms of debt financing. |
| Seller Financing | In some cases, the owner and seller of the target company may be willing to finance a portion of the acquisition. This is known as seller financing, and it can help bridge the gap between the purchase price and the amount of capital that the Success Fund has raised. |
| Earnout | An earnout agreement is a financial arrangement in which a portion of the purchase price is contingent upon the performance of the acquired company. This can be used to bridge the gap between the purchase price and the amount of capital that the Success Fund has raised. |

| Mechanism | Summary |
|-----------|---------|
| Phantom Equity | Instead of giving the seller actual ownership in the new company, the company could propose phantom equity and convince the seller that a "second bite of the apple" will be larger as you grow the company. Phantom equity gives the seller the right to receive cash payments equal to the value of a certain number of shares in the new company. This means that if the company does well and its share price goes up, the seller would receive a cash payment that reflects the increase in the company's value. The key difference between phantom equity and actual equity is that phantom equity does not give the seller any voting rights nor ownership. It is simply a way for the new company to reward the seller for their hard work and incentivize them to continue to contribute to the new company's success. |
| Mezzanine Financing | Mezzanine financing is a hybrid form that combines elements of both debt and equity financing. Mezzanine financing can be used to bridge the gap between the equity investment and the purchase price of the target company. |

"I'm glad you explained this, Coach," Christina said. "When we first spoke, I was terrified that I'd have to come out of pocket to purchase a business. It's a relief to know there are so many good options. But how do you know which one is best?"

"Cash is king," he replied. "But you will formulate a deal structure using multiple financing mechanisms to reach the purchase price. You'll account for risks of the business and whether the business owner wants to roll their equity or cut all ties and walk away. You'll have a much better idea as to which options to choose once you've reviewed all the financial documents and in your conversations with the seller.

"For instance, let's say your target company has a large percentage of revenue from one-time, project-based customers rather than recurring revenue from customers. This creates a risk and you will utilize future payments to the seller to account for this risk, such as an earnout. Contrarily, if the business has 100 percent recurring revenue secured by contracts and a history of working with the same customers, this will require more cash at close and you may include seller financing secured on the assets of the business. Investors and lenders love recurring, predictable revenue. Risk factors are how you will structure the deal. I've put together a deal structure worksheet to help you."

He put an example of the Anatomy of a Deal on the board:

| | | |
|---|---|---|
| **Total Purchase Price** | $20,000,000 | |
| **Acquirer Funds Provided at Closing** | $15,000,000 | |
| | $7,320,000 | Cash from the acquirer |
| | $6,600,000 | Senior debt (44% of the "cash" offered) |
| | $1,080,000 | Subordinate debt (7.2% of the "cash" offered) |
| **Earn-Out** | $3,000,000 | |
| **Seller's Note** | $1,500,000 | |
| **Rolled Shares Value at Closing** | $500,000 | |

"As Christina mentioned, the cash for the deal will come from your investors, so we will also discuss the acquisition from the investors' point of view, such as senior and subordinated debt. Understanding how and why an investor is interested in this approach is critical to your coursework. As the CEO of the business, you will have "skin in the game," aka equity in the business; so will the investors. As you grow the business, you will create value for the whole team. In baseball terms, investors are happy with doubles and triples; home runs aren't necessary, and these stock options give them what they need to be successful as long as you're successful. We will cover the investors' point of view and how the stock is structured in your homework. I will be structuring this with investors for each of you. What's most important for you is structuring a winning deal with the seller."

The Success Coach handed out a worksheet with greater detail from the investors' point of view.

"For now, using the example in your coursework, I want each of you to create a letter of intent to express your interest in acquiring a small business. Follow the guidelines we've discussed and use the provided information on this handout as a reference. You have thirty minutes to complete your first LOI before sharing with the class."

Instructions:

1. Choose a hypothetical small business that you would like to acquire. It could be a gym, coffee shop, construction business, or any other SME.

2. Write a letter of intent addressed to the owner of the chosen small business. Make sure to include the following elements:

Subject: Letter of Intent to Purchase [Company Name]

I am writing to express my strong interest in acquiring [Company Name], a small business operating in [industry/sector]. After careful consideration and analysis, I believe that [Company Name] presents an excellent opportunity for growth and aligns with my long-term business objectives. This letter outlines my intentions and serves as a non-binding proposal for the purchase of [Company Name].

Introduction and Background:

a. Briefly introduce yourself and your background in the industry or complementary skill sets.

b. Provide a summary of your business experience, your value system, your accomplishments in athletics, and any other relevant accomplishments.

Purchase Terms and Conditions:

a. Specify the proposed purchase price and the payment structure (e.g., cash, seller financing, etc.).

b. Mention any proposed adjustments to the purchase price based on due diligence findings or other factors.

c. Outline any additional financial terms, such as a proposed deposit or an escrow arrangement.

Assets and Liabilities:

a. Detail the assets and liabilities that will be included in the purchase, such as tangible assets, intellectual property, contracts, and any outstanding debts or obligations.

b. Clarify any specific assets or liabilities that will be excluded from the transaction.

Due Diligence:

a. Express your intention to conduct a thorough due diligence process to evaluate the business's financial, operational, and legal aspects.
b. Specify a reasonable timeline for completing the due diligence process.

Confidentiality:

a. Highlight your commitment to maintaining the confidentiality of any proprietary or sensitive information shared during the negotiation process.
b. Request that the recipient treat this letter and its contents with the same level of confidentiality.

Exclusivity and Negotiation Period:

a. Request a period during which you will have the opportunity to negotiate exclusively with the seller and not engage in discussions with other potential buyers.
b. Specify the duration of the exclusivity period.

Desired Transition and Support:

a. Outline your expectations for a smooth transition, including the involvement of key personnel and any support or training you may require from the seller.

Additional Terms:

a. Include any other terms or conditions that are crucial to the proposed transaction but have not been covered above.

Closing Remarks:

a. Express your enthusiasm for the potential acquisition and your willingness to engage in further discussions to finalize the transaction.
b. Provide your contact information for any queries or to arrange a meeting.

Please note that this letter of intent is nonbinding and is intended to facilitate further negotiations and due diligence. It does not create any legal obligation on either party until a definitive purchase agreement is executed.

Thank you for considering my proposal. I look forward to the opportunity to discuss the potential acquisition of [Company Name] in more detail.

Sincerely,

[Your Name]

3.   Submit your completed letter of intent to your instructor for evaluation.

"Just thirty minutes?!" Kai felt anxious. He wanted more time.

"Thirty minutes. You'll get the hang of it after one or two times, I promise. We'll be filling these out all week, so don't sweat it."

"Easy for you to say," Kai joked. "You've done this thousands of times now, right?"

"Yes, and once you've done it a few times, it becomes second nature. Just like throwing a football."

Out of nowhere, Kai had a flashback of a time the year before when Bryce gave him an unreasonable one-hour deadline late one Friday on a holiday weekend. It felt like an impossible task, but out of sheer determination, Kai met the deadline with several minutes to spare. It wasn't the same as a hard-fought win on the gridiron, but it was a nice boost to his ego, nonetheless.

"Freakin' Bryce," he mumbled to himself, then chuckled at the realization that he was in a *far* better situation in the athlete-entrepreneur accelerator than his pencil-pushing former nemesis.

The truth was, since joining the program, Kai's athletic identity had slowly started to come back to him. He was remembering who he was and what he was capable of. He could more readily admit his flaws and faults. And he had a new community with the same goal—to succeed at buying a business and creating a legacy he was proud of.

He was at his best when faced with a challenge and new information to learn, and this business boot camp had stretched his brain and comfort zone in ways he hadn't experienced since college. Even his parents had noticed the changes in his life and were proud of the steps he was taking to ensure a better future for himself.

Robin, who had finally started accepting his phone calls again, had begun to take notice too.

## 19

# MODULE 6: DUE DILIGENCE

It was the start of the next week of the accelerator program, and the Success Coach was looking forward to his weekly meetings with each mentee to hear their thoughts and discuss progress and feedback. At seven weeks, they were halfway through, and he could see immense strength, growth, and potential in each one.

They had become more confident, more self-aware, better communicators, and deeper thinkers, in addition to the shifts toward better health for several members. But what he loved most was seeing how they worked together, supported each other, and became not just a cohort of like-minded business leaders, but a room of friends who were invested in each other's lives.

Although he had high hopes each mentee would be successful in the quest to buy a business, he knew there would be challenges during the process and only the most resilient and driven would succeed early on. The collective group would make sure all ten mentees achieved success one way or another. Sports teaches that, and he knew that's what athlete-entrepreneurs do.

As he walked the hallway from his office to the classroom, he paused briefly to listen in on the chatter, everyone catching up after the weekend. Above the conversation, he heard Christina's melodical laughter. She reminded him so much of his own daughter. Strong and smart, compassionate and kind. She was going to be an excellent business owner.

The class took their seats as the Success Coach found his customary location at the front of the room. "Are you ready for more sports analogies?"

"Yes!" they said in unison.

"This week, we're talking about due diligence, which is all about asking the right questions, getting people on the same team, working through financial and legal first, and then going operational, and getting as much information as you can. It is a collaborative process between two parties. Just as much as I can ask you questions, you can ask me questions, because you, as the owner, want to know who you are selling to. We typically review the trailing three years of information, and it's up to you to set up a secure digital data room clearly organized with the files you will be requesting.

"Imagine you're preparing for a big game against a tough opponent. Just as you would study their strategies, strengths, and weaknesses to gain an edge, due diligence in buying a small business involves conducting a thorough investigation to understand the business's strengths, weaknesses, risks, and opportunities. Here's how we can explain it in seven steps.

"First, you **scout the business**. Before entering the game, you gather information about your opponents. Similarly, in due diligence, you 'scout' the business by reviewing its financial statements, contracts, customer base, and operational processes. This helps you understand the business's current state, historical state, and potential. That's everything we've been working on the last few weeks.

"Next, **understand the team**. You analyze the team's players, their skills, and their roles on the field. Similarly, in due diligence, you assess the business's team members, including the owner, key employees, and their roles. A tenure report is where you will find this. This helps you understand the team dynamics and the potential impact on the business's performance."

"Coach?" a hand raised. "Is it ever advisable to let some people go when you buy a business? I know it happens all the time but is that a best practice for small businesses, or should we avoid it?"

"Great question. My preference is to keep the culture intact as long as possible. You don't want to come in and tear the business apart. Some private equity firms developed a bad reputation for doing exactly that years ago. They didn't care about the employees. They'd make promises to get the deal done, then come in and rip the business apart, fire people, get it down to its bare bones, run it for a few years, and then sell it again for a ton of money. I personally think that's a terrible approach if you want to maintain a good reputation and clear conscience. After all, culture eats strategy for breakfast, and the team is number one!

"As you begin to review the team, you may very well find a few employees who are not pulling their weight or who are detrimental to the team dynamics. With good collaboration, the owner will disclose this as well. I suggest not firing or replacing them but letting the dust settle and allowing the employees to get to know you better. This also gives them time to turn around. Sometimes it can't be avoided, especially if there are HR issues. But otherwise, I like to wait. And I tell the business owners that too. They are always concerned about their employees and whether a new owner will slash and burn what they've built. They've seen it happen. You can put them at ease by telling them you won't make any major changes for a full year."

"Thanks, Coach."

"So next, you will **review the playbook**. Just as you study your team's playbook to understand its strategies, in due diligence, you review the business's marketing strategies and competitive advantages. This gives you insights into how the business operates and its plans for growth and success.

"Next, **examine the stats**. In sports, analyzing statistics helps you understand a player's or team's performance. Similarly, in due diligence, you've already examined the business's financial statements. You now want to research sales trends, customer acquisition costs, lifetime of each customer, recurring customers versus one-time customers, and other key metrics. This helps you evaluate the business's financial health, profitability, and growth potential.

"Then, you'll **assess the playing field**. Before a game, you assess the field conditions, weather, and other factors that can impact the game. In due diligence, you assess the industry landscape, market trends, competition, and regulatory environment. This helps you understand the external factors that can influence the business's success.

"Along with that, you want to **identify risks and opportunities**. Remember, due diligence is a collaboration with the owner, not an investigation. Keep the conversation alive and continue to develop trust with each other. Just as you anticipate risks and opportunities during a game, in due diligence, you identify potential risks such as high client concentration, unpredictable cash flow, and high employee turnover. Additionally, you look for opportunities. One huge opportunity among many baby boomer businesses is digital transformation. You might be able to implement new sales and marketing techniques and tools that are readily available, switch to a new CRM, add automations and artificial intelligence at redundant points of the business process, etc. This is a great time to notate any areas of missed opportunities that you can capitalize on as the new owner.

"And finally, as you work your way through due diligence, finding opportunities and spotting the weaknesses, you'll be working with our investors or the bank to **line up the financing** to close on the deal. It's critical to keep the owner up to speed on the financing portion of the deal and work together to get the deal across the finish line. Our attorney will draft the final paperwork. Your job is to use your team-oriented mentality to keep the deal alive and energized. Manage your side of the deal, the owner, the attorney, the financing, the transition plan. Be enthusiastic and energized. I can't stress it enough."

"Have you ever made a bad business deal?" the basketball player asked.

"Several. Things fall apart for a number of reasons, but just as your college coach gave you advice on how to win based on his or her experience, I'm doing the same here as your business coach. As you saw with your failure resume, there are always lessons learned. And I can guarantee you that I've won far more than I've lost—and you will too."

He leaned forward. "Hear me when I say you *will* make mistakes. That's part of the process of learning and evolving. But as long as you continue to push forward and learn from those mistakes, you'll come out ahead.

"It's all part of due diligence when buying a small business. It involves conducting thorough research, analyzing the business's performance, asking the right questions, understanding the industry landscape, and assessing risks and opportunities. This process allows you to make informed decisions and increase the chances of a successful acquisition, just like winning a game becomes easier with a well-prepared strategy. Nearing the end of due diligence, and as your financing to buy the company is set up, you will prepare a transition plan and messaging to the employees. Work with the seller on this. Oftentimes, the seller will stick around and transition the business for many months with you after the close of the deal. Remember, you are teammates with the seller, not competition. Our team will be with you every step of the way as you are a newly minted CEO.

"For the rest of this week and next, you'll be doing your due diligence, not just with the financial statements but with entire company profiles I've created for you, using our internal database as a guide. You'll be given resources like sample financial statements, online customer review platforms, industry reports, contracts, and other relevant business documentation.

"Two weeks from now, you'll begin crafting your final thesis to present to me and my board, and you'll need to be fully prepared to execute all of this knowledge into a solid business plan for your acquisition goals.

"So, for now, I want you to divide yourself into two groups of five. We'll repeat this exercise four times today. You'll have thirty minutes each time to find the information I'm requesting from your team, which could include financial statements, contracts, customer reviews, competitor analysis, industry trends, and legal documents. I want you to analyze the information and discuss its significance in assessing the overall health and potential of the business. You'll then debrief the class on your findings."

"It sounds like a scavenger hunt," said Christina.

"It is exactly that."

"What's the prize? Scavenger hunts always have prizes, right?" asked the tennis player.

"Puppies!" shouted the swimmer, just to get a rise from her classmates.

"Even better," said the Success Coach. "The gift of learning and upleveling your skill set." After he delivered all of the packets and data to both teams, he clicked the timer on his watch, and the work began.

## 20

# *MODULE 7: DEVELOPING YOUR WINNING GAME PLAN*
## Crafting Your Thesis

Every week of the program, the stress levels, classwork, and homework had intensified. And each week, the athlete-entrepreneurs continued to crush the content. The remaining time would be dedicated to determining their future and making big choices about industries, location, and goals. These were some of the biggest decisions the mentees would ever make, but they wouldn't walk through it alone. The Success Coach—along with their CEO mentors and the board—would be guiding them every step of the way to ensure each offer was smart and solid.

"As athletes, you understand the importance of strategy and planning to achieve success in sports," the Success Coach said, standing at the whiteboard. "The same principles apply when it comes to developing a winning game plan for acquiring and operating a business.

"This week, I will guide you through the process of crafting your athlete-entrepreneur thesis in athletic terms. This is the most important document you will produce. You have the remaining three weeks to make your final decision as to which industries you'll pursue and where, solidify your research, and create a thesis to present to the board that explains why your choice perfectly aligns with your skill set, interests, and goals. You've got *one* shot at convincing the board that you and your thesis are worth millions of dollars of investment. This is game day. Prepare like it.

"If you win over the board, you'll spend the remainder of your two years on the move with your head down, researching and reaching out to those thousand business owners, having conversations, making meaningful connections, reviewing financial documents, and doing due diligence, until you make a successful purchase. The goal is to purchase it in well under two years and elevate yourself to CEO. The faster, the better. I'm cheering each one of you on and am your coach during the process. I know you are highly qualified to lead a business. And I'm excited to see your next steps."

A hand raised. "I hope we all stay in touch after the program. I know we still have a long time to go but I'm going to miss seeing everyone every day," said Christina thoughtfully. "This has been some of the hardest but most rewarding work I've ever done. And I'm so thankful for each of you. We really have become a team."

"We *are* a team of athlete-entrepreneurs!" the track star agreed. "I know the time will fly by, but I promise I will stay in contact with everyone."

"Me too," the tennis player smiled.

"Ditto," offered the baseball player.

"Don't forget—you still have weekly meetings with me during your search, and our coaches will assist you in your new role as a CEO, so you're never alone" said the coach.

"I don't see why we can't meet regularly as a group too," said the rugby player. "I say we have at least a quarterly video call, maybe even monthly, to check in after this part of the program is complete."

"That's a great idea," said the Success Coach.

"I'm on it," the rugby player smiled, looking far more fit and healthier than when he joined the program.

With a game plan for continued communication solidified, the coach clicked a slide onto the screen with a list of steps to summarize creating the thesis.

**Overview:** An athlete-entrepreneur's thesis in an acquisition serves as a road map that guides the search process and facilitates the evaluation of potential acquisition targets. It aligns the athlete-entrepreneur's objectives with those of potential investors and helps maintain focus throughout the search and acquisition phases.

**Industry Focus:** The thesis defines the industry or industries of interest for potential acquisition targets. It outlines the rationale behind the chosen industry, such as growth potential, personal expertise, or market dynamics.

**Company Size and Characteristics:** It specifies the desired size and characteristics of the target company, including revenue range, profitability, geographic location, and other relevant factors. This helps narrow the search and aligns with the searcher's skill set and investment criteria.

**Investment Parameters:** The thesis outlines the financial parameters and investment criteria for target companies. This may include the desired level of equity ownership, minimum and maximum enterprise value, acceptable leverage ratios, and return expectations.

**Competitive Advantage:** It identifies the athlete-entrepreneur's competitive advantage or unique value proposition that can be leveraged in the acquisition and subsequent operation of the target company. This could include specific industry knowledge, operational expertise, digital transformation, or network connections.

**Growth Strategy:** The thesis outlines the growth strategy that will be pursued post-acquisition. This may include organic growth initiatives, strategic partnerships, geographic expansion, or potential add-on acquisitions.

**Management Team:** It defines the desired management team structure and outlines the athlete-entrepreneur's plan for involvement in the day-to-day operations of the target company. This helps assess the fit between the athlete-entrepreneur's skill set and the existing management team or the need to recruit additional talent.

**Deal Sourcing Strategy:** The thesis describes the approach for sourcing potential target companies. It outlines the athlete-entrepreneur's plan for networking, leveraging industry contacts, engaging with owners and intermediaries, and/or utilizing other deal sourcing channels.

**Financing Strategy:** It discusses the financing strategy for the acquisition, including the use of ETA capital, external investors, bank debt, and/or other funding sources. This helps outline the financial structure and feasibility of potential acquisitions.

**Exit Strategy:** The thesis includes a plan for the eventual exit from the acquired company, which may involve selling to a strategic buyer, a financial buyer, or pursuing an IPO. It demonstrates the searcher's forward-thinking approach and alignment with potential investors.

**Personal Goals:** Lastly, the thesis may incorporate the athlete-entrepreneur's personal goals and motivations for undertaking the ETA process. This helps provide context and highlights the searcher's commitment to the long-term success of the target company.

"First things first—before you begin any research, **assess your athletic skills**. I want you to reflect on your athletic journey and identify your strengths, skills, and experiences. Consider the discipline, teamwork, leadership, resilience, and goal-oriented mindset you developed as an athlete. Recall your transformation in the mindset courses. Remember who you are. An athlete. An entrepreneur. A graduate of the athlete-entrepreneur accelerator and now an athlete-entrepreneur. We are unique Champions of Business. And think about how these skills can be translated into the world of entrepreneurship and business leadership.

"Next, **scout the field**. This is when you'll begin to conduct market research to identify potential industries and sectors that align with your athletic characteristics, the soft skills and technical ones. I know you each have a pretty good idea of what you'd like to choose, so now it's time to solidify that decision. Analyze market trends, growth opportunities, and competitive landscapes in those industries. Look for areas where your athletic skills and experiences can give you a competitive advantage."

"And my undeniable charisma," said the track star, intentionally causing a few lighthearted groans.

"Never forget, you are playing to win. When it comes to crafting your thesis, set specific criteria for the types of businesses you want to target and SMART goals. Consider factors such as size, industry, growth potential, and cultural fit. Align your thesis with your athletic values, highlighting how your skills can be leveraged for success in the business world.

"Starting now, you are building your winning team. You are surrounded with a supportive network of coaches, advisors, and industry experts. Seek guidance from individuals who can provide insights and expertise in areas related to your athlete-entrepreneur thesis. And leverage your athletic network to build relationships and gain valuable insights from successful athletes who have become successful entrepreneurs.

"Finally, you will **execute your game plan**. That means you will develop a step-by-step plan to execute your athlete-entrepreneur thesis. A thesis is only good if you act upon it with purpose and tenacity. I want you to outline strategies for sourcing potential acquisition targets, conducting due diligence, and structuring deals. Set goals for yourself, create milestones, and track your progress as you navigate the athlete-entrepreneur process. And for several examples of what this thesis might look like, you can refer to the coursework.

"Remember, just like in sports, developing a winning game plan takes time, effort, and continuous improvement. Stay focused, leverage your athletic skills, and be prepared to adapt your strategy as you pursue your entrepreneurial goals. I'll be cheering you on all the way."

"And don't forget, Coach. You promised to bring Twister to the last class," the swimmer nearly whispered.

"Man, I'd break a hip if I tried to bend that way. My body is not a pretzel," Kai said.

"What I hear you saying is that you're already planning on losing. Is that right?" the swimmer said, turning to Kai with a playful smirk on her face.

The tennis player shouted, "That's really good active listening right there!"

Kai raised an eyebrow, trying not to laugh, then shook the swimmer's hand across the table. "Challenge accepted."

## 21

# *WALKING THE WALK AND TALKING THE TALK*

## Living an Inspiring Life While Creating a *Monumentous* Future

For the remaining few weeks of the accelerator boot camp, the mentees stayed highly focused and extraordinarily busy, doing research, analyzing market trends, networking, and crafting their theses to present to the board for feedback and approval. Utilizing all their new mindset elements and business knowledge, each mentee was quickly becoming the very best version of themselves—versions they'd never dreamed possible months before.

Confidence was at an all-time high, as was their dedication to health and wellness—mentally, physically, and emotionally. And as change began to take place on the inside with knowledge and understanding, it was only a matter of time before it permeated every facet of their personalities and lifestyles. The Success Coach could see they were athlete-entrepreneurs through and through.

Each student felt a huge surge of confidence, energy, and a renewed identity. No longer were their best days behind them; they had found a new identity and game to win. They knew, without a doubt, who they were and what they stood for. And they were proud of the sacrifices and progress they'd made in a short time. Regardless of the struggles they'd endured after leaving competitive sports and transitioning into the workforce, they were on top of the world now, and back at the top of their game.

Some noted that their previously difficult relationships were undergoing a transformation. Undesirable habits or patterns had been replaced by new perspectives and positive actions. And areas where the mentees felt weak at the start of the program were being reinforced with consistent action and encouragement, as the ten grew to become a team, rooting for each other, cheering each other's successes, and calling out old mindsets and beliefs when they popped up. Unfortunately, no amount of cheering could help Kai's poor balance as he lost at Twister, on the last day of class, to the swimmer.

At the completion of the three-month athlete-entrepreneur accelerator, all ten mentees successfully presented and defended their theses. And as promised, the rugby player set in motion monthly calls and quarterly meetups to keep the synergy and camaraderie high as the real work began: researching and connecting with *at least* one thousand business owners. Time was of the essence—and they were ready to meet the challenge.

———

As for Kai, his world had changed so much over the three-month accelerator, often feeling like a roller coaster. It was enough to make his head spin and his heart quicken. He was convinced his best days were ahead of him. Robin had not only read the letter, she'd written one back. Even better, she agreed to fly to New York to meet Kai for dinner one night, a week after the completion of the first three months of the program. This was his one last shot to make things right, and he knew it.

He brought two dozen roses, thoughtful gifts for her and Mia, and another letter he'd written and fine-tuned over several weeks to read to her. At a corner table at Robin's favorite Italian restaurant overlooking the river, the couple gingerly hugged, then sat facing each other, unsure of what the night would bring.

There, under the darkening sky, surrounded by twinkling lights and a warm breeze, Kai exposed his heart fully for the first time in their entire relationship and read his letter to her. He was raw and honest, admitting his shortcomings, flaws, and faulty thinking, recognizing her hard work and her many wonderful attributes, thanking her for everything she did for him and their daughter, asking for forgiveness, and transforming his stern athlete-self into a new man.

"I can't change the past, although I wish I could," he read, wiping away a tear, allowing Robin to witness his emotions in a way he'd never dared before. "I would have done so many things differently. I would have been a better husband, a better father, more present and aware of our daily lives—and especially your needs and wants. I would have listened when you had concerns instead of brushing them aside. And I would have worked on myself and transitioned from football to life much sooner. All I truly want is to provide for you and Mia and live our dream life like we talked about."

For the first time, Robin heard him take responsibility without pointing out any areas she should improve, which had been his regular tit-for-tat response when they argued. Tears streamed down her face as she fought to maintain her composure. This was what she'd needed to hear, what she'd wanted from him for so long. A true life partner.

"I've made a lot of changes since being in the athlete-entrepreneur program and had a lot of time to reflect. I'm a better man than I was and I want you with me, by my side, as I step into this new season. I can't promise I'll be perfect. But I can promise I'll fight with everything I have to be the man you deserve and to create a new foundation for our family that is built on trust, open communication, and respect. I'm asking you for one more chance. Please."

He reached across the table with his hand open, hoping for a new beginning with the woman he still deeply loved.

Instead, she jumped out of her chair and fell into his arms, both of them in tears. Both relieved. Both thankful for second, third, and even tenth chances.

"I love you and Mia so much, baby," he whispered into her neck as they hugged tighter. "I promise you I am committed to doing the work to ensure our marriage is strong and happy, and that we're both happy."

"Me too," she said, amid muffled sniffles.

It was a promise they both kept.

---

After the completion of the three-month accelerator, Christina decided to take a break from dating so she could fully focus on the program, the work ahead, and herself without needless distraction. She knew her best days were ahead of her. And then, when she least expected it, she found herself sitting next to a handsome and charismatic man on one of her flights back to NYC. While their relationship started off slowly and cautiously, they built something remarkable together, a healthy relationship based on respect, great communication, and quality time. He proved to be a huge source of encouragement and calm energy through her transition of buying a company and stepping into the CEO role.

After they'd been dating for a while, Christina went home with him one weekend to Idaho to meet his family for the first time. They welcomed her with open arms, and from the moment she walked through the door of their farmhouse, she felt at home and at ease among his two sisters and three brothers—all former athletes—who were eager to get to know her better.

Back home, she'd begun to make a name for herself as a young and headstrong visionary CEO. But here, amid acres of farmland, as she sat down at the large dinner table with her boyfriend's family, she was simply Christina, the kind young woman who had captured the oldest brother's heart.

That night as the family gave thanks before dinner, he squeezed her hand under the table, and she opened her eyes slightly, peeking around the table at a big happy family who all loved and supported each other. No cross words. No shaming. No abuse. Just love. Her heart leapt in her chest. A true family—it's what she'd been dreaming of her whole life.

On Saturday night after dinner had been cleared away, she and her boyfriend sat on the front porch swing in silence, listening to the crickets and doves sing lullabies to the land. The only other sounds were the light, rhythmic squeaking of the swing, and conversation often punctuated by laughter from inside the house. Out of the corner of her eye, Christina noticed him staring at her and turned to ask what he was thinking.

With a kind smile, he said, "Do you ever wonder what your life will look like in five or ten years or even fifty years?"

"Five years, yes. I have it sketched out with goals, timelines, and a vision board. But fifty? I haven't thought that far into the future. What do you think yours will look like?"

He chuckled at that. Her vision, organization, and planning were just a few of the many things he loved about her.

"I can't be sure, but I hope it looks just like this." He reached over and took her hand, intertwining his fingers with hers, then pulled the back of her hand to his lips for a kiss. They sat on the porch together late into the night, talking and dreaming about what a future could look like together.

## 22

# FROM THE ATHLETE-ENTREPRENEUR ACCELERATOR TO BECOMING BUSINESS OWNERS

By the end of the accelerator program, eight athlete-entrepreneurs were able to purchase a business within the allotted two-year time-frame. Of the remaining two, the basketball player was placed as an operating partner at previously acquired businesses Success Coach Jack and his team were invested in, a route to leadership and ownership in great businesses the basketball player loved.

Knowing how the process works and how others find value in businesses, the track star decided to start a business with the goal of selling it, ideally to an athlete-entrepreneur.[42]

After the athlete-entrepreneurs acquired businesses, they continued to speak weekly with the Success Coach and his team, surrounded by teammates, coaches, and a network helping them to achieve their goals.

Jack partnered each one with a Peak Performance coach and operating coach to guide them on their journey to the championship in business.

Jack Merrick is finalizing the next round of the athlete-entrepreneur accelerator, with another ten handpicked mentees who are eager to learn and ready to change the world.

———

Kai became the business owner of a thriving accounting company in Houston, Texas, and is enjoying the new challenges and lessons of being his own boss. He is completely in control of his destiny and is excited about the future every day. The game of business is his new passion. He has channeled his athletic mindset into becoming a stellar CEO, and his best days are no longer behind him. His reputation as a trustworthy business buyer has brought more sellers to him in the accounting industry, and he is evaluating the add-on acquisitions to his current firm. He has thrived as a leader using the mindset elements within his own firm, even doing a few speaking engagements on the importance of bridging the identity gap for student-athletes after graduation and transitioning into a leader in business.

His marriage to Robin is stronger than they ever imagined, thanks to great communication and the athlete-entrepreneur performance coaches that guide him as a CEO as he prioritizes his new life. They love their new four-bedroom home in the suburbs of Houston, and recently finished decorating the nursery for their new arrival, a baby boy, only a few months away. Until then, Robin is working as a part-time teacher's aide, a job she absolutely loves, at an elementary school only six minutes from their new neighborhood.

With Kai's salary and equity as a CEO and the laser-focused drive of an athlete-entrepreneur, they've already been able to pay off their medical bills and are shopping for a vacation home in the Caribbean. The whole family is thriving.

Every morning before Kai's workout, he writes a gratitude list in his journal, where the athlete-entrepreneur accelerator has a permanent spot among the top five slots. Kai often marvels at how quickly change occurs when the heart and mind are aligned. And he relies on his business boot camp training daily to make impactful decisions as a proactive leader. He has regained his identity and then some, proving to himself that what may seem impossible at the start is *absolutely* possible with hard work, belief in yourself, and a supportive team.

He's forever grateful to Jack, the Success Coach, for taking a chance on a cocky former athlete, seeing his potential, and calling him to step into his own greatness.

———

Christina made quick work of research, networking, and dialoguing with owners, and at the seventeen-month mark, she purchased a digital media company with a portfolio in athletics headquartered in Seattle. With the help of the Success Coach, her mentors, and the existing leadership at her new company, she stepped into her leadership role like it was made for her and was warmly welcomed by the employees. (The former owner agreed to stay on as a consultant for the following two years to ease the transition.) Christina's athletic skill set and lessons learned made her an excellent CEO who quickly gained trust among her advisory team and the company at large, and frequent praise from the former owner who was thrilled to have found such a bright and determined leader to continue his vision as he transitioned into retirement.

As she had hoped, she's able to work remotely from her loft in Weehawken, New Jersey, but travels frequently for networking and meetings. At the first company-wide meeting, four months after she became CEO, she challenged and encouraged the entire team to dream even bigger, as she talked through what the next three to five years could look like if they worked together toward their goals of excellence and expansion. Her employees respect her and look to her for new ideas, encouragement, and dedication to the tasks ahead for growth and expansion. And she empowers them to do their best work while remaining focused on the big picture.

She's still able to play soccer with her recreational team on weekends when she's in town. And her friend group remains as supportive as ever. She also has made wonderful new connections within her industry and the media.

In control of her life, her finances, her mindset and thoughts, and her goals, she wakes up every morning with peace of mind and a deep sense of belonging, regardless of how busy the day might be. She knows that whatever obstacles arise, she is more than capable of working through them, using the mindset elements and all the knowledge gained from the athlete-entrepreneur accelerator program. Ever the cheerleader and champion for celebrating others, she frequently keeps in touch with her cohort and loves seeing how everyone has flourished in their new roles.

Here she is, in her mid-thirties, a thriving business owner with a six-figure salary, a loving boyfriend, and a supportive community of friends—including her athlete-entrepreneur team—to count on. She is living the dream and knows this is just the beginning of an incredible life—one that she controls and guides. One she is immensely proud of.

She is ready to give her best every day—and she can't wait to see what lies ahead.

# *YOUR TURN: THE FUTURE IS ATHLETE*
## Apply to Become an Athlete-Entrepreneur Today

Following Kai and Christina's transformation stories to success should get you fired up about the potential—your potential—for greatness. There are thousands of former athletes in their exact positions, struggling with the ever-present identity gap, ready to work hard and dream big, yearning for guidance and a path forward to chase the Championship in Business. If you are one of these people, know that your very next step or next opportunity could be the one that propels you into becoming the best version of yourself.

Data proves that as an athlete, you have innate skills that perfectly align with the entrepreneurial spirit and apply well to leadership roles. You show up daily. You understand risks and rewards, resiliency, emotional stability, team orientation, and performance under pressure. You also know it takes a lot of hard work, deprogramming, reprogramming, shifting perspectives, and gaining knowledge to make it to the championship level of life. You are no stranger to a challenge, to early mornings, late nights, blood, sweat, and tears. When coaches were on your ass, you still showed up to practice when you didn't want to. And because of your dedication to the game, to your craft, and to your teammates, you are no stranger to victory.

If, while reading the stories of the athlete-entrepreneurs, you saw yourself in their struggles and in their wins, I'd encourage you to apply to become an athlete-entrepreneur in the next accelerator program. Just as it was laid out in the book, the program begins with a three-month, in-depth business boot camp that will challenge and inspire you to step into your greatness, reignite your true identity, and accept the role you were born to play, as a leader.

As you've seen in this story and in your day-to-day life, far too many people are content to spend their days working for someone else, aligning their schedule and finances to support someone else's priorities and dreams, hitching their wagon to another person's North Star and thinking it's good enough to get by.

But if you are ready to completely uplevel your life, create a living legacy, and make real change in the world, I'd love to have you on the team. As your mentor and coach, I'll be by your side the entire time, as will my team, guiding and teaching every step of the way, as you step into the victory circle. From there, the sky truly is the limit.

Attention, aspiring athlete-entrepreneurs
and ambitious business enthusiasts!

Are you ready to succeed in your transition from sport
and level-up your business game by joining a community
of like-minded individuals who are passionate about
thriving in the world of athlete-entrepreneurship?

Look no further!

We invite you to join our community of former athletes and
unlock a world of unparalleled expertise, support, and resources.

As a member, you'll gain access to a wealth of benefits
that will turbocharge your journey toward a successful
transition from sport and entrepreneur, including:

**Access to Unparalleled Expertise**
**Research-Backed Mindset Strategies**
**Peak Performance Coaching**
**Step-by-Step M&A Education**
**Exclusive Network**
**Deal Sourcing and Evaluation**
**Due Diligence Support**
**Investors and Funding Support**
**Mentorship and Support**
**Post-Acquisition Integration**
**Live Coaching and Events**

Visit www.SuccessCoach.com and sign up today. Your journey awaits!

# *APPENDIX*

## Unlocking the Neuroscientific Benefits of Athletics for Business Success: 10 Principles

In a world where businesses constantly seek innovative ways to enhance performance and thrive in a competitive landscape, an unexpected source of inspiration emerges: athletics.

Research has substantiated the direct impact of soft skills on the performance of organizations. Neff and Citrin (2001) asserted that success hinges on 90 percent soft skills and 10 percent hard skills. Additionally, Vasanthakumari (2019) recognized "soft skills attributes" to include values, motivation, behavior, habits, character, and attitudes. The world of sports, as shown by research-backed evidence, reveals a treasure trove of principles that can revolutionize the way businesses operate, innovate, and succeed. Studies indicate that athletes possess unique cognitive and neural advantages that extend beyond the playing field, impacting business dynamics in profound ways. Below we explore ten principles supported by research that illustrate how athletes have the potential to drive financial performance, foster innovation, inspire teams, navigate challenges, and create a culture of excellence within the business world. Moreover, the neuroscientific benefits of athletics serve as a catalyst, propelling these principles to redefine business success.

## CREATIVE THINKING

Participating in athletics demands a delicate balance of mental and physical effort, fostering hand-eye coordination while igniting the flames of creativity. These activities activate the parietal lobe, the very source of creativity. According to research by McKinsey, creative companies had 70 percent above-average total return to shareholders.[43]

This intersection of athletic engagement and business leadership is profound. Athletes, through their dynamic experiences, learn to cultivate a creative mindset that is profoundly transferable to the corporate landscape. This creative outlook empowers leaders to not only navigate the ever-changing currents of the market but also to confront challenges with ingenuity and seize opportunities that might otherwise slip through the cracks. It's the fusion of these attributes that sets the stage for extraordinary business success, as recognized by business leaders and supported by research in creative industries.

## RESILIENCE

The athlete's brain, particularly the prefrontal cortex, is instrumental in bolstering resilience, cognitive flexibility, emotional regulation, and stress response. Such cognitive enhancements enable athletes to bounce back from setbacks effectively. Making the connection to industry, research published by *Global Business & Finance Review* indicates that resilient leaders are better equipped to steer businesses through disruptions, adapt to change, and inspire teams to overcome obstacles, ultimately driving organizational success.[44]

## CURIOSITY

Curiosity is a cognitive attribute that athletes actively cultivate through sports involvement. The intersection of sports and business serves as a fertile ground where the pursuit of excellence in athletics nurtures curiosity, and, in turn, where business leaders who wholeheartedly embrace curiosity tend to be more successful in navigating the complexities of their industries. The activation of the hippocampus in athletes is linked to curiosity, contributing to lifelong learning skills. When it comes to commerce, firms who embrace curiosity, as indicated by research cited in *Harvard Business Review*, perform higher and have greater adaptability in the ever-evolving landscape of the business world.[45]

## RELIABILITY

Athletic training emphasizes meticulous practice, honing the prefrontal cortex's top-down control. This attention to detail mirrors the leadership quality of focusing on precision, which greatly benefits project planning, organization, and execution. Research published in *Harvard Business Review* highlights that the capacity to consistently deliver results is the most influential among the four crucial CEO behaviors. CEO candidates demonstrating a strong track record of reliability are twice as likely to secure the role and have a higher likelihood of succeeding in it. This unwavering focus on accuracy not only aligns with athletic discipline but also drives higher-quality outcomes, operational efficiency, and overall business performance, making it a trait highly esteemed by boards, investors, and employees for its steadiness and predictability.[46]

## INTRINSIC MOTIVATION

Intrinsic motivation in sports is cultivated through a combination of enjoyment, autonomy, competence, relatedness, challenge, rewards, feedback, self-determination, a learning mindset, and passion. These factors can collectively contribute to the development and sustenance of intrinsic motivation in sports, where the role of dopamine in the brain's reward system mirrors athletes' intrinsic motivation, promoting attentiveness and behavioral engagement. The intrinsic motivation instilled by sports carries over to business environments, where motivated leaders spur employee satisfaction, growth, and performance. Research published in the *Academy of Management Journal* established that leaders setting challenging goals and encouraging personal growth amplify overall business success.[47]

## EMPATHY

Sports activate mirror neuron systems, fostering empathy in athletes. This empathetic nature translates to business leadership, creating a positive organizational culture that boosts employee trust and satisfaction. In business, leaders who embrace and demonstrate empathy earn greater trust from their followers, resulting in improved performance and outcomes. Empathy is a cornerstone of transformational leadership, known for its effectiveness and ability to inspire. Such leadership fosters motivation, enthusiasm, and commitment, ultimately reshaping environments for the better.[48]

## LEADERSHIP

The leadership skills exhibited by athletes, reinforced by neuroscience insights, can be transformative. Athletes lead by example and their actions inspire others. Similarly, understanding the brain's functions and their influence enhances leadership in business. Recognizing the significance of their experiences, collegiate student-athletes acquire crucial skills and traits that contribute to business success, enhancing their leadership behavior and interpersonal skills. Studies have indicated that collegiate student-athletes develop skills and qualities that are vital for success, positively influencing their leadership behavior and interpersonal abilities.[49]

## COMPETITIVE MINDSET

Research has revealed that a specific area of the frontal cortex, the anterior cingulate cortex, is involved in competitive decision-making. Further research found that this area of the brain was enlarged in athletes versus nonathletes. A second experiment looked at how these brain areas talk to each other when the brain is at rest. Results showed that the connections between these brain areas were stronger in basketball players compared to nonathletes.[50]

This may explain how athletes' strong sense of competition propels them to consistently improve, a trait transferrable to business environments. The importance of a competitive mindset in business cannot go understated, and the book *Inside the Competitor's Mindset* by John Horn emphasizes predicting and positioning for success in competitive markets.[51]

## METACOGNITION

The prefrontal cortex's role in metacognitive skills—critical for athletes' self-evaluation and performance optimization—transcends sports to business contexts. Metacognition fosters better decision-making and problem-solving. Author Geoff Colvin, in *Talent is Overrated*, emphasizes top performers' systematic self-observation, a practice that nurtures self-awareness, enhances decision-making, and drives excellence in both sports and business.[52]

## COACHABILITY

Playing sports imparts valuable life skills that extend far beyond the field or court. One of the most crucial lessons learned through sports is how to be coached. It's a skill that seamlessly transitions into the world of business. The ability to receive feedback, adapt, and continuously improve is a cornerstone of success. In business, the capacity to learn and be coached is a distinguishing factor that sets high achievers apart. It not only fuels personal growth but also drives exceptional performance, as it enables us to refine our strategies, enhance our skills, and ultimately reach new heights of success.

In conclusion, the intersection of athletics and business unveils a wealth of principles underpinned by research-backed evidence into the neuroscientific benefits of sports. From analytical and creative thinking to resilience, curiosity, empathy, and leadership skills, athletes possess a cognitive advantage that can revolutionize the business landscape. By embracing these principles, businesses can harness the power of sports to drive financial performance, foster innovation, inspire teams, overcome challenges, and cultivate a culture of excellence.

# ACKNOWLEDGMENTS

Sincere and heartfelt thanks to the countless former and current athletes we spoke to, for sharing so generously your inspiring stories of trials, triumphs, mistakes overcome, lessons learned, perseverance applied, hard-won wisdom gained—both in your sport and in the business world—and for all that you have continued to achieve . . . *after the game.*

Particular thanks goes to Alice Sullivan, whose keen character observations and depictions brought the people in this book to life. Brad Budde for sharing his spirit to play at a higher level after sports. My family for their unconditional love. I am also especially appreciative of Geraldine Anathan's contributions analyzing the neuroscience behind athletes' post-career ventures and decisions. This book would not have been complete without their collaborative spirit and expertise.

# *NOTES*

1. P. Lally, "Identity and Athletic Retirement: A Prospective Study," *Psychology of Sport and Exercise* 8, no. 1 (2007): 85–99.

2. G. M. Murphy, A. J. Petitpas, & B. W. Brewer, "Identity Foreclosure, Athletic Identity, and Career Maturity in Intercollegiate Athletes," *The Sport Psychologist* 10, no. 3 (1996): 239–46.

3. S. Park, D. Lavallee, & D. Tod, "Athletes' Career Transition Out of Sport: A Systematic Review," *International Review of Sport and Exercise Psychology* 6, no. 1 (2013): 22–53, https://doi.org/10.1080/1750984X.2012.687053.

4. V. Hosek & J. Zipp, "Identity Loss and Recovery in the Transition from a Professional Sports Career," Qualitative Research in Sport, *Exercise and Health* 11, no. 2 (2019): 205–20.

5. C. K. Harrison & S. M. Lawrence, "African American Student Athletes' Perceptions of Career Transition in Sport: A Qualitative and Visual Elicitation," *Race Ethnicity and Education* 6, no. 4 (2003): 373–94.

6. Lally, "Identity and Athletic Retirement: A Prospective Study."

7. Park et al, "Athletes' Career Transition Out of Sport: A Systematic Review."

8. V. Ratten, "Sport-based Entrepreneurship: Towards a New Theory of Entrepreneurship and Sport Management," *International Entrepreneurship and Management Journal* 7, no. 1 (2011): 57–69.

9. Kirill Pervun, *Essays on CEO Personal Characteristics and Corporate Outcomes: Athlete CEOs and Foreign CEOs,* "Appendix B: Athlete

Profile, Table B.1, Characteristics of Athletes—Narrative Evidence in Literature," March 23, 2021, Dissertation for Kate Tiedemann School of Business and Finance, Muma College of Business, University of South Florida.

10. "Baby Boomers: Incredible Numbers Buying and Selling," California Association of Business Brokers, https://cabb.org/selling-a-business-in -ca/baby-boomers-incredible-numbers-buying-and-selling.

11. "Table 7. Survival of private sector establishments by opening year," 1995–2022, U.S. Bureau of Labor Statistics, https://www.bls.gov/bdm /us_age_naics_00_table7.txt.

12. Some of what I experienced was an example of a phenomenon known as *social contagion*. Your behaviors, actions, and emotions spread spontaneously through groups: your team, your friends, and your family. For more info on social contagion, see N.A. Christakis and J.H. Fowler, "Social contagion theory: examining dynamic social networks and human behavior." *Statistics in Medicine*, 32 (2013): 556–577, https://doi-org.ezp-prod1.hul.harvard.edu/10.1002/sim.5408.

13. Building wealth for others is usually not at the top of the list for most retired athletes. Many athletes share the same personality traits as those of successful entrepreneurs, according to the Enneagram methodology. Perhaps you are one of them. To learn more, see https://www .enneagraminstitute.com.

14. While the divorce rate of collegiate retired athletes is only 20 percent compared to the average US average of 25 percent, the rate of divorce for professional athletes is 78 percent. For more, see: Marlene Y. Satter, "High divorce rate plays havoc on athletes' retirements," *Benefits Selling*, August 14, 2014, https://www.proquest.com/docview/1553340718 /abstract/D5A282C303654C06PQ/1.

15. EQ stands for Emotional Quotient, or a measure of your emotional intelligence. Having a solid EQ is essential in business; it is your ability to recognize and understand your own emotions, as well as the emotions of others. Daniel Goleman, the "father of EQ," outlines five components: self-awareness, self-regulation, motivation, empathy, and social skills. You can develop your EQ over time, which will help you

meet goals and targets, as well as create a happier and healthier life. For more, visit www.Gottman.com.

16. As an Enneagram type 3, Christina is an Achiever: "Threes are self-assured, attractive, and charming. Ambitious, competent, and energetic, they can also be status-conscious and highly driven for advancement. They are diplomatic and poised but can also be overly concerned with their image and what others think of them. They typically have problems with workaholism and competitiveness." https://www.enneagraminstitute.com/type-3.

17. In studies of more than 11,000 people who had retired from athletics, more than 97 percent of subjects suffered what is called "loss of identity." Symptoms of identity loss include negative self-talk, feelings of betrayal from your community, transforming the way you act in various settings, a low level of self-care, and lack of passion for the things you used to love doing. It is essential to fill the identity gap through education and guidance, as it can lead to long-term depression. For more, see Park, "Athletes' Career Transition Out of Sport."

18. Feelings of powerlessness at work are precursors to stress, anxiety, and burnout. When team members feel that their expertise is valued, good things happen. Acknowledging and appreciating a team member who takes such a risk—offers a new idea, admits an error, asks a question—is a powerful tactic for inspiring others to follow suit, and is a key component for high-performing teams. For more on this, see: Amy Edmondson, *Teaming: How Organizations Learn, Innovate, and Compete in the Knowledge Economy* (San Francisco: Jossey-Bass Pfeiffer), 2012.

19. Social media is great, but use it wisely. Your digital imprint is forever. LinkedIn posts and community engagement will demonstrate your credibility, help you network with the right people, and boost your reputation as a team player.

20. "Intercollegiate athletes report greater alcohol consumption and more alcohol-related problems than their non-athlete peers. Even higher rates of binge drinking have been documented for collegiate athletes in comparison to their non-athlete peers. Athletes may benefit from feedback regarding their alcohol use in the off-season, as athletes tend

to consume more alcohol outside their season of competitive play. This is especially true for male athletes high in Win Orientation and female athletes higher in Goal Orientation." (Brenner & Swanik, 2007; Leichliter, Meilman, Presley, & Chasin, 1998; Nelson & Wechsler, 2001; Wechsler, Davenport, Dowdall, Grossman, & Zanakos, 1997.)

21. Park et al, "Athletes' Career Transition Out of Sport: A Systematic Review."

22. Writing down your thoughts, feelings, and to-dos is what we casually call a "brain dump." From a neuroscience perspective, a brain dump can be helpful because it allows the brain to externalize thoughts and ideas, thereby reducing cognitive load and freeing up working memory. Writing down thoughts and ideas engages multiple areas of the brain, including the prefrontal cortex, which is involved in executive function and decision-making. This process also stimulates neural connections and can enhance creativity and problem-solving abilities. Give it a try next time you feel overwhelmed.

23. "Doubt" is hardwired into our DNA. It's our mind's automatic protective mechanism, a response to the possibility of incoming change. However, there is a term called "negativity bias," which means we tend to believe the negative voice in our head more than we believe the optimistic one. Thinking back, can you imagine how mundane your life might be had you not taken some of those past risks?

24. Christina's deep dive into Jack's online presence is what's called *social proof*. Also called social influence, the term was coined in 1984 by author Robert Cialdini in his book *Influence*. Essentially, it's the idea that people copy the actions of others to emulate behavior in certain situations—so if Jack has great reviews, and a high online presence, Christina will feel even more secure in her decision to work with him. On your way to becoming an entrepreneur, think of your social media posts as "social proof," representing who you are, what you believe in, and how you can benefit those around you. Think of yourself as a brand. Surveys show that 95 percent of consumers read online reviews before they buy, and 58 percent say they would pay more for

the products of a brand with good reviews. ("Brand Rated: 'Nine out of ten customers read reviews before buying a product,'" *Globe News-wire*, January 13, 2022, https://www.globenewswire.com/news-release /2022/01/13/2366090/0/en/Brand-Rated-Nine-out-of-ten-customers -read-reviews-before-buying-a-product.html.).

25. Michael Strahan with Veronica Chambers, *Wake Up Happy: The Dream Big, Win Big Guide to Transforming Your Life* (New York: 37 INK, 2015).

26. R. M. Arce-Mujica et al., "Relationship between physical activity, psychological well-being, and academic performance in college athletes: The role of growth mindset," *Sustainability* 13, no. 7 (2021): 4133, doi:10.3390/su13074133.

27. Shirzad Chamine, *Positive Intelligence: Why Only 20% of Teams and Individuals Achieve Their True Potential AND HOW YOU CAN ACHIEVE YOURS* (Austin, TX: Greenleaf, 2012).

28. Carol S. Dweck, PhD, *Mindset: The New Psychology of Success* (New York: Random House, 2006).

29. The 6 Human Needs Narrative Exercise is available at https://barrie fht.ca/wp-content/uploads/2021/01/The-6-Human-Needs.pdf.

30. Park et al., "Athletes' career transition out of sport: a systematic review."

31. For one resource among many for meditative breathing techniques, see Brianna Majsiak and Claire Young, "7 Ways to Practice Breath Work for Beginners," Everyday Health, reviewed June 23, 2022, https://www.everydayhealth.com/alternative-health/living-with/ways -practice-breath-focused-meditation/.

32. Michael Breus, "Chronotype Quiz," Sleep Doctor, last updated December 13, 2022, https://sleepdoctor.com/sleep-quizzes/chronotype-quiz/.

33. F. Guillén & S. Laborde, "Higher-order structure of mental toughness and the analysis of latent mean differences between athletes from 34 disciplines and non-athletes," *Personality and Individual Differences*, 60 (2014), 30–35.

34. Pete Carroll and Yogi Roth, *Win Forever: Live, Work, and Play Like a Champion* (New York: Portfolio, 2011).

35. R. Tang, K. J. Friston, and Y. Y. Tang, "Brief Mindfulness Meditation Induces Gray Matter Changes in a Brain Hub," *Neural Plast*, November 16, 2020, https://www.ncbi.nlm.nih.gov/pmc/articles/PMC7704181/.

36. Kobe Bryant, *The Mamba Mentality: How I Play* (New York: Farrar, Straus & Giroux: MCD, 2018).

37. Kirill Pervun, *Essays on CEO Personal Characteristics and Corporate Outcomes: Athlete CEOs and Foreign CEOs*, "Appendix B: Athlete Profile, Table B.1, Characteristics of Athletes—Narrative Evidence in Literature."

38. Pervun, *Essays on CEO Personal Characteristics and Corporate Outcomes*.

39. "Baby Boomers: Incredible Numbers Are Buying and Selling Businesses," California Association of Business Brokers.

40. "Baby Boomers: Incredible Numbers."

41. For a sample letter of intent (LOI), visit https://docs.google.com/document/d/1kf-mFSUCOREwEExzGgsjRf_ki2qtZtbo/edit?rtpof=true&sd=true.

42. M. Mackay, "The Correlation Between Sports and Entrepreneurial Success," Unpublished manuscript, Manhattan College School of Business.

43. Marc Brodherson et al., "Creativity's bottom line: How winning companies turn creativity into business value and growth," McKinsey, June 16, 2017, https://www.mckinsey.com/capabilities/mckinsey-digital/our-insights/creativitys-bottom-line-how-winning-companies-turn-creativity-into-business-value-and-growth.

44. *Global Business & Finance Review* 27, no. 4 (August 2022): 17–26, https://doi.org/10.17549/gbfr.2022.27.4.17; Elena Lytkina Botelho et al., "What Sets Successful CEOs Apart," *Harvard Business Review*, May–June 2017, https://hbr.org/2017/05/what-sets-successful-ceos-apart.

45. Francesca Gino, "The Business Case for Curiosity," *Harvard Business Review*, September–October 2018, https://hbr.org/2018/09/the-business-case-for-curiosity.

46. Elena Lytkina Botelho, Kim Rosenkoetter Powell, Stephen Kincaid, and Dina Wang, "What Sets Successful CEOs Apart: The four essential behaviors that help them win the top job and thrive once they get

it," *Harvard Business Review*, May-June, 2017, https://hbr.org/2017/05/what-sets-successful-ceos-apart.

47. Amy Colbert et al., "CEO Transformational Leadership: The Role of Goal Importance Congruence in Top Management Teams," *Academy of Management Journal* 51, no. 1 (February 2008).

48. *The Journal of Student Leadership* 3, no. 2 (2019), https://journals.uvu.edu/index.php/jsl/issue/view/46.

49. E. T. Pascarella & J. C. Smart, "Impact of intercollegiate athletic participation for African American and Caucasian Men: Some further evidence," *Journal of College Student Development* 32 (1991): 123–30.

50. X-Y Tan et al., "Morphological and Functional Differences Between Athletes and Novices in Cortical Neuronal Networks," *Frontiers in Human Neuroscience* 10 (2016), https://www.frontiersin.org/articles/10.3389/fnhum.2016.00660/full.

51. John Horn, *Inside the Competitor's Mindset: How to Predict Their Next Move and Position Yourself for Success* (Cambridge, MA: MIT Press, 2023).

52. Geoff Colvin, *Talent Is Overrated: What Really Separates World-Class Performers from Everybody Else* (New York: Penguin, 2010).

# ABOUT THE AUTHOR

**Jay Dixon** is a former college athlete turned entrepreneur, investor, and coach. After multiple exits of his own, Jay consulted with entrepreneurs nationwide on the process of buying, growing, and selling businesses. He started an elite accelerator for athletes to transition their skill sets to entrepreneurial ventures using a time-tested, research-backed, and athlete-approved playbook, with courses and coaching to go from winning athlete to thriving entrepreneur. Jay played football at the University of Nevada and pursued his MBA at Columbia Business School in New York City, where he holds a certificate of Business Excellence in Venture Capital/Private Equity. He earned a certificate of completion of BAM alongside the most exceptional accelerator managers from 500 Global, Silicon Valley's leading program for accelerator managers. He is a sports enthusiast, an adventurer, and the father to an amazing daughter. Learn more about Jay by visiting www.JayDixon.com.